Recent criticism of Eliot has ignored the public dimension of his life and work. His poetry is often seen as the private record of an internal spiritual struggle. Professor Cooper shows how Eliot deliberately addressed a 'North Atlantic' manufacturing fearful of social disintegration during the politically turbulent 1930s. Almost immediately following publication, Four Quartets was accorded canonic status: a work that promised a personal harmony, directed from the disharmonies of the emerging postwar world. Cooper conveys cultural agenda. He aimed to reinforce established social structures during a period of painful political transition. This powerful and original study re-establishes the public context in which Eliot's work was received and understood. It will become an essential reference work for all interested in a wider understanding of Eliot and of Anglo-American cultural relations.

T. S. ELIOT AND
THE IDEOLOGY OF
FOUR QUARTETS

T. S. ELIOT AND
THE IDEOLOGY OF
FOUR QUARTETS

JOHN XIROS COOPER

University of British Columbia

 CAMBRIDGE
UNIVERSITY PRESS

Published by the Press Syndicate of the University of Cambridge
The Pitt Building, Trumpington Street, Cambridge CB2 1RP
40 West 20th Street, New York, NY 10011-4211, USA
10 Stamford Road, Oakleigh, Melbourne 3166, Australia

First published 1995

Printed in Great Britain at the University Press, Cambridge

A catalogue record for this book is available from the British Library

Library of Congress cataloguing in publication data

Cooper, John Xiros, 1944–
T. S. Eliot and the ideology of Four quartets / John Xiros Cooper.
p.   cm.
Includes bibliographical references and index.
ISBN 0 521 49629 2 (hardback)
1. Eliot, T. S. (Thomas Stearns), 1888–1965. Four quartets.
2. Eliot, T. S. (Thomas Stearns), 1888–1965 – Political and social
views.   3. Literature and society – United States – History – 20th
century.   4. Literature and society – England – History – 20th century.
5. Social problems in literature.   I. Title.
PS3509.L43F642   1995
821'.912–dc20
95-6019   CIP

ISBN 0 521 49629 2 hardback

SE

For Kelly and David

This is an evil time.

The Times (26 September 1938)

. . . it was you
who, not speechless from shock but finding the right
language for thirst and fear, did much to
prevent a panic.

W. H. Auden, 'To T.S. Eliot on his Sixtieth Birthday' (1948)

When we read *Four Quartets* we are left finally not with the thought of 'the transitory Being who beheld this vision', nor with the thought of the vision itself, but with the poem, beautiful, satisfying, self-contained, self-organized, complete.

Helen Gardner, *The Art of T.S. Eliot* (1950)

Contents

Acknowledgements   *page* x
List of abbreviations   xiii

1   *Ash-Wednesday* and the transition to the late candour   1

2   Provisional delusions: crisis among the mandarins   28

3   The society of the mandarin verse play   61

4   Representing *Four Quartets*: the canonizers at work   100

5   *Four Quartets*: the poem proper   122
    i.   Burnt children   122
    ii.   Rehearsing renunciation   141
    iii. Freedom in history   169

6   White mythology: the comedy of manners in Natopolis   182

Notes   198
Works cited   216
Index   228

Acknowledgements

Many people and institutions have helped me in the making of this book. I am grateful for their many efforts on my behalf. I would particularly like to thank the librarians, archivists, and staffs of the Main Library at the University of British Columbia, the British Library, Faber & Faber Ltd, the University Library at Cambridge, the libraries of King's and Magdalene Colleges, Cambridge, University of Victoria Library Special Collections, the Humanities Research Centre at the University of Texas, the Vancouver Public Library, the Bennett Library at Simon Fraser University, the McKimmie Library at the University of Calgary, and the many other library catalogues and indexes I 'visited' electronically during the making of this book.

I am also grateful to many people who listened to my ideas about Eliot and who discussed them with me over the years. In particular, I would like to acknowledge the help of Cheryl Cooper in the initial stages of the research. I would also like to thank the members of two graduate seminars at the University of British Columbia in the last four years, one on Eliot's later work and another on British poetry in the 1930s. Our discussions helped me to focus my ideas more clearly and the seminar presentations and papers provided me with an opportunity to hear what various other critical intelligences made of this material. I am grateful also to audiences, other panellists, and respondents of meetings in various academic places, Vancouver and Hamilton in Canada, Merano and Urbino in Italy, Orlando and San Francisco in the United States, who were kind enough to listen and respond to parts of this work during the years of its composition.

It is always a little bit dangerous naming names of individuals whose conversation, casual remarks, encouragement, and scepticism helped me in more ways than I can set down. Of course, none of them are responsible for what you will find here, but each was indispensable to its making. In particular, I would like to thank Keith and Joan Alldritt,

Stephen Battersby, Ted Bishop, Rob Browning, Ronald Bush, Andrew Busza, Peter Childers, the late Frantisek Galan, Phillip George, John de Gruchy, Michael Holquist, Nick Hudson, Andrew Klobucar, Ira Nadel, Peter Nichols, Grove Powell, Peter Quartermain, Roger Seamon, Kay Stockholder, Steven Taubeneck, Demetres Tryphonopolos, and Michael Zeitlin. I want to acknowledge separately my father, Norman Cooper, and my late and much missed mother, Hariclea, whose personal memories of the 1930s and 1940s, evoked the day to day life of a fascinating period.

Finally, my most important debt is owed to Kelly Cooper, whose understanding and strength assisted me in a difficult time, and who gave birth to our son David during the later stages of composition. Hearing their happy voices filling our house made all the difference, and I would like to dedicate this work to them.

All quotations from T. S. Eliot's poetry and plays are taken from *Collected Poems, 1909–1962*, Faber & Faber, 1968 and *Collected Plays*, Faber & Faber, 1969. Quotations from Eliot's prose works are taken from the Faber & Faber editions of *For Lancelot Andrewes*, 1970, *The Idea of a Christian Society*, 1962, *Notes towards the Definition of Culture*, 1972. All quotations from W. H. Auden's poetry are taken from the Faber & Faber editions of *Collected Shorter Poems, 1927–1957*, 1969 and *The English Auden: Poems, Essays, Dramatic Writings, 1927–1939*, 1986. All quotations from the poems of C. Day Lewis are taken from *Collected Poems 1954*, Jonathan Cape, 1970. Quotations from the works of Louis MacNeice are taken from *The Strings Are False*, Oxford University Press, 1966 and *Collected Poems, 1925–1948*, Faber & Faber, 1954. Quotation from a poem by Stephen Spender is taken from *The Still Centre*, Faber & Faber, 1939.

Abbreviations

T. S. ELIOT

ASG	*After Strange Gods* (1934)
BN	'Burnt Norton' (1936) in *CP*
CP	*Collected Poems, 1909–1962* (1963)
DS	'Dry Salvages' (1941) in *CP*
EC	'East Coker' (1940) in *CP*
FLA	*For Lancelot Andrewes* (1928)
FQ	*Four Quartets* (1944)
Idea	*The Idea of a Christian Society* (1939)
Letters	*The Letters of T.S. Eliot.* vol. 1. (1988)
LG	'Little Gidding' (1942) in *CP*
Notes	*Notes towards the Definition of Culture* (1948)
OPP	*On Poetry and Poets* (1957)
Plays	*Collected Plays* (1962)
SE	*Selected Essays: New Edition* (1950)
TCC	*To Criticize the Critic* (1965)
WL	*The Waste Land* (1922) in *CP*

OTHER

CP 1925–1948	Louis MacNeice, *Collected Poems, 1925–1948* (1949)
CP 1954	Cecil Day Lewis, *Collected Poems, 1954* (1954)
CSP	W. H. Auden, *Collected Shorter Poems* (1966)
EA	W. H. Auden, *The English Auden* (1977)
TLS	*The Times Literary Supplement*

CHAPTER ONE

Ash-Wednesday *and the transition to the late candour*

Reading *Ash-Wednesday* today is a relatively simple matter. We under-stand its place in Eliot's *corpus* and in his biography. We at least have *Four Quartets* as the *terminus ad quem* towards which we can now see the earlier poem pointing (cf. Gardner, *T. S. Eliot* 78). But in 1930 *Ash-Wednesday* was a difficult and curious performance for a poet celebrated as the supreme ironist of his generation (Howard, 'Mr Eliot's Poetry' 146), a poet able to raise the most fashionable neuroses to the level of lyric song, and one noted also for his curious learning and the snooty inabil-ity to resist showing it off (Lucas, review of *The Waste Land* 116). He was celebrated enough to provoke nasty parodies that could lead a pub-lisher, like Ernest Benn for example, to invest the money in producing a book he thought he could sell to an appropriately amused and knowing audience. Herbert Palmer's parody of Eliot in 1931 called *Cinder Thursday* reminds us that one way of gauging a celebrity's standing 'in the world' is to measure the amount of capital that is invested (always, of course, with a view to being able to turn a profit) in the enterprise of derision:

THE SAHARA
(With apologies to T. S. Eliot)

The wilderness shall blossom as a rose,
But with cactus.
Look backwards and forwards and into the air.

'Sir, Sir, Oh Sir,
You are quiet in your chair,
Did you not hear me as I reached the highest stair?
I have left my shopping parcel,
I have left my combinations,
I have left them on your chair
When I came to ask some questions.
For certes you are learned and curiously wise.' (13)

And so on. The derision recognizes Eliot's success in his time.[1] There were still many like Palmer, even in 1931, who felt that he was the author of 'The most stupendous literary hoax since Adam . . .' (17), yet a hoax about which they were willing to say that it was still 'in some abysmal way creative, / Even in its disintegration . . . (17). In 1930, dragging that kind of reputation behind him, Eliot published *Ash-Wednesday*, in which the sympathetic readership he had done so much to acclimatize to a new era of feeling was given what seemed on the surface, at least, a plain poem of religious conversion. Even Eliot's partisans were genuinely puzzled by this new direction and found its intent difficult to fix.

Certainly those who knew Eliot's work in the late 1920s would have been aware of a change of direction. If nothing else the three Ariel poems, published just before *Ash-Wednesday*, would have suggested the suddenly obvious interest in religion. But those familiar with his earlier poetry and criticism would have been justified in asking whether this new interest was an interest as such or an interest in using religious materials for the making of impersonal verse. The personal element would have been further obscured by the fact that two of the Ariel poems are dramatic monologues. Because we read with the knowledge of his whole career to guide us, we no longer find the seriousness of Eliot's faith a matter of much dispute. This is a critical luxury readers in the 1920s did not have.

It was the publication of *Ash-Wednesday* that made the intent of the Ariel poems very clear. The new poem solidified not only a new theme, but also a new approach to style. What exactly passed through a sceptical reader's mind when he or she stopped reading *Ash-Wednesday* is now impossible to say. Whatever it was, the poem by all accounts *was* precisely what it seemed to be and not another volute in the irrepressible ironies of old. It was not a *more* candid poem than *The Waste Land*. *The Waste Land* has a candour and daring all its own that is very different from the self-exposure of *Ash-Wednesday*.

Notwithstanding the tonal effects on the poetry of his own personal crisis during *The Waste Land* period, a good deal of what that early candour is about must be put down to Eliot's involvement in the advent of the modernist movement on the margins of British literary culture. More specifically, *The Waste Land*'s alternating currents of hyacinthine aetherialism, satirical sharpness, and visceral disgust can be related to the poem's position, on one level at least, as a kind of bohemian remonstrance aimed at the literary and critical establishment of the day, a series of rude noises in the drawing room of polite society. The candour of *The Waste Land* is certainly personal, but the candour of, so to speak, the real person is obscured by the more visible display of the poetic personae, the lyric wincing of the masks.

The masks and tonalities of *The Waste Land* engage with materials that are certainly candid as topics of public discussion, the casual sexuality of the lower orders for example, the negative erotics of neurosis, the breakdown of the micro-institutions of society like marriage and virtue, the quixotic quest for spiritual regeneration on the wasted margins of a sterile world, and so forth. The confessionalist presentation is not, in the end, personal confession. It is a style which uses candour as a rhetorical scheme, principally as a shock effect, but also as a way of pushing consciousness to the edge of personal exposure, that is to say, the symbolic enactment of self-exposure, rather than the thing itself. The influence of this presentational mode has been profound, especially on American poetry, all the way from the sweated nudities of *Howl*, through the unveilings of Sylvia Plath, to the poolside bareness of John Ashbery.

Eliot, of course, never confessed in print, never set down his own account of the life-altering changes he underwent in the 1920s. Not that it matters, because we have come to know the episodes and personalities involved rather well. What is missing is some indication of Eliot's own attitude towards these episodes and personalities, towards himself and his career progress. Nowhere in the corpus is one line set down of explicit reflection on these events, not one line of justification or rationalization of his actions, say about his inexcusably shameful treatment of Vivien for example, or later his callousness towards Emily Hale, nor a word of reflection on his own success as an author and businessman,[2] a success achieved much to the amusement of his old bohemian friends, Wyndham Lewis and Ezra Pound (Ackroyd, *T. S. Eliot* 220). But of course this is too much to ask of any public celebrity.

Some feel it necessary, however, to provide history with an account of their own lives, not necessarily to establish the facts, but to convey the meaning of the life as that meaning is glimpsed from the inside. We have come to understand about such texts that they constitute not the truth of the subject, but one more interpretation of the text of the life. Such an interpretation has a special kind of authority no doubt, but, as interpretation, it does not supplant the discerning insights of an outsider. Eliot was a public man with no sense of obligation to convey his own sense of the meaning of his life, or a justification of his actions. He once told Ottoline Morrell that 'he always felt more at ease among strangers; no doubt he disliked the idea of being "known" and "talked about"' (Ackroyd 216). He was a man who achieved a certain public celebrity, and he guarded his privacy tenaciously. Yet what did he think of his own place in the world of letters? What did he think of his own fate in the England to which he migrated? What did he think of his own personal difficulties, with respect to his wife, with respect to his conversion, with respect to those who saw him simply as a schemer, a careerist, and a fraud? In our time, we have come to recognize that we do not need explicit answers to such questions in order to get a feel for the slants of the inner life. Ironically, it was Eliot himself who schooled us in this sort of inferential explication.

The poetics of impersonality conveniently deflected attention from the opacities of everyday life towards the work, towards the higher transparencies of language, form, and tradition. But it is possible, as many critics have noted, to find in Eliot's formal work statements that reveal something of the man. In his criticism, especially, there are passages in some essays which suggest more than a professional interest in the subject at hand; they press on us the weight of personal affinities. They suggest that Eliot has recognized something of himself in the particular work, personality, or events which he has found in the life of writer or thinker who interests him; early on it was Jules Laforgue and John Donne for example, or Lancelot Andrewes and Niccolò Machiavelli from the *Ash-Wednesday* period, or, later, Blaise Pascal, and Baudelaire, or Charles de Foucauld and, of course, the Dante of *La Vita Nuova*. There are passages in all these essays which critics have recognized as being written with a sharpness and passion that suggest that something more is going on than disinterested commentary on another writer's work. For example, in 'The *Pensées* of Pascal' the paragraph in which he discusses the French philosopher's 'knowledge of worldliness and [his] passion of asceticism' (*SE* 363–64), Eliot could very well be looking into a mirror. His commendation of Pascal's 'honesty' in facing 'the *données* of the actual world' (*SE* 363) reads very much like a comment which Eliot might wish to have said about himself. He certainly can, he seems to be saying, like Pascal and Montaigne, endure very much reality.

One passage though that has not been identified as carrying the sort of oblique autobiographical interest of the above comes in the important 1944 essay 'What is a Classic?', a passage about Virgil's 'unique position' in the Roman world and about the meaning of Aeneas in Virgil's epic (but see Reeves, *Virgilian* 159). The passage comes in a discussion of Virgil as the poet who realizes the singular 'destiny' of the Roman Empire and the Latin language (and this from London, the capital of a contemporary Empire and in the hegemonic language of his own day).

This sense of destiny comes to consciousness in the *Aeneid*. Aeneas is himself, from first to last, a 'man in fate', a man who is neither an adventurer nor a schemer, neither a vagabond nor a careerist, a man fulfilling his destiny, not under compulsion or arbitrary decree, and certainly from no stimulus to glory, but by surrendering his will to a higher power behind the gods who would thwart or direct him. (*OPP* 68)

It is the list of all those things which Aeneas is *not* and the aside about glory that reveal, in brief, the merest nervous twitch of a reticent public celebrity who believes his motives have been misunderstood.

We do well to remember that Eliot had been stung on a number of occasions on the matter of his sincerity, and not always by enemies. Even friends like Wyndham Lewis had 'misinterpreted,' or so Eliot would have thought, his new allegiances. Eliot, by the time *Men Without Art* was published in 1934, was being seen as a kind of traitor to art in terms that accused him publicly of being a wily schemer, an arrogant social climber and thoroughly insincere in his new professions.[3]

In the matter, then, of the candour of *Ash-Wednesday*, it comes down to a difference of tone and to the composition, during the 1920s, of a new voice, more suited to the emotional changes which the later poem enacts (Ricks, *Eliot and Prejudice* 225). Eliot's passage from one to the other in the 1920s is a very interesting, even exemplary, episode in the modern history of bourgeois sensibility. The stations of the discourse in this stylistic *via dolorosa* are, of course, 'The Hollow Men', *Sweeney Agonistes: Fragments of an Aristophanic Melodrama* (1925–26), 'Eyes that last I saw in tears' (1921), 'The wind sprang up at four o'clock' (1921–24), plus the Ariel poems. The parallel stations of the life are to be found in the existing biographies. Lyndall Gordon's *Eliot's New Life* gives us the events, the raw chronology of affliction, of that transition, even though her interpretations of the significance of these events and her earnest estimation of the moral worth of her subject belong more to the century of Cardinal Newman and Matthew Arnold than to the century of Antonin Artaud and Georges Bataille.

Of course, as Eliot changed, the resulting mutations of voice cannot be explained as a simple technical revision of verbal style, or a change of style to more accurately convey the course of convulsive inner struggles. The best stylistic accounts of the poem – those of Helen Gardner, Hugh Kenner, David Moody, and Ronald Bush – tend to make Eliot's personal agony the determining context for their judgements (see also Leavell, 'Eliot's Ritual Method' 149–52 and Ricks 222–28). But there is more to the making of a style than is to be found in the isolated individual subject. By taking subjectivity as the fountain of personal meaning, as the source of a personal voice, we ignore those aspects of inwardness that are inescapably social and intersubjective, like language itself. Style does not simply serve, in Ronald Bush's words, 'to repress, channel, and adapt' the impulses of inner being (*Study in Character and Style* xiii); it takes us across the barriers of individual identity out into the social world. Style is not a seismograph recording the psychic tremors below the surface, but an effect of the way the individual chooses to find him or herself in the world, a world in which one is free to act, but never in circumstances of one's own choosing.

No matter how intense Eliot's personal dilemmas were during his career there was never a time (except perhaps in *The Elder Statesman* period) when he did not maintain a keen interest in the external social world, and, further, maintain himself as a commentator, spokesman and impresario of certain social and cultural values which he promoted, increasingly publicly, after 1930. And those engagements are just as important in making the late style as is the inner turmoil. Eliot's recent sympathetic critics have focussed our attention on the man's inwardness and lost sight of his outward faces: the public moralist, the drily aggressive controversialist, the contented social climber, and, above all, the successful London editor and publisher.[4]

This is not to say that from *Ash-Wednesday* on, Eliot abandons the practice of impersonality in verse in order to speak in his own voice; the force of unwilled, external circumstance never allows it.[5] The voicings of *Ash-Wednesday* are still derived from a range of literary sources. The very first line remembers Cavalcanti's 'Perch'io non spero di tornar gia mai . . .' and, no doubt, also Lancelot Andrewes' Ash Wednesday sermon in 1619 (Moody, *Poet* 137). The echo of Cavalcanti harmonizes with Eliot's continuing interest in the Italian *trecento* and Dante, the perfect poet, in particular. In addition the turn towards the Tuscans and the *Vita Nuova* puts into practice the changes in Eliot's re-assessment of the literary history of Europe as sketched in the Clark Lectures of 1926, where the *trecentisti* replace the Metaphysicals as the leaden rule of literary value. Eliot was still composing a poetic voice from traditional materials, so that the confessional element of his new style was not something as simple as speaking in his own voice, but the more difficult matter of making poetry out of one's personal beliefs.

The candour of *Ash-Wednesday* lies precisely here, in the man's convictions. The voice of the poem, composed from a number of historical and social sources, is no longer exploited in order to create an ironic distance both from the poem's readers and from the poem's own professions. All the potential for irony, which was so thoroughly and surely exploited in the early poetry, is no longer projected in the same way. It is wrong to say that *Ash-Wednesday* is not ironic; there is irony there, but its aim and function are quite different from the superciliousness of 'Portrait of a Lady' or the snickering which accompanies the perplexed pratfalls of Prufrock. The ironies of the new style are directed not at the poetic persona as a type, the emblem of a culture rotted through by relativism, but at the believer himself. Not the persona, but the concrete believer now endures the poem's ironies. This is the concrete believer who lives in history, whose actual inner struggles, the struggles of faith and belief and commitment, are performed in and completed by the composition of the poem. There are still 'the police' done, more or less, in different voices, but now they use irony as a way of exposing the believer, not the speaker in the poem. The poem becomes a kind of structure over which the author increasingly relinquishes control, primarily over the matter of how the poem is to be read.

One might say, then, that *Ash-Wednesday* is a less deliberate poem than *The Waste Land*, or at least, deliberate in a different way. *The Waste Land*'s ambiguities are ambiguities generated by the poem's fragmented surface cohesiveness; the poem's designs on its readers, however, are clear and precise and can be retrieved when the poem is fully contextualized. The surface cohesion of *Ash-Wednesday* is subverted again and again by the shifting focus of the poem's deeper ironies, now directed towards the believer, as self-lacerating and unstable gestures of authenticity, and no longer designed to deconstruct a hegemonic discourse. *The Waste Land*'s subversions underlined and helped amplify the crisis of direction and meaning into which European thought had begun to slip after Kierkegaard and Nietzsche (Dreyfus, *Heidegger* 289–91). I think this was an inadvertent effect of Eliot's poem, but it has often been read as contributing to that crisis. I don't believe he intended any such thing. I agree with Gordon's argument throughout *Eliot's Early Years* that his work as a student of nineteenth-century idealist philosophy and his later religious affirmations are perfectly consistent. This suggests that he did not see his own thinking in terms of post-Nietzschean nihilism.[6]

In a decisively non-modernist, even anti-modernist, manoeuvre, Eliot turns away from the central philosophical dilemma of the twentieth century. His Christian avowals in the mid-1920s, however, positioned him to re-enter authoritatively the metaphysical debate in the 1940s, during the general crisis of nihilism occasioned by the collapse of

Europe. *Four Quartets* will speak to that crisis in a time when his reader-ship, the intelligentsia of his day, which initially found the quixotic behaviour of the late 1920s oddly out of character and, then, with a shrug, irrelevant, would itself turn empty-handed from the inescapable facts of contemporary history, the terror bombing, the torture chamber, and the wasted humanity which emerged from Treblinka, and would want to listen hungrily to the Christian poet in a destitute time.

For Eliot, 1930 culminates a movement towards new personal and social allegiances. Such a transformation allows us to see the interaction of style, psychological disposition, and socio-political commitments as a whole strategic activity. The voice of *Ash-Wednesday* has as much to do with Eliot's position as a publisher and businessman, or his opinions about the Tudor Church, Mallarmé and the Tory party as it has to do with his spiritual agonies or with the deliberate elimination of the social voices and mythic framework which characterize *The Waste Land*. In fact, the recourse to myth in *The Waste Land* can be approached in two ways, on the one hand, as a makeshift scaffolding for the disorganized and crumbling epistemology of the poem, and, more simply, as a species of more or less deliberate literary opportunism.

Myth, the occult, the new anthropology, the studies in hysteria, the popularizing of Freud, the crisis in humanism all represented the dis-cursive currencies of the first three decades of the twentieth century. Eliot was not above spending them to the limit. It connected him, for the time being, to the post-war avant garde and allowed him to establish himself as an authentic, authoritative voice with his own generation, from the waste lands of a failed society. Having earned his credentials on the margins, it was not long before he began the social trek from the bohemian periphery to the centre of established society, a trek that did not pass unnoticed among former colleagues like Ezra Pound. And it was not long before the modernism of the first London Vortex, duly domesticated, was transformed by the publishing programme of the Faber company into the secondary, and tamer, modernism of the Auden generation, a generation of writers among whom Eliot acted as talent scout, mentor and, eventually, spiritual guide. Only William Empson, I believe, from within that generation, intuited the psychological hold Eliot exerted over them as both poetic mentor, the literary source of the formulaic 'wastelandism' of the Auden group in the beginning, and the calculating impresario, who had the power to put young men on the map, to make or break them. 'I don't know how much of my own mind he invented . . .' Empson writes in 'The Style of the Master' (1948); it was, Empson continues, 'a very penetrating influence, perhaps not unlike an east wind' (35).[7]

We cannot know with certainty when Eliot decided that his use of myth in *The Waste Land* was no longer a viable aesthetic practice. It probably coincided with the crisis in his personal life in 1923 (Gordon, *Early Years* 123–25) and with the influence, perhaps, of William Force Stead, who placed in Eliot's hand the sermons of Lancelot Andrewes in that year (Gordon, *Early Years* 125).[8] In any case, it was in the five-year period between the publication of the famous *Dial* review on the 'mythic method' of Joyce's *Ulysses* (1923) and the publication of *For Lancelot Andrewes* (1928) that Eliot committed himself to Anglo-Catholicism and to the institution of the Church of England. It was a quixotic step and it took everyone, everyone who knew Eliot as a public reputation at least, by surprise. But it made sense in terms of social mobility, because it was so disarming a gesture when respectability and social acceptance were the goals.

It also made sense intellectually. The visible Church gave him a thoroughly historical social locus which neither the notion of myth nor the dehistoricized Hegel of Bradleyan idealism contained (Eagleton, *Criticism and Ideology* 150–51). Yet the Church, also, offered a transcendental signified that raises the Church's spiritual and cultural significance beyond mere contingency: it is both of the world and not of the world in a way that can adequately illuminate the relation of the historical *and* transcendental in a single visible unity. Neither the Bradleyan 'felt whole in which there are moments of knowledge' (Eliot, *Knowledge and Experience* 155) nor a mythological framework could work with the same social efficiency and authority. Later, Eliot was to conceive of the 'man of letters' in similarly paradoxical terms: he is both the product of history, and yet at the same time is able to negate that set of conditions which has produced him. As Michael North has put it, 'The man of letters can take the "longer view" because he is both in and out of society . . .' at the same time (*Political Aesthetic* 111).

To the historical and spiritual synthesis that the institution of the Church and its body of doctrine represented for Eliot, we must also add an aesthetic element. Eliot's was certainly not a puritanical Anglicanism; he was converted to the Anglo-Catholic tendency of the Church of England. On the second page of *For Lancelot Andrewes*, the volume in which his new allegiances were announced, and trenchantly defended, we find the Church under Elizabeth described in terms of a beautifully constructed *objet d'art*, 'a masterpiece of ecclesiastical statesmanship' that

reflects the 'finest spirit' of Tudor England (12). He identifies this spirit as
the foundation of the Tudor state, embodied most flawlessly in the figure
of the Queen herself. Her intuition, her intellect, her poise made her
politically invincible, and gave to the whole Tudor polity an equilibrium
that was only disturbed by the alien vexations of the subsequent reigns.

In these opening pages, the Church is presented metonymically; in it
we are asked to see reflected the whole of late Tudor culture. Eliot's
description finely captures the connoisseur's avidity in the presence of
astonishing beauty, but pulls back from mere aestheticism by the concrete polemical purpose which it serves. This purpose can be summarized in a few words: the parenthetical aside to 'other religious impulses'
that asserted 'themselves with [great] vehemence during the next two
reigns' (12) and which eventually led to the disfigurement of the
Elizabethan 'masterpiece' are not mentioned solely in the interests of
historical fidelity and completeness. Later in the volume Eliot aggressively attacks those narrowing tendencies in English cultural history that
led to the isolation of the Church from European Latinity, and the
Protestant sectarianism that conspired, either wittingly or unwittingly, to
deface the Church as the 'masterpiece' he claims it was in late Tudor
times.[9]

The England Eliot loved is plainly told in the opening pages of *For
Lancelot Andrewes*, the third section of the opening movement of 'East
Coker' and the whole of 'Little Gidding'; it is this aetherial, Cavalier text
of England that he took in. What he loved was a mixture of the real and
the possible, a brilliant, responsive, but peculiarly domesticated civilization, anchored in faith to its central, generative institution, the National
Church, a civilization rising, not in ostentatious Baroque opulence, but
closely knit in a finely sensible common culture, rooted in Latinity, rising
on the banks of the Thames, and, through the clear-voiced agency of an
independent, but obedient intelligentsia, radiating to every parish in the
realm the imperatives of an achieved authority. The utopian vision was
ravishing, but it resembled too closely the visions of Don Quixote to be
of much use in an England where most castles had already become inns
and no amount of strenuously ironic polemic could turn them back into
castles.

When we put back Eliot's text of Elizabethan England in the time in
which it was composed, we notice it was the period – the 1920s – when
revisionist historians like R. H. Tawney were having their first great
impact, not only on the study of history, but on the popular conception
of historical periods. Tawney's own revolutionary study of the Tudor

epoch, *The Agrarian Problem in the Sixteenth Century*, although published in 1912, was read widely in the 1920s for the first time, as a consequence perhaps of the impact which his *Religion and the Rise of Capitalism* had when it appeared in 1926 and of Tawney's own visibility as an adviser on educational matters to the Ramsay MacDonald government, before the General Strike.[10]

One of Tawney's principal contributions to this reassessment was to purge historical thinking in England of its essentialist and idealist orientation, and instead look more to political economy, to the infrastructural processes and contradictions of society. In the mutations of dominant and subordinate modes of production and the material relations which they determine, Elizabethan and Stuart society hardly offered to Tawney the aesthetically pleasing and settled prospect Eliot chose to find.

Eliot was certainly not alone in reading English Renaissance history as an achieved serenity, only to be disturbed later by some ill-bred malcontents (the 'little upstarts', *FLA* 29). By opening *For Lancelot Andrewes* with a vision of the Elizabethan church and society in calm equilibrium, he knowingly aligns himself with an essentially conservative historiography. Keith Feiling's *History of the Tory Party, 1640–1714* (1924) speaks of the Tudor period in exactly the same metaphors of balance and equilibrium. His book provides a typical account of the time from this ideological perspective. The parallel visions are not surprising. Eliot, in his account of the Elizabethan church (and by extension Elizabethan society) in Andrewes' time, simply puts, in more elegantly incisive sentences, precisely the same Tory narrative of the past. Feiling's evocation of the 'satisfied glory of Elizabeth's reign' (43) ought to remind us of Eliot's characterization of the Anglican church in her time. Feiling's attentiveness to the order and balance of Elizabeth's reign as arising 'from the fact that all [the] great influences – chivalry and a semi-medieval monarchy, mythology and the classics, Protestantism and the new learning – were for a brief halcyon season in equilibrium' (43) is echoed by Eliot all through the positive avowals of *For Lancelot Andrewes*. Even Eliot's commendation of Andrewes' prose style can be applied, with the apt substitition of terms, to the composedness of the Elizabethan State: 'In this extraordinary prose, which appears to repeat, to stand still, but is nevertheless proceeding in the most deliberate and orderly manner, there are often flashing phrases which never desert the memory' (*FLA* 22). There were many men and phrases 'seizing the attention and impressing the memory' in Elizabeth's time. This vision of the

past was not restricted, incidentally, to the learned, but was the interpretative norm of the whole Tory press, from *The Times* to *The Daily Mail*.
British nationalism, asserting itself against the internationalist inclinations of liberal and leftist thought, required it. Eliot's historical sensibility
was even more fully in tune with Tory historiography than the above
might suggest. The following passage not only reminds us of Eliot in the
1920s, but ought also to remind us of the first movement of 'East Coker'
in the 1940s.

Round the village church still gathered the immemorial habits of the common
people. Sir Thomas Overbury's Franklin 'allows of honest pastime, and thinks
not the bones of the dead anything bruised or the worse for it, though the
country lasses dance in the churchyard after evensong: Rock Monday and the
Wake in summer, shrivings, the wakeful catches on Christmas eve, the Hokday
or Seed-cake – these he yearly keeps, yet holds them no relics of Popery'.
Edward VI's Injunctions had bidden the clergy teach their people that they
might in harvest-time work on holy days, to 'save that thing which God hath
sent', and the Catholic Sunday as opposed to the Jewish Sabbath was one mark
of the Churchman. The parish of Bishop's Canning in Wiltshire, which 'could
have challenged all England for music, ringing, and football play', could also,
led by its parson, produce a masque for Anne of Denmark; respectable
Gloucestershire squires would dance every Sunday 'at the Church-house': the
pipe and tabor, maypole and morris-dance, Twelfth-night, mummings and
Whitsun ales, processions and 'mothering-Sunday' – these were some of the old
customs which saintly George Herbert approved . . . No explanation of the
Restoration, no reading even of Queen Anne's reign, would be adequate that
did not take into account the immensely conservative power of this body of
ancient moralities, built into a people still predominantly made up of villagers
and yeomen. (Feiling 43–44)

There was much to approve in this pastoral, timeless world in which civil
harmony was maintained without explicit constitutional exertions (cf.
Ellis, *The English Eliot* 84). But, from the perspective of Tawney and his
students, it was in large part a nostalgic fiction, a rewriting of the past in
idealized terms in order to base the claims of political Toryism in the
1920s on what was always described as the natural conservatism of the
English people in general.

It was to permit the richer play of these deeper allegiances in the
common people that Eliot went out of his way to name the impulses in
contemporary British culture which obscured them: 'the *British Banner*,
Judge Edmonds, Newman Weeks, Deborah Butler, Elderess Polly,
Brother Noyes, Mr. Murphy, the Licensed Victuallers and the
Commercial Travellers' (*FLA* 59), and to attack the debased romantic

inwardness which promoted in the swinish masses a kind of destructive narcissism, but called it humanism: 'The possessors of the inner voice ride ten in a compartment to a football match in Swansea, listening to the inner voice, which breathes the eternal message of vanity, fear, and lust' (*SE* 16). Not only is the political message of such sentiments clear enough, but it is also clear that Eliot (as a newly minted Englishman) knew very little about the culture of industrial Britain, notwithstanding the pub fragment of *The Waste Land* and the Marie Lloyd essay, both evidence of little more than upper-middle-class paternalism. The inadvertent contradiction between the communalism of 'ten in a compartment' and the implied individualism of 'the inner voice' marks one of the many limits of his understanding of his adopted country. His knowledge of English working-class culture had not improved much sixteen years later when he came to write inanities about the industrial proletariat as an alienated and hypnotized 'mob' in *The Idea of a Christian Society* (21) and to assert, quixotically, in April 1938 that 'the real and spontaneous country life . . . is the right life for the great majority in any nation' (*Criterion* 483). These polemics define the political skirmishing lines between conservative and left-liberal versions of the past in the 1920s.

Which representation is correct is not my concern here. What is important is that Eliot's radiant vision of the Tudor Church and, by extension, of Tudor society appears at precisely the moment when revisionist historians, like Tawney, are bringing to light not a static, comfortably poised, imperturbable civilization, but a dynamic, untidy, materially and ideologically divided one. What this insurgent and assertive historical materialism tends to do to a conception like Eliot's, one dealing in essences and ideal forms, is switch a bright light on the way such a conception represents the cohesion of the system it totalizes. In other words, it illuminates the logic by which the society's critical elements and levels are connected. What is it that keeps a static society, such as the Elizabethan is presented as being, unified, coherent, and complete? Clearly the answer Eliot and a host of largely Tory historians and thinkers have traditionally given in England is a socio-ethical one – loyalty to, obedience and trust in the paternalistic authoritarianism which a governing elite practises in the context of a scrupulously divided and ranked hierarchical society (O'Sullivan, *Conservatism* 82–118; Nairn, 'Literary Intelligentsia' 57–83, especially 78–79; Boutwood, *National Revival* 38–80).

Mutual and absolute trust, actualized in practice in an intuitive social network of intermediate loyalties encompassed by the larger, public rituals of fealty (people to monarch, monarch to God) naturalizes authority and the efficacy of the divisions and ranks of society. This efficacy is established by a divinely supported confidence that social divisions and ranks conform, without exception, to the rule of Reason and to an essentially incontestable notion of Nature. That Eliot seriously believed that such a community could be nourished again on the banks of the Thames in the face of a modern England that was decisively set on a radically different course is a quixoticism so profound, and moving, that it must be taken as the sign of a love for late Tudor culture as deep, as passionate as Alfonso Quixana's love for the radiant world he found in the chivalric romances on which he gorged his mind, his feelings, and his speech (cf. Ackroyd, *T. S. Eliot* 166).

This naive, quixotic note is new in the 1920s and sharply contrasts the worldly knowingness of the neurasthenic dandy who has wearily seen through everything. In *The Waste Land* period, the tonal contrast to the dandy was heard in the 'thunder' of mythic consciousness and its prophetic-visionary forms of expression. However, this contrast – dandy/visionary – was constructed within the framework of a particular bohemian expressive style adapted to certain practical demands, principally the uncompromising disruption of the humanist text of inwardness in a particular historical moment.

That moment, and its stylistic requirements, had passed by 1928. In *For Lancelot Andrewes*, there are new commitments and allegiances that go well beyond the naming of his 'general point of view . . . as classicist in literature, royalist in politics, and Anglo-Catholic in religion', in the preface. As is evident from what follows in the preface, Eliot was very aware of the impression such a profession could make on a sceptical audience he had helped accustom to irony and the placing pauses of the eloquent unsaid: 'I am quite aware that the first term is completely vague, and easily lends itself to clap-trap; I am aware that the second term is at present without definition, and easily lends itself to what is almost worse than clap-trap, I mean temperate conservatism; the third term does not rest with me to define' (7). Having taught his generation how to juxtapose the hollowness of the conventional humanist and the pieties of liberalism against the cacophonies of the present, Eliot now opens himself to the gibe of irrelevance. His agile qualifications, with their edge of bad-tempered exasperation directed at readers tuned to hearing the inevitable false note in all professions of sincerity, acknowledge the risk of appearing ridiculous. After all, as the author of 'The Hippopotamus' (*CP* 51–52), he had already struck a hilarious flat note in his generation's attitudes towards the very Church he now said he sincerely embraced.[11] The question of his sincerity in these avowals was as evident to him as it was to the startled expectations of his original readers. The occasionally cranky and rudely aggressive outbursts in the prose of the 1920s and 1930s, a measurable change from the controlled ironies of the early literary criticism, suggest a new defensiveness.[12] His satiric, gibing voice fell short of mastering the imperatives of his new allegiances. It consequently withdrew from the poetry permanently and by *Ash-Wednesday* it was no longer audible.

C. H. Sisson reads this change of tone as 'crucial for Eliot's subsequent development' (*English Poetry* 142), identifying the 'moral duty to be ironical' as the element which has now been 'subtracted' from the early poetry. The subtraction, he writes, leaves a difficult interpretative sum for the critic to calculate. It involves the reckoning of a believer's integrity in acceptance of the Christian faith, and the value of this acceptance we cannot really know anything about. Instead, the 'question for the critic is whether we have in *Ash-Wednesday* an expression of belief that carries us with it.' The new rhythm and tension of *Ash-Wednesday* probably cannot carry us with its expression of belief, because the poem is too unsure of its own figurative footing, is too much an attempt to find a new aesthetic equilibrium before the ungainly fact of the public profession of religious belief, is too audibly listening to its own candour and its new approach to the common intuitive life, which now, as opposed to 1922, has Eliot's own previous reputation lying awkwardly across it. He finally achieves this new poise in 1935 in 'Burnt Norton'. However, *Ash-Wednesday* is another matter.

First of all, it stammers.

> Because I do not hope to turn again
> Because I do not hope
> Because I do not hope to turn (*CP* 95)

It is not exactly clear what Eliot hopes to convey by this procedure; if it simply enacts in the manner the matter of the opening line, it is a rhetorical mannerism well below the demonstrated capacities of his technical skill. But in this new context, where only the purest simplicity will sustain the poem's professions, such a device is perhaps not inapt. Indeed the suggestion of a suspended or defeated floridness, a rebuke to both the smart glibness of the sceptical cosmopolite of the 1920s and the yawning rotundities of Victorian devotional style, seems particularly appropriate in the context of a resurrected passion and vitality. The marks of this simplicity are everywhere in the poem – in the narrowing, for example, of vocabulary to the small words with the greatest resonance: love, goodness, honour, brightness, hope. There is also a significant narrowing in the learning the poem wears. Its range of reference is drawn from the common texts of his new allegiance: Shakespeare's sonnets, *The Book of Common Prayer*, the *Hymnal*, the language of the Thirty-Nine Articles, the *The Anglo-Catholic Prayer Book*, the Cavalier devotional tradition, and, of course, on the horizon, the master texts of Dante. The direct, sinewy, anti-figurative presentational simplicity of imagism is also turned to a new purpose in the composing of this new rhythm and tone (cf. Gardner, *T. S. Eliot* 102; Kenner, *Invisible* 229–30). Gone also is the social ventriloquism and the feeling we have in his early poems that he spent a lot of time listening to the conversations in the next room.

We might apply to Eliot's style after his conversion what Erich Auerbach wrote of Augustine's after his. Auerbach's remarks about Augustine include his classic formulation of the effect of Christianity on the discursive practices of antiquity. Christ had not appeared to mankind as a king, hero, or rhetorician, but 'as a human being of the lowest station'.

Nevertheless, all that he did and said was of the highest and deepest dignity, more significant than anything else in the world. The style in which it was presented possessed little if any rhetorical culture in the antique sense; it was *sermo piscatorius* and yet it was extremely moving and much more impressive than the most sublime rhetorico-tragical literary work. (*Mimesis* 72)

Augustine 'may well have been the first to become conscious of the problem of the stylistic contrast between the two worlds' (72–73) and accommodated his own impressive periodicity, acquired in the best rhetorical tradition, to the requirements of his new spiritual commitments.[13] *Ash-Wednesday* may stammer, but the stammering is the music of an unassailable candour.

This style illustrates also the wry disclaimer of Montaigne's about his own work, that, in his *Essayes*, he was trying to make a book without affectation, 'genuine, simple and ordinarie' (Florio, *Essayes of Michael Lord of Montaigne* xxvii). As a matter of rhetorical planning, an opulent, recondite, artful presentation of the inescapably direct truths of human existence runs dead against the spirit of their simplicity. Eliot was as conscious of the need to avoid the appearance of 'contention, art or study' in order to recommend Christian truths in an age of elaborate liberal-humanist claptrap, as Montaigne had been in exposing, with his sober humanism, as a mere matter of tinsel and paste the verbal and emotional profusiveness of Counter-Reformation Catholicism. Apart from the well-known literary references and allusions (like the Cavalcanti and the Shakespeare echoes with which the poem opens), I would agree with David Moody that 'Eliot's critical consciousness of the literary tradition is not prominent in [much] of the sequence' (*Poet* 138). The presence of Dante though is indisputable. Moody has put it well, '[Dante's] presence is all pervasive, and operates at all levels. He is behind the opening allusion to Cavalcanti, as the implicit master of love poetry. There are everywhere specific images, phrases and effects borrowed from him; at certain moments a feeling of the *terza rima* informs the verse; and the separate poems appear to be modelled more nearly upon the sonnets and canzone of the *Vita Nuova* than upon the Catholic liturgy or anything else I can think of' (139). One can excuse the impressionistic woolliness of this by saying that one knows what Moody is talking about here. Eliot felt close to Dante all through his career as a poet and critic, but it was in the sensitive years surrounding the conversion proper that Dante meant more to him than words could say.

Eliot's general intellectual and emotional debt to Dante, and his reliance on the Christian experiences of penitence and resurrection in the theology of the poem, have all been well studied as the foundations of both a new sense of poetics and a personal faith (Gardner, *T. S. Eliot* 113–14, 126). What I would like to attempt is to situate the poem's verbal style within social discourse. First impressions suggest that such an approach to an essentially private poem, a poem of private devotion and confession, will yield next to nothing of value. I think this is a blinkered view.

Private devotional discourse is as thoroughly social as a sermon delivered from the pulpit to a congregation of churchgoers. For one thing, the poem constructs from its materials a concrete subjectivity, which can be located in the contemporary history of the subject. The fact that the subject is construed here with an eye on the devotional style of a seventeenth century divine does not make the poem less social in our time, but more so. It would not have escaped Eliot's notice that the manner and matter of the poem he was writing, irrespective of his own personal struggles, would have perplexed most of his readers in 1930. It would not have escaped his notice that the style of *Ash-Wednesday* would have entered social discourse at a slant, a style that readers, shaped by the dominant secularist culture, would have most probably considered unimportant, innocuous, or irrelevant, once they had realized that none

of this was meant to be taken ironically. Eliot's awareness of this situation is discernible in the alternating defensiveness and aggression of *For
Lancelot Andrewes* and later of *After Strange Gods*, and, of course, the perplexity of some readers was recorded in many of the reviews of the
poem.

The poem also represents a new twist in a stylistic mannerism that
would have been familiar in a different form to Eliot's earlier readers. In
his early poetry, Eliot begins to subvert the traditional sense of mastery
which the master poet, since the Renaissance at least, is meant to possess.
The deployment of the perverse dialectic of mastery and incompetence
is a deliberate strategy in all of Eliot's poetry. Of course, it changes its
character as his work develops thematically. In the early poetry it
appears in the monologues as an aspect of the persona's submission to
paralysis. For example, there is Prufrock's incompetence in finding a
stable ego, and thus the springs of action, or the speaker's 'self-posses-
sion' guttering 'in the dark' in 'Portrait of a Lady' (*CP* 21) or the horrified
male 'I' in 'Hysteria' hoping to concentrate his 'attention with careful
subtlety' to the task of stopping 'the shaking . . . breasts' of his female
companion at tea and, thus, collecting 'some of the fragments of the
afternoon' (34), or the more famous 'fragments' that conclude *The Waste
Land* (79), and the matter of the 'Notes' to that poem which silently jeer at
readers whose competence in recognizing their own cultural inheritance
is called mockingly into question, make the theme dominant in the early
poetry. But, one should add that with *The Waste Land* the situation begins
to change.

The poem itself begins to enact stylistically the incompetence which
the earlier poetry deflects into the psychic conduct of specific monologu-
ists. In *The Waste Land*, Eliot plays a kind of peek-a-boo game with his
reader, in which he not only speaks about breakdown as theme, but
enacts it in the texture of the verse. This is both a technical refinement
and also, more importantly, a calculated gesture of authenticity.
Prospero is the model here (not surprisingly for a poem which engages
more than once with *The Tempest*), but the magus's relinquishing of his
power is primarily an ethical act at the conclusion of the play, whereas
the verse ruin at the end of *The Waste Land*, which aims at psychological
truth, achieves instead the thorough inauthenticity of the psychological
manipulator. One of the reasons for Eliot's debunking comments about
the poem later in his life, I believe, comes from his own recognition of the
game he was playing there. The stammering at the beginning of *Ash-
Wednesday* redeems the dialectic and brings it to its final and most impor-

tant stage, the master poet's public display of renunciation of his mastery, embodied as a new style for expressing in the public sphere the need for personal salvation, aiming at a surrender that is unassailable.

Ash-Wednesday finds its way into social discourse in other ways as well. Eliot uses the strategy of appropriation of an unfamiliar style to confront both the secular humanist unbeliever and the conventional Anglican among his readers. After all, the verbal style of *Ash-Wednesday* is pastiche. The intent may not be satirical or ironic, but the adoption of some of the verbal mannerisms of Lancelot Andrewes (the use of certain rhetorical figures like ploce and polyptoton for example) constructs a stylistic artifice that is, first of all, foreign enough, yet possessing an impeccable English pedigree, not only to take us by surprise, but to admonish us as well.

> As I am forgotten
> And would be forgotten, so I would forget
> Thus devoted, concentrated in purpose. (*CP* 97)

Eliot's comments on Andrewes's 'extraordinary prose' in the title essay of *For Lancelot Andrewes* describes uncannily the making of the pastiche in *Ash-Wednesday*.

Andrewes takes a word and derives the world from it; squeezing and squeezing the word until it yields a full juice of meaning which we should never have supposed the word to possess. In this process the qualities which we have mentioned, of ordonnance and precision are exercised. (*FLA* 20)

And so section V of *Ash-Wednesday*:

> If the word is lost, if the spent word is spent
> If the unheard, unspoken
> Word is unspoken, unheard;
> Still is the unspoken word, the Word unheard,
> The Word without a word, the Word within
> The world and for the world . . .   (*CP* 102)

The foreignness of this procedure on twentieth-century ears also enacts the *Verfremdung* (estrangement) necessary to awaken those sensibilities sedated by the anaesthesia of modern prose in decline:

To persons whose minds are habituated to feed on the vague jargon of our time, when we have a vocabulary for everything and exact ideas about nothing – when a word half-understood, torn from its place in some alien or half-formed science, as of psychology, conceals from both writer and reader the utter meaninglessness of a statement . . . Andrewes may seem pedantic and verbal. (*FLA* 19)

He may seem so, but he isn't, *and* he is the product of a thoroughly English development, holding 'a place second to none in the history of the formation of the English Church' (*FLA* 26).

The presence of Andrewes in the poem can be heard also in the pragmatics of rhythmic variation. The use of the line break for essentially rhythmic purposes suggests a further technical refinement in the writing of free verse which Eliot has learned from the rhythmic effects of Andrewes' punctuation, although the verse precedent for this accumulative style of presentation, minus the conceptual lucidity, 'the ordonnance and precision', of Andrewes, is Walt Whitman. Eliot's further comments about the rhythm of Andrewes' prose casts a good deal of light on the technical vehicle of the poem. First, Eliot on Andrewes' fine mastery of sentence length:

And then, after this succession of short sentences – no one is more master of the short sentence than Andrewes – in which the effort is to find the exact meaning and make that meaning live, he slightly but sufficiently alters the rhythm in proceeding at large . . . (*FLA* 21)

And, again, the short sentences concluding the poem's second movement:

> This is the land which ye
> Shall divide by lot. And neither division nor unity
> Matters. This is the land. We have our inheritance.

With section III Eliot proceeds 'at large', altering the rhythm.

Not only the carriage of the verse in *Ash-Wednesday*, but also the imagery contributes to the making of the pastiche. Eliot was struck from the start by Andrewes' use of images in an essentially non-figurative style. Andrewes carefully rations them out, so that when they appear in the sermons, they carry an extraordinary imaginative charge. Eliot is immensely impressed by the discipline of restraint – as opposed to Donne's 'wantonness' (*FLA* 26) – which Andrewes demonstrates.

Phrases such as 'Christ is no wild-cat. What talk ye of twelve days?'. . . do not desert us; nor do the sentences in which, before extracting all the spiritual meaning of a text, Andrewes forces a concrete presence upon us. (*FLA* 22)

and again, about Christ's birth, Eliot quotes a passage at length, '. . . How born, how entertained? In a stately palace, cradle of ivory, robes of estate? No; but a stable for His palace, a manger for His cradle, poor clouts for His array' (quoted in *FLA* 23). It is those 'poor clouts' which press a concrete presence upon us. In this procedure Eliot glimpsed a method by which the concrete immediacy of the image as practiced in the period of imagist anthologies could be turned to effect for a new rhetorical occasion. The accumulative verbal structure of the Andrewes sermon concentrates and steadies the reader for the decisive arrival of the image which fixes the attention on some definite object, 'Christ is no wild-cat'.

> White light folded, sheathed about her, folded.
> The new years walk, restoring
> Through a bright cloud of tears, the years, restoring
> With a new verse the ancient rhyme. Redeem
> The time. Redeem
> The unread vision in the higher dream
> While jewelled unicorns draw by the gilded hearse. (*CP* 100)

Admittedly, Andrewes would have resisted the opulence of the final image, but in Eliot's poem we are dealing with pastiche, so that the informing sensibility cannot always unerringly stop its ears to the siren song of excess.

The implicit assumption that writing of the greatest value culminates in the achievement of 'concrete presence' both links Eliot to the London modernism of his earlier poetry and to the ontological dilemma which European metaphysics, a metaphysics of presence, has confronted all through the twentieth century. Of course adherence to Christian metaphysics banishes the philosophical post-Nietzschean nihilism with which all speculative Western philososphy has grappled in our time. Modernist aesthetics is predicated on the efficacy of the image as an ontological anchor in a symbolic order that increasingly came to be thought of as separated from the ground of being in Nature. Imagism is the shorthand ontology of verse practitioners, not philosophers. Eliot's reading of Andrewes reveals how that assumption of literary value is transposed by Eliot from the secularist ontology of modernism to the new ontology of the Christian convert. The comfort of belief in the twentieth century lies precisely in believing that the ontological link between the symbolic order and things cannot be broken.

There is another, more curious, way in which *Ash-Wednesday* occupies a place in social discourse. The poem enters a socio-historical context in the 1930s which Eliot understood to be inimical to such professions. 'Thoughts after Lambeth' (1931) makes this plain enough, the peroration especially so:

The World is trying the experiment of attempting to form a civilized but non-Christian mentality. The experiment will fail; but we must be very patient in awaiting its collapse; meanwhile redeeming the time: so that the Faith may be preserved alive through the dark ages before us; to renew and rebuild civilization, and save the World from suicide. (*SE* 342)

The poem must steel itself to the probability that it will lose many readers the further they go into it. The reader, schooled by a moderate Christianity and a secular culture, and, to complicate matters, schooled also by Eliot's earlier work, will not normally accept that such 'an expression of belief', to quote Sisson again, can 'carr[y] us with it'. The poem loses both the unbeliever and the Broad-Church Anglican who finds the Anglo-Catholicism distasteful and suspect. They may read to the end, but both kinds of reader will grow more alienated from the poem, the more openly the poem prostrates itself before the strange God of the ardent Anglo-Catholic.

The poem is unbending in its avowals; it even makes aesthetic appreciation difficult. The nearness of the believer – 'And let my cry come unto Thee' (*CP* 105) – cancels the distance in which an aesthetic response might take shape. This strategy of deliberate alienation, of pushing away the sceptically minded, was a necessary step for Eliot in establishing his seriousness and his sincerity. But it creates a problem. Even those who might be sympathetic, but are not yet desperate enough for assent, might want to linger with the poem on other levels before they are willing to let the essential message carry them with it. For Eliot the problem is one of establishing priorities. His own inner struggles take precedence; the problem of making a poem that might carry others with it, especially the less sanguine, is put to the side as Eliot establishes his new style of presentation in verse practice and in the remaking of himself as an historical subject.

It is this problem which *Four Quartets* will not have to face. First of all the socio-historical situation will change. The collapse of Europe in the late 1930s and 1940s will not only bring about a general political crisis, it will also devastate the spirit, and particularly the spirit of the mandarinate – the intelligentsia and the higher officials – who act as the intelligence and conscience of the directive elites in the governance of society. The humanist and utilitarian norms by which the mandarinate participates in managing secular society will be vanquished not by arguments pro or con the perfectibility of Man or the primacy of Reason, but by the death factories at Auschwitz and Sobibor, by the mad science of Josef Mengele, by the incineration of Dresden, and by the zero degree of nihilism we will glimpse in the mushroom cloud over Hiroshima. The 'dark ages' will have arrived with a vengeance. But humanism, as the intellectual and moral steering mechanism of civil society, did not die in the ovens with a million Jews, it had died earlier. It had died even earlier than the thousands of corpses on the banks of the Somme in 1915–16, although there its death was undeniable to anyone who had eyes to see. The modernists understood the new position of Man in the 'contrived corridors', the 'wilderness of mirrors' (*CP* 40, 41) at Versailles. 'Gerontion' ought to be our guide in these new latitudes of the human prospect. By 1945, 'To lose beauty in terror, terror in inquisition' (*CP* 41) was no longer a neatly turned anadiplosis which provided nihilist *frissons* for a mandarinate that had not yet caught up emotionally to the devastation. The meaning of a phrase like 'terror in inquisition' came to mean something rather new for the human spirit in the era of the Gestapo and the NKVD. *Four Quartets* spoke about the spirit in the midst of this new crisis and, not surprisingly, there were many readers who would not only allow the poem to carry them with it, but who also hungered for it. *Four Quartets* also solved the *Ash-Wednesday* problem of the alienated reader in another way. By 1940 Eliot had put something like fifteen years as a serious Christian behind him; he had learned in 1931 that 'we must be very patient . . . so that the Faith may be preserved alive' until that conjunction of history when the people *must*, will *want* to, listen. Moreover, he no longer had to deal with the 'bad boy' persona of the revolutionary, avant-gardist author of *The Waste Land*.

By 1940 he was comfortably settled in the very heart of British society, enjoying all the privileges which the obedient servant of power – the mandarin – can enjoy in a stable, well-policed, class-divided society. *Four Quartets* reflects in its manner the comfort, even serenity, of not only the man who has arrived, but of the man who has been there for a while. So, the poem can provide some aesthetic space for the sceptical, even though its professions of faith and belief have only deepened and been extended since the time of *Ash-Wednesday*. In fact, the poem can take on board the whole question of aesthetics, even the whole issue of aestheticism, as a principal theme and examine it in relation to the spiritual life without the anxiety and guilt we sense in *Ash-Wednesday* whenever the believer gets too close to the distractions of art:

> The broadbacked figure drest in blue and green
> Enchanted the maytime with an antique flute.
> Blown hair is sweet, brown hair over the mouth blown,
> Lilac and brown hair;
> Distraction, music of the flute, stops and steps of the mind over the
>   third stair,

Fading, fading; strength beyond hope and despair
Climbing the third stair.

Lord, I am not worthy   (*CP* 99)

In this matter of feeling 'comfortable', I am not talking about the immediate comfort of Eliot's domestic arrangements at Shamley Green in Surrey during the war (Gordon, *New Life* 122) where he wrote the last two quartets, but the psychological comfort that comes from final arrival in society and the social acceptance that accompanies it.

He had carefully felt his way into English society, well up in the hierarchy, though Lyndall Gordon tries to suggest that what gratified Eliot most was his acceptance among 'groups of ordinary people' (136). But 'ordinary' here means people like 'retired Indian majors' (136) and, at Shamley Green, the rather well off family of an English novelist, which included 'the nightly ventures' of one member of the household who had to go after her pekinese 'who took to chasing rabbits by moonlight' and 'where conversation centred on the importance of the vet (who was constantly needed for the over-fed dogs)' (Gordon, *New Life* 122). As 'the prize domestic pet amongst the old ladies' of 'Shambles', Eliot lived through 'the shared danger' of the Battle of Britain and the Blitz. It seems that like everything else in a society constructed around power and privilege, the distribution of the privations of war tend to be as unequal as the distribution of goods and services. By the feeling of comfort in *Four Quartets*, then, I mean a quality of the style of the poem, a quality missing from *Ash-Wednesday*.

In terms of literary history, *Ash-Wednesday* represents an important mutation in another sense, especially in the composition of a poetic voice. It acknowledges Eliot's stylistic commitment to the 'classicizing' tradition of High Modernism and to the centrality of music as the telling metaphor of the highest form of aesthetic cognition available to the mature, European artist. By this I mean that he more clearly adopts and develops the approaches of Baudelaire and Mallarmé to the question of poetic language. Their concern to make a literary, and 'purified' dialect comes to preoccupy Eliot after *Ash-Wednesday*, but in a different way from his two mentors. Eliot's 'dialect' carries with it a firm grasp of the connection between writing and society. He works towards a dialect which neither dissolves utterly in the many social voices of everyday life, nor exhibits that degree of artificiality and distance from the everyday we hear so palpably in the poetic diction of the lesser Augustans.

The stripping away of romantic poetic diction which exercised him in his early work led to the polemical use of social voices. Eliot did not intend to develop a naive aesthetics of the common tongue, that is, to develop a poetic language which makes exclusive use of social voices and the discursive practices of everyday life. In other words, he was no William Carlos Williams. His use of such language was always in the service of a particular social and cultural critique. The small lyrical passages in *The Waste Land* tentatively restrain the poem from its own social ventriloquism and the drift to the musical use of the many sound-shapes of actual speech. There is a Low Modernist tradition, however, which has, in fact, taken that course; its point of departure lies in the verbal practices of Arthur Rimbaud. It has culminated in our time in the work of American poets like Frank O'Hara at one end, and the 'talk' poems of the Beats or of David Antin at the other.[14]

With *Ash-Wednesday* and its acclimatization of the lyrical voice of *The Waste Land* to the dictions and tonalities of Christian scripturality, Eliot moves decisively to the High Modernist tradition. His theoretical and practical efforts in this direction are well known. His recurring interest in the definition of the 'classic' and 'the music of poetry', for example, are really explorations of the possibility of coining a poetic language that has the colloquial suppleness of the everyday, projecting a voice that is not narrowly the voice of a single class, and yet a language formal enough that it achieves an authentic, and 'high' seriousness (Kenner, *Invisible* 229; but see Condon *Classical Norm* 176–178 and Kwan-Terry, 'Ash Wednesday' 159). Some have argued that Eliot won through to just such a 'purified dialect' in *Four Quartets*.[15] By this term Eliot does not mean something like the making of a *poésie pure*, but something approaching the primary refinement of a classic work or a classic literature. By the term 'classic', he came to mean in 1944 a literature and culture distinguished by maturity. Stable and rooted in the past, a classic culture, he writes, is not limited to a barren chronicle of documents, people, and events. Instead he speaks of its development as an essentially unconscious history of verbal refinement, a splendid 'progress of language' realizing to the full, in countless small acts of discernment, all its possible aptitudes (*OPP* 55–56).

But maturity is only half the story. Eliot means a maturity which culminates in what he calls 'a common style'. By this he did not mean that in a classic period all writers are the same. Differences are not fewer, they 'are more subtle and refined' (57). These distinctions, then, define 'a community of taste', rather than a flavourless conformity. '[T]he age in which we find a common style', he continues, recalling in his choice of words his earlier vision of the Elizabethan masterpiece, 'will be an age when society has achieved a moment of order and stability, of equilibrium and harmony.' Periods which manifest extremes of style, on the other hand, will simply parade their childishness and decline into senility. The testing of these possibilities, the making of such a 'classic' dialect, in which the personal, the communal, and the sacred are perfectly balanced, begins in earnest with *Ash-Wednesday*.

The practical accommodation, his own small acts of discernment, of new religious commitments in *Ash-Wednesday* is very striking. Eliot draws widely on the corporate or common style of the Christian account of religious experience. The alteration of diction, syntax, and rhythm through the pull of the discursive practices of the English Church, and of Lancelot Andrewes, is, of course, not simply a stylistic choice. If it is to count as more than one more extreme of 'manner', it must work as the sign, he would say, of obedience and conformity to a higher Reason. The texts of the Church contain the essential wisdom which the Church has to offer, but they are not simply that wisdom distilled to the lowest common denominator; they are not 'provincial' (*OPP* 69). The simplicity of their presentation is as much a mark of their authority as is their profundity (cf. Kenner, *Invisible* 227). The characterizing rhythms, tonalities, and formulary phrases of *The Book of Common Prayer* or the Jacobean Bible or the Creeds embody more than a set of beliefs; they vivify a whole way of life and express its 'finest spirit'. An individual lyric voice, within the compass of this all-embracing cosmos institutionally settled in the doctrines and formulas of an historical confession, no longer needs an anthropological-mythic framework in order to legitimate its speech. *Ash-Wednesday* accepts, conforms to, the discipline of an ecclesiastically established spirituality as sufficient legitimation of the lyric voice, now no longer in need of defining its authenticity by the semantics of its distance from an institutional order contaminated by liberal-humanist ideas.

As several commentators have noted, the poem enacts the conversion process itself; that is, it enacts the convert's metaphorical 'death' to one way of life and his 'rebirth' in the new (Gardner, *T. S. Eliot* 113–121; Unger, *Moments and Patterns* 53). This includes, of course, the death of a certain kind of poetry ('[bear] / Away the fiddles and the flutes' [100]) and the birth of some new kind (parts IV and V). This rebirth requires also a new voice to express it. For Eliot this voice was not an easy invention, simply because it did not sound itself in a private silence. By the late 1920s, Eliot was already a celebrity, a public man of some stature. So the invention of a new voice occurred in both the private sphere, as he moved haltingly towards the subjective and verbal disciplines of belief, and in the public sphere. In the glare of the public world, he had to contend with his own celebrity, his own severe anti-humanism, his own glib ironies.

An account of the change in tone and voice in *Ash-Wednesday* cannot limit itself to recording a few stylistic mannerisms. A verbal style synthesizes, is composed of, many disparate elements. For Eliot, it is 'composed' in another, psycho-ethical sense as well. By this I mean the achievement of a new authority and confidence based, now, on the discovery within himself, below the public exhaustions of irony, of the inner composure of a Don Quixote, of a naive quixoticism. The old poetry gained its authority and power through his daring explorations of the psyche's wasted lands; in *Ash-Wednesday* he finds an idiom and a tone of voice that will carry him toward his final masterpiece, *Four Quartets*: will carry *him*, even if it did not always carry, by which I mean convince, his earliest readers, schooled by 'Prufrock', 'Gerontion', *The Waste Land*, and 'The Hollow Men' to other tonalities, other disciplines.

CHAPTER TWO

Provisional delusions: crisis among the mandarins

In the previous chapter my discussion has seemed to assume that Eliot was primarily a writer with a British audience and British affiliations. Of course, this is not the whole story and especially not so as his fame grew from the mid-1930s on. He was an American who established himself in England, and it is important to remember that during his later years, the years of fame, he was also a transatlantic personality. Eliot's career embodies the coherence of the Atlantic community in the 1940s and after. In recognizing Eliot's special position in this respect, the Ackroyd and Gordon biographies very rightly underscore Eliot's American origins. Moreover, the work of Eric Sigg, *The American T. S. Eliot*, proposes a reading of the early writings which emphasizes Eliot's indebtedness to American intellectual history, as one might expect, but also the enduring impact of Eliot's family relations on his creative evolution.[1]

Eliot's Americanness is now a familiar critical given (and acknowledged by Eliot himself in many places but most significantly in 'The Dry Salvages' and his amusing mini-allegory of the migrating American robin in *To Criticize the Critic* 50). The question of whether his *work* is primarily American or English, or European, in influence and character is not the issue I want to raise. There is another reason for keeping Eliot's transatlantic connections before us. My argument about the later poetry and plays depends on recognizing the extent of Eliot's authority as a cultural figure in his later years and in bringing to light his 'natural' audience, the particular audience to which his work seems to be primarily addressed. This is the readership in the North Atlantic world which esteemed him, not simply as one literary voice among others, but as perhaps the most authoritative voice in English letters.

The evidence of Eliot's extraordinarily influential position in his later years is not difficult to find. It seemed evident enough to a close friend who lectured on Eliot, to overflowing crowds, at the Institut d'Etudes Anglaises in Paris in 1948.

Despite the years of intellectual darkness, it was clear that Eliot had become for them a revered figure. For the French, the early years of the war had brought Charles Morgan to the fore, as he seemed the one English intellectual prepared to stand by them, with his 'Ode to France', etc., but by the end of the war, the figure who had come to stand not merely for France but for the entire civilized order of the West was undoubtedly Eliot.[2] (Tomlin, *A Friendship* 156)

Eliot was able to speak to a diverse audience in different countries and his work was the subject of wide public exposition, appreciation, and debate. But what does 'wide' mean in this context?

This is difficult to say with any precision. But some numbers might help to put the matter in perspective.[3] Faber printed the relatively large number of 9,030 copies of the first Faber edition of 'East Coker', a thin pamphlet in yellow paper covers, in September 1940. Five months later Faber issued the first separate edition of 'Burnt Norton' in a press run of four thousand copies. There were, however, over ten thousand copies of the first appearance of the latter poem, in *Collected Poems, 1909–1935* (1936), in circulation in England and America already, plus an unknown number of reprinted copies. The first edition of 'The Dry Salvages' was published as a separate pamphlet by Faber in September 1941 in an edition of 11,223 copies. 'Little Gidding' appeared in December 1942 in an edition of 16,775 copies. *Four Quartets*, as a sequence, was published in New York by Harcourt Brace in May 1943 and Faber in October 1944 in first editions which totalled over ten thousand copies. Later reprints considerably increased these already high numbers. Finally in July 1959 Faber reprinted the sequence in its 'Faber Paper Covered Editions' series in an edition of 58,460 copies.

With Eliot's celebrity as a poet at its zenith in 1948, Faber and Penguin co-operated in producing an edition of Eliot's *Selected Poems* which, between the year of publication and 1967, put well over 120,000 copies of the selection in circulation on both sides of the Atlantic. Those were initial print runs; reprints of the four original states in paper and cloth editions would have no doubt increased the numbers considerably. Even more remarkably, in 1950, the initial print runs for *The Cocktail Party* put over 50,000 *cloth* copies of the play in circulation in England and America. In the late 1930s and early 1940s the only poet whose print runs even remotely approached Eliot's was W.H. Auden, a career Eliot himself had sponsored and marketed at Faber & Faber. But the expansion in Eliot's readership during the 1940s and 1950s (and well into our own time) outstripped all other serious poets in the Atlantic world, including Auden. Today all of Eliot's poetry and a good deal of his criticism are still widely available in a variety of cheap editions, collections, selections, and other product packages.

The situation of Eliot's criticism, less likely to be of interest to general readers, nonetheless underwent a similar surge of interest and sales. In July 1941, for example, Faber published 4,000 copies of the John Hayward selection of Eliot's literary and cultural criticism, a book which in England bore the title *Points of View*. It was later updated and expanded by Hayward and published by Penguin Books in 1953, as *Selected Prose*, in an edition of approximately 40,000 copies, a ten-fold increase, and reprinted, again in 1953 (the first edition having sold out), and in 1958, and, again, as a Peregrine paperback in 1963 in an edition of 25,000 copies. These very large print runs in the late 1940s and 1950s for a 'difficult' author like Eliot are quite remarkable, especially when set against the figures for the previous decade.

In the 1930s, Eliot was a 'successful' author, as successful as an intellectual can usually expect to get, especially a 'modern' author with a reputation for being obscure and even, at times, incomprehensible, qualities which tend to radically limit one's readership to a group of readers that might be loosely called 'avant garde'. If the reviews are anything to go by, he appealed to a sizeable, but not large, audience of well-educated, culturally engaged and intellectually active readers. His print runs in the early 1930s were respectable for a relatively successful, serious poet who was well known in intellectual and artistic circles, but they were not particularly high. *Ash-Wednesday* (1930), for example, was issued in editions of 2,000 copies each in London and New York. *Anabasis*, in the same year, was printed in '1650 sets of sheets' (Gallup 40). The Ariel poems, capitalizing on Eliot's fame in the late 1920s as the poet of *The Waste Land*, especially among the intellectually inclined younger generation, were issued in runs of 2,000 to 3,500 copies at a shilling apiece. These poems at popular prices probably help in giving a rough estimate of Eliot's whole readership among all kinds of readers, among the committed, the somewhat interested, the pseuds and the merely trendy. The print runs of his *Selected Essays* in 1932 match these figures, three thousand in England, 3,700 in America, and might be taken to indicate the outer limit of his audience, including an older, well-educated readership, a readership with money, or at least those who could afford the 12s 6d which the book cost in that year.[4] At the less numerous end of his readership, the subscribers' list for the *Criterion* in the 1930s, never rising above nine hundred, probably identifies roughly the bedrock of committed readers on which Eliot could depend. Thus, when these earlier figures are set against the later ones, the story they tell is more or less self-evident.

By the 1950s, his fame had spread enormously, and even though he remained 'difficult', this was now seen as merely a feature, so to speak, of the product, possibly even a selling point for an era when 'Mr. Eliot's per-plexing profundities', as T.S. Matthews put it in *Life* magazine in 1954, were no longer an impediment to the enjoyment of his work. Those peskily difficult themes – like 'the mystery of reality, and loneliness, and love' – did not intrude themselves in 'any painful or even provocative way' on Eliot's American readers in the Eisenhower years. Indeed Eliot's *The Confidential Clerk*, Matthews writes, 'is a much slicker article' in making difficult themes – the mystery of reality etc. – more beguilingly entertaining than his earlier work (56). No doubt 'brainy was beautiful' that year on Madison Avenue.

The production figures convey in general terms at least the extent of Eliot's audience in the decades after 1930. For an intellectual figure, his readership in the late 1940s and after was very wide indeed. And within that larger audience, one could still make out the smaller but still rather sizeable cadre of intellectuals, academics, artists, the more culturally attentive Oxbridgians from the professions, the civil service and journal-ism who had come to his work in the late 1920s and 1930s, the readers who had puzzled over the Ariel poems and *Ash-Wednesday*, purchased the *Selected Essays* in 1932, and wondered about Eliot's politics and loyalties in the years of historical turmoil and war. It was like the small, but influen-tial, social formation Paul Valéry had identified in 1925 in the social land-scape of modernized societies as 'l'Intelligence-Classe,' a company that in addition to 'la caste des lettres' embraced 'Mandarins, clercs, doc-teurs, licencies' ('Propos sur l'Intelligence' 1056). It was this smaller group of readers in England and America, and increasingly in Europe as well, who found in *Four Quartets* both a psychological refuge and the out-lines of a new kind of subjectivity better suited to the new world order, and the new situation of power politics, at the end of the German war. One could still make out these readers, even with an expanded reader-ship, because Eliot never stopped speaking specifically to them. He may have dealt with general ideas and concepts in art, politics, and culture, but how he framed those ideas, the effectiveness of the rhetoric of their presentation owed as much, if not more, to his sense of the audience he wanted to address, and to the historical situation of that audience, as it did to the calibre of his temperament or to the icy ferocity of his private struggles.

His audience after the war was also international. It was composed, horizontally, across national boundaries, rather than vertically from among people of different social classes. Eliot was as authoritative a cultural presence in certain intellectual and academic circles in Mexico City, say the circles in which the writer and diplomat Octavio Paz moved, as he was known and admired, in similar intellectual groupings, in Rome or Delhi or Montreal. If we turn to the title page of the Richard March and Tambimuttu homage of 1948, *T. S. Eliot: A symposium . . .*, produced to commemorate the poet's sixtieth birthday by Editions Poetry in London, we find tributes and contributions from America, England, half a dozen European states and from India. Eliot came to appeal to similar kinds of people, the same social fractions, in each of the countries where he was celebrated as a sage. I believe this is something that Eliot himself understood very well. He knew that his work was aimed at a small 'number of conscious human beings' within a mass society which was otherwise 'largely unconscious' (*Idea* 28) and disposed to intellectual sloth (14).

His audience was constituted principally of sections of the literary, academic and professional servants of power in the North Atlantic world and in the parallel social formations among the culturally subordinated intelligentsias of colonized nations like India. They are the closest equivalent that correspond, in actually existing societies, to Eliot's utopian ideal of a cohesive 'Community of Christians' in *The Idea of a Christian Society* (37–38), with, of course, the national Christian framework missing. This is what I am calling the North Atlantic mandarinate, large segments of which in the 1930s passed through a crisis of conscience and political uncertainity that almost rendered them incapable of maintaining their traditionally secure and often cosy relationship with the governing elites. It was the beginnings of this crisis in the 1920s that provoked Julien Benda to refer to their socio-political apostasy as 'la trahison des clercs' in the book of the same name, a book Eliot read with admiration. Benda accused the 'clercs' of turning their backs on their true callings and hankering after involvement in the sordid matters of political life. To the general accusation of having abandoned their proper tasks, the clerks, in their turn, answered that in times such as these, their 'treason' was the only honourable course intellectuals could take.

For some, like Eric Blair, the old Etonian and former Imperial policeman, the crisis meant a life-change so profound that a new persona and, with it, a new name, George Orwell, had to be invented in order to weather the crisis. It was for him a rebellion against the established order that could not be reversed. For others, the rebellion was little more than youthful idealism and, when you came right down to it, a simple case of callow posturing from which, later, it became necessary to find the proper stratagems of escape. When they had had their fill of politics, with its betrayals and illusions, in the 1930s, it was Eliot's *Four Quartets* which showed the way back. Panicky, middle-aging mandarins were led to abandon the frozen gestures of the revolutionary politics of the past. They were guided through the new curriculum, of contrition, detachment, transcendence and, finally, reconciliation with the established order, by a new pattern of subjectivity, cut from the cloth of a Virgilian stoicism, more suited to the stressful demands of post-war political realities. In the end, they found themselves again in history, but this time more protectively fledged for the new ice age, more fully adapted for survival in the pantomime of grimaces during the Cold War.

I understand that the word 'mandarin' has a specialized meaning in England. It usually refers to the permanent senior civil service in Whitehall and it is still very much in use in this sense today (see 'Reassuring Sir Humphrey' in *The Economist* 68). My adoption of the term entails a wider range of reference than this. I should add that it was also a word which Cyril Connolly applied to the prose style of the generation of writers against which the writers of the 1930s reacted. The 'new vernacular' of Orwell, Isherwood and others was fashioned to displace the 'mandarin dialect' of writers like Walter Pater, Henry James and Lytton Strachey (*Enemies* 9–16, 58–72). Although my use of the term cannot be neatly separated from certain matters of style and rhetoric, I am not adopting Connolly's programme of purely literary definition.

I use the word 'mandarin' and 'mandarinate' primarily in a sociological sense, to identify Eliot's primary readership as a loosely organized social group. I am adopting the term in this sense on the authority of John Hayward, one of Eliot's closest companions and a literary collaborator during the years in question (for the use of the word 'mandarin' with respect to Eliot see also Lewis, *Men Without Art* 65). It was Hayward who used the term 'mandarins' to describe this group and he often talked of their 'civilizing mission among the masses' (Hayward 47, and quoted in Hill, *TLS* 1274). This mission to keep the symbolic order intact in the heads of the masses was only one of its tasks. There were others, particularly in the area of serving the diverse needs of the governing elites of established society. Eliot's work in the 1930s speaks directly to a demoralized mandarinate shaken by the economic wreckage of the Great Depression, by the impotence of the 'democracies' in resisting totalitarianism, by the indifference of the powerful to the plight of the masses and to the humiliation, finally, of the events at Munich in the autumn of 1938, events that pained a disconsolate Eliot into bringing the *Criterion* to an end in January 1939, as the frontiers of Europe began to close. It was also this unhappy conjunction that led him to devote his Boutwood lectures at Corpus Christi College, Cambridge in March 1939 to the theme of the redemption of a morally bankrupt land.

That 'terrible Munich week' (Connolly, *Enemies* x) was, of course, the crucial event; even as tenacious a believer in the established order of things as E.W.F. Tomlin, a British Council mandarin and one of Eliot's friends, was shaken by the events of 1938. He recalled Eliot's particular sense of anguish and shame:

What particularly shocked him, from then [summer 1938] until the outbreak of the war, was the repeated humiliations heaped on Czechslovakia [sic], especially at the Munich conference in September. For although Britain, France, Germany, and Italy had guaranteed the frontiers of that country (minus the Sudetenland) at that same conference, the Czech Republic was fragmented a few weeks later, and by the following March Germany had completed her design by totally absorbing an independent state. Eliot felt that at Munich there had been a betrayal which seemed to demand an act of almost personal contrition. It was in this mood that he decided to bring *The Criterion* to an end. (Tomlin, *A Friendship* 106–107)

Eliot himself referred to the affect of these events on him in the composing of the lectures which eventually became *The Idea of a Christian Society* (63–64). The Munich crisis also shook the younger literary mandarins to the core. It provoked from Louis MacNeice his best work, *Autumn Journal*. Hugh Sykes Davies recalled years later, that in 1938, the *annus horribilis* of the peace, he knew in his bones, that 'the game was up' for the radicals of the 1930s (quoted in Deacon, *Apostles* 129).

It was to people like Tomlin, MacNeice and Sykes Davies, the small 'number of conscious human beings' (*Idea* 14), that Eliot felt compelled to speak. Their full integration into the culture of the governing elites led Eliot to his patient mentoring of many younger writers and thinkers in the 1930s and 1940s, in order, he would say, that they might serve the higher aims of a civilized order. His nurturing of the careers of MacNeice, Spender and Auden in particular, and of his success in turning them, finally, after their youthful radicalism, to ends that came to resemble his own, is a well-known story.[5] It is this kind of person whom Eliot has in mind when, beginning *The Idea of a Christian Society*, he describes his proper reader as someone 'to whom one speaks with difficulty, but not perhaps in vain' as opposed to those whose 'invincible sluggishness of imagination makes them go on behaving as if nothing would ever change' (14).

The mandarinate, then, wavered, for a time in the late 1920s and 1930s, in its commitment to the preservation of the existing socio-political order. 'The old world is a sinking ship', Cyril Connolly told his mandarin readership in 1938 (*Enemies* 69). The mandarinate lost the sense of the settled obviousness of the old order, or as Rex Warner put it in 1947, looking back to the beginnings of the political radicalism of *l'entre deux guerres*, 'It began to seem to many people that the governing class was unfit to govern . . .' (*Power* 21). One result of that process of estrangement provoked the recognition that intellectuals were an essentially sequestered class and that the confines of their position ought to be overcome in action, compelled to enact 'the role of human decision in history' (Trotter, *Reader* 122). W.H. Auden, in a letter to E.R. Dodds, conveyed the general frustration.

I am not one of those who believe that poetry need or even should be directly political, but in a critical period such as ours, I do believe that the poet must have direct knowledge of the major political events . . .

I feel I can speak with authority about la condition humaine of only a small clan of English intellectuals and professional people and that the time has come to gamble on something bigger. (Quoted in 'Introduction,' *EA* xviii)

Auden's sense of the time as 'a critical period' is very important here. The urgency to act is a matter of responding to the general crisis and Auden feels himself trapped within 'a small clan of English intellectuals and professional people', the group I am calling the mandarinate. Finally, the need 'to gamble on something bigger', to break out of the privileged enclave and connect with the 'bigger' forces of history, will be a wager that will not pay off in the long run. The safe haven, with its familiar and comfortable liberties,[6] under the wings of power, will seem awfully attractive when he finds himself out there in the cold, the shivering captive of the bigger, and more frightening, freedoms of history. But that moment would come later.

The unease about the direction society was taking had begun much earlier. The mandarinate – in government, in the professions, in the academy, in the established church – had already begun to turn liberal and socialist ideas and ideals into policies and institutions after 1918. This is a mandarinate that began to believe in rational solutions to socio-economic problems, in large scale planning, social engineering, reform of the traditional institutions of government, education, religious life, in the making of a meritocracy, in equal opportunity, the democratic opening of society, and even, in some cases, in the necessary overturning of the established order.

It was in response to the deepening crisis of Europe in the 1930s that this critique of the old order took on a greater urgency, an urgency that sometimes pushed political civility to the limits. The historian and writer Guy Chapman recalled in his memoirs that the 'brilliantly amusing and fluent' lectures at the London Schoool of Economics of that 'nihilistic physician,' Harold Laski in the early 1930s, were no doubt 'a maleficent influence on the undergraduate body':

[H]is jeering asides were designed to suggest, and did, that the whole country was being run by dishonest men, a moral scepticism he enjoyed pressing into the soft wax under his thumb. He once wrote that politics is a combination of high principles and low manipulation: in his lectures he left the impression on immature minds that only the manipulation exists. (*Survivor* 135)

Laski's critical voice was not alone; there were other teachers of great force and presence at the School, although most were less malicious in Chapman's estimate: people like R.H. Tawney, Eileen Powers, Lionel Robbins, Evan Durbin, M.M. Postan. It was the intellectuals and teachers of this generation, and their mentors the Fabians, that Rebecca West spoke of as presuming 'that there was nothing in the existing structure of society which did not deserve to be razed to the ground and that all would be well if it were replaced by something different as possible' (173–74). They steered a whole generation of students into a political activism of the left which was intended, finally, to transform England. Its greatest moment and opportunity arrived in May 1945. It ended in the disillusions of 1951; its work only fractionally concluded, and with the old Tory England still more or less intact.

Of course, this mandarinate was a complex social formation, made up of intellectuals who not only served the needs of power directly as scientists, technologists and civil servants, but those who also contributed to the maintenance of the symbolic order (even as its critics) as men of letters, clergymen, journalists, artists and scholars, the group Martin Weiner calls the professional subclass that emerged in English life in the closing years of the nineteenth century (*Culture* 14–16). By the 1930s and 1940s this subclass had developed a sense of its own character and its position and function within society. This is especially true of the socially unattached intellectuals, those who did not enjoy inherited privileges in class society (Berger and Luckmann, *Reality* 22). This group was far more conscious of itself as bound to the directive elites, not as a matter of ingrained class allegiance, but rather by negotiation, on the basis of merit and performance. As a group, the meritocrats lobbied the State in order to be taken seriously. Karl Mannheim and the sociologists and social thinkers who surrounded him come immediately to mind, principally because of Eliot's involvement in the Moot circle and his vehement opposition to their case for governance by a *nomenklatura* of trained experts (Kojecky, *Criticism* 163–97, 237–9).

Mannheim's notion that it was necessary to unite the intelligentsia, not in opposition to those in power, but as a force for persuasion in reminding the powerful of their responsibilities, was put forward with great persuasive force and with an astonishing naivety. His influential *Man and Society in an Age of Reconstruction* (1940) was the fullest statement of the ideas he had circulated in a series of short papers to the Moot and to which Eliot responded explicitly, within the Moot and beyond it, in his *Notes towards the Definition of Culture*. I think it safe to say that both Eliot and Mannheim were in agreement about many issues; they worked towards the same, essentially conservative, vision of society. They generally disagreed on the methods of achieving it. Both recognized the central importance of intellectual elites in the production and preservation of culture, and both saw that intellectual elites must play an important consultative and exemplary role in maintaining the bond between the clever mandarin and the governor. If that link is broken, the whole of society suffers, and with it good order: the nation's culture declines, and, among the governors, one begins to see the deterioration of ethical behaviour and discernment.

For Mannheim, merit must determine the character of an elite. Clearly Mannheim's own turbulent experiences in central Europe in the 1920s and his exile from Germany in 1933, led him to emphasize the need for meritocratic advancement of the best and brightest into the relevant specialized elites. He argued for a thorough training of men and women who would then be able to enter these functional elites from any position in society. It ought to be the useful ideas in a person's head and his or her ability to work with them, rather than 'blood, property, and [then] achievement' (89), that mattered.

Eliot answered Mannheim by insisting that the making of mandarin elites on the basis of merit was a suspect thesis. It is not enough merely to be the cleverest boy in the school, one must also inherit certain predispositions, 'contacts and mutual influences at a less conscious level, which are perhaps even more important than ideas' (*Notes* 38). Culture is not merely a collection of diverse activities and functions, 'but a way of life' (41). Specialists and technicians may be very clever indeed, but their cleverness does not guarantee that they are also cultured and, therefore, able to enact the refinements of an elite, one of which is the capacity to transmit the culture they have inherited. Classes are important to this process of transmission. For Eliot, social class, not abstract intelligence, ought to constitute the horizon of inclusion for an elite. A class preserves and hands down a vital culture, certain 'standards of *manners*', rather than mere 'ideas' (42). Functional elites are no doubt composed of many eminent individuals from different stations in life, but, Eliot argues, 'in the past the repository of this culture has been *the* elite, the major part of which was drawn from the dominant class of the time, constituting [also] the primary consumers of the work of thought and art produced.' It is important then, in his estimation, that the members of the dominant class who make up the heart of the cultural elite 'must not . . . be cut off from the class to which they belong'.

An elite must therefore be attached to *some* class, whether higher or lower: but as long as there are classes at all it is likely to be the dominant class that attracts this elite to itself. (*Notes* 42)

In the 1930s, the divisions between the mandarinate and the dominant class widened, not only socially, in the making of new avant garde or bohemian artistic enclaves, but politically, as a radical movement of opposition to the continued dominance of the traditional governors. Eliot was highly conscious of this falling away of the mandarinate from its traditional easy solidarity with power. The increasing isolation which this caused led to a radical repositioning of intelligence and talent on the socio-political landscape.

For example, in the bilingual periodical *Solidarity* (published in French and English), edited by the Free French intellectual Jacques Métadier in London, in its 1943 annual number (Volume IV) a contributor writing under the *nom de plume* 'Homo Sapiens' bemoaned the 'social bondage of the Intelligentsia' (25). In spite of the fact that 'all economic, industrial and cultural vantage points' in society are under the direct control of intellectuals, these scientifically trained experts do not control the destiny of the community, but are subordinated to the political authorities.

The subservience of the intellect to the powers that be has . . . far-reaching and nefarious consequences. For the State is in a position to mobilize the conscience of its legal experts, the benediction of its priests, the eloquence of its poets as easily as its man-power, and make them serve ends inimical to their ethos. This forced apostasy of the Intelligentsia is equally debasing for those who decree it as for those who submit. (26)

The article goes on to set out an agenda for the inclusion of the intelligentsia in the exercise of power. The article culminates, quixotically, in a call to deliver all power to the intelligentsia (30). It proposes with astonishing innocence and naivety a 'Programme' for doing so (32–35). Of course, it came to nothing.

In the 1930s, as a response to the Depression, not only academics and leftists, but even businessmen, like Israel Sieff of Marks and Spencer, began to promote regulation of the 'haphazard and potentially destabilizing market forces' of capitalism in the interests of planning. These initiatives were influenced by what was seen as the increasing national efficiency in command economies like the Italian and the Soviet ones. After 1933 the American New Deal had an enormous impact on British planners. But even before that the need for some kind of common action in Britain was recognized. The *Week-End Review* in February 1931, for example, devoted a long supplement to the theme of 'A National Plan for Britain' compiled by Max Nicholson.

Nicholson's article attracted the support of a diverse group of intellectuals, such as the biologist Julian Huxley, the educationalist Kenneth Lindsay and the economist Arthur Salter, and also progressive businessmen, like Sieff, all of whom were seeking an appropriate political focus for their anxieties about the drift into decline. (Newton and Porter, *Modernization* 78)

These social thinkers and businessmen represented the white collar technocrats. The various liberalizing '-isms' of the centre and left in Britain were widely influential in the whole intelligentsia. It is this liberalizing mandarinate whose optimistic ideas Eliot explicitly attacks in his cultural criticism. He did this principally in *The Idea of Christian Society*, *Notes towards the Definition of Culture* and in the Moot forums where, as mentioned above, notions of planning and the making of a meritocratic elite were being urgently advanced by Mannheim in the late 1930s and 1940s (Kojecky 169–170). But the experience of the collapse of Europe after 1938 subverted the optimism.

The crisis affected the mandarins in different ways. Some found themselves so maddened by the idiocy and obtuseness of the traditional governors in the established order of things, they went to extremes. Personalities like Oswald Mosley, the Cambridge traitors of the 1930s and 1940s and the atomic spies in America are the more dramatic embodiments of the crisis in commitment right across the Atlantic world. In 1955, Eliot had the Cambridge spies particularly in mind when he wrote to the American conservative Russell Kirk about the need for firm moral instruction in education. An education not founded in moral training, he said, 'leads to the view that so long as a man performs satis-factorily the work he is given to do, the rest of his life is his own business – a debilitating principle which ends by giving us in public life our Macleans and Burgesses' (quoted in Kirk, *Eliot* 367). That he should give the two traitors as his example is significant. Setting aside their 'crimes', they are notable because they were conspicuous failures in the otherwise generally successful absorption of the British mandarinate to the system of power at home. Even their homosexuality, which Kirk brings up in a nasty little footnote, would not have mattered much in England had they not taken the irreversible step into treachery. Burgess and Maclean were mandarins who cut the traditional moorings and who acted, in the only way they could, against the dominant oligarchy. Their capacity to act was prepared for by the more widespread disillusionment with and hatred of the traditional socio-political and cultural arrangements of the North Atlantic system. Of course, outright treason was not the rule; the more typical, angst-ridden mandarin response can be found in writers like Louis MacNeice and Delmore Schwartz, not in the example of a Kim Philby or an Anthony Blunt. It was among those whose opposition did not spill over into significant action, clandestine or otherwise, that Eliot's counsels had their greatest affect.

A significant section of privileged sons and servants of the governing elites of America, Britain and France, for a time, turned against their mentors and masters. Not all of them were very serious, especially as a particular kind of political rebelliousness began to acquire a superior chic in the 1930s: Auden's 'Consider this and in our time' (*EA* 46–47) neatly surveys the more typical gestures (and cf. Cunningham, 'Marooned' 4). For many, opposition meant little more than revision of one's style of life, a matter, in the end, of narcissistic self-absorption con-cealed by a stylish radicalism. The *Express* columnist Tom Driberg (who wrote under the *nom de plume* William Hickey), later to enter the Commons as a Labour member, responded to the sense of a failed society which had betrayed its own highest principles, by resort to polit-ical and personal behaviour that for a time brought him to the attention of the American and British intelligence services (Wheen, *Tom Driberg* 158–60, 315–18). But it became very clear, very quickly, that those of Driberg's generation were more likely to play at rebelliousness than to rebel. They alternated political, social and sexual unconventionalities depending on the occasion and the audience in question. Driberg for one learned to play the game cannily enough; he finished up in the House of Commons with a safe Labour seat after a life in London's seamier psychosexual bohemias of rent boys, male prostitutes and black-mailing pimps (Wheen 168). And in case one is puzzled by the fact that a Tom Driberg could sit comfortably as a Labour MP in the 1940s and 1950s, rising in fact to the Party Chair, while engaging in the most outrageous private behaviour, then this attests, firstly, to the blind eye of party leaders and journalists when dealing with someone in the mandarinate who knew how to keep up appearances, and secondly, to the nature of the British power structure, which protects all of its children, as long as they are part of the family, even as they coyly set themselves up in the public sphere as critics and renegades.[7]

By contrast, others of that generation, like Brian Howard, who never mastered the finer points of living as a house rebel, living an opposition that did not matter, were finally consumed by the psychosexual ambiguities they cultivated (Green, *Children of the Sun, passim*). Having gone too far, Howard never found his way back to reliability in Whitehall or Fleet Street or the garden flat in a quiet Chelsea square. Anthony Powell's *Books Do Furnish a Room* anatomizes accurately enough the post-war version of these chic but ineffectual bohemias. Eliot addressed this group, much of it on the margins of metropolitan literary society, as well as the more serious mandarins. And his later work ought to be seen as an attempt to remind both the pretend radicals and the wavering or defecting mandarins of their duty in the name of the highest cultural and spiritual values.

Inevitably, the contradictions of mandarin 'radicalism' would out. The mandarinate came to an internal crisis of its own in the late 1930s and during the period of the Second World War, when its meliorist faith in 'humanity' was shaken by the despair of total war and by the disclosure, in the general terror, of the true position of 'Man' in our time. In Britain, this liberal, humanist mandarinate wavered, but did not collapse in the way their French counterparts had, in the spirit of the defeatist slogan of May 1940, 'pour qui, pour quoi?' – for whom was one defending France, the walls of May asked, and for what reason?

Before them, of course, their German colleagues had already succumbed to the armed might of the totalitarian state. Many had resigned themselves psychologically to such an eventuality well before the Wehrmacht crossed into Poland in 1939, men like Ernst Junger,

Gottfried Benn, Martin Heidegger and Wilhelm Furtwängler. With the outbreak of war itself and the terror bombing of cities, social criticism, rational argument and the optimistic reading of human nature no longer sufficed in ministering to a more profound crisis. Eliot's authority in the 1940s was based on his efficacious resuscitation of what seemed now a matured inwardness that met the spiritual needs of an intelligentsia newly defeated by history.

Eliot's work in this path extended even to the task of reclaiming the German intelligentsia after the fall of Berlin and the Allied conquest of Germany. As James Fenton has remarked, on the occasion of another, more recent, conquest, 'It appears to be an idea common among conquerors that what a fallen city needs is a good injection of culture. After the capture of Berlin, every sector was immediately featuring Russian dancing and lectures by T. S. Eliot' (*Places* 94). Eliot, in fact, did play a part in the denazification of the Germans after the Hitler war. As the most prominent North Atlantic literary man of the time, he addressed, first on the radio and then in print, the German intelligentsia in the 1940s on the coherence of European culture and on the theme of the importance of the German contribution to its unity. *Die Einheit der Europäischen Kultur* was published in Berlin, in 1946, in the ruins of war, by the Carl Habel Verlagsbuchhandlung. The book as such was never published in England or America, although the text is to be found as an appendix to *Notes towards the Definition of Culture*.

This is a text which is little read today, but if one looks at Eliot in the context I am sketching here it takes on a new colouring. It was originally a series of three broadcast talks from London aimed at German listeners and clearly from the subject matter it was primarily addressed to the German mandarinate. The first talk discusses the unity of European culture through a general consideration of how language and poetry draw the nations of Europe into a common culture. English is offered as an example of a language which embodies European unity: to the Germanic foundation, a Scandanavian element was added after the Danish invasions; the Normans brought French influences and as a result, through them, Latin and Greek entered the cultural mix of England. Each of these additions has modified the literary culture of England, especially the writing of poetry, and joined England to the European homeland (*Notes* 111).

The second talk is more personal in that it discusses Eliot's experience as the editor of the *Criterion*. 'We produced the first number of this review in the autumn of 1922, and decided to bring it to an end with the first number of the year 1939. So you see that its life covered nearly the same period that we call the years of peace' (115). He goes on in this talk to recommend to his German auditors the importance for European culture of intellectual contact across national boundaries. Eliot suggests that one of the best ways of assuring that this contact occurs at the highest intellectual level leads through the medium of the independent literary review, and he lists a number of reviews – Eliot is careful to include two German periodicals – which during 'the years of peace' made it possible to maintain 'the circulation of ideas while they are still fresh' (116) in Europe. He also asserts the importance of personal contact among the editors and regular contributors of such a network of important cultural institutions; they 'should be able to get to know each other personally, to visit each other, to entertain each other, and to exchange ideas in conversation'.

He makes special mention of a friend and contributor to the *Criterion*, the German critic Theodor Haecker (116), who opposed the Nazis from within Germany and suffered for it, and produced one of the more moving accounts of that blighted time, *Journal of the Night*. Gareth Reeves has characterized Haecker's 'resolute opposition' to the Nazi regime in the following terms:

He condemned the Third Reich because of its limited historical perspective, its blindness to the traditional reality of Western Christendom: the Nazis 'think the hegemony of the West will fall to them? But, my friends, then it would not be the West any more!' (Reeves, 'Empire' 200)

In his introduction to Haecker's *Journal*, Alexander Dru comments that 'the central theme of the *Journal* is the relation of Christianity and culture or more accurately, a momentous instance of their divorce – the *apostasy* of Germany' (xxxiii, and quoted in Reeves). The mention of Haecker in Eliot's talk suggests the kind of thought he hoped would revive in Germany, by which Germany would be able to find its way back into the West, back towards the North Atlantic culture from which it had separated itself. But the point of Eliot's story of his review and of its network of regular contributors and contacts, men like Haecker, is not of its partial successes, but of its ultimate failure, attributable 'to the gradual closing of the mental frontiers of Europe' in the 1930s (116).

He sketches the chronicle of the disaster for the spirit of Europe in the individual exiles, deaths, confusions, and tumults of a destitute time. But he does not alienate his German audience by laying the blame at their feet; his sadness at the past tragedy acknowledges the responsibility of all for the general failure, including France, and to complete the rhetoric of inclusive sympathy, England as well: 'England though manifesting some symptons of the same malady, remained apparently intact' (117). The conciliatory note, the inclusive stroke occurs in that deftly positioned 'apparently' which seems to shift in the blink of an eye some of the general blame onto English shoulders as well as ascertaining that the mental damage done by the folly of those years spared no one.

The disintegration of the literary coherence of Europe which damaged all Europeans is, then, read by Eliot as having its origin, not in literature, but in politics. This point, the real heart of the message to the German intelligentsia, disengages questions of politics from questions of culture.

A universal concern with politics does not unite, it divides. It unites those politically minded folk who agree, across the frontiers of nations, against some other international group who hold opposed views. But it tends to destroy the cultural unity of Europe. (117)

This is the message, not only to the Germans, but to the English, and indeed to the North Atlantic mandarinate as a whole.

It hardly needs saying that his argument assumes a relation of culture to politics which is essentially false; political conflict is not simply the contest of particular parties or political ideas. It has its roots in the array of localized social formations – of class, community, local region, ethnic group – which make up a society. It is the visible and organized action of the group in its contests with other groups within the artificial boundaries of the nation-state. Each of these 'political' formations embodies a concrete subculture of its own, one that defines the historical and anthropological reality of the abstraction.

The concepts of a 'national culture' and 'the culture of Europe', on the other hand, are ideological abstractions with important political implications. Culture, in this abstract sense, does not exist as a texture of immediate lived relationships and did not exist until the foundation of the nation-state. Culture, in this form, is part of a modern apparatus of control and domination which provides important legitimatory abstractions for the prevailing directive elites of the nation-state. It provides also a kind of artifice, a learned protocol, as a list of canonic texts (Eliot's notion of 'the tradition' is crucial here), to which the national intelligentsia, Gramsci's organic intellectuals (5), whose fate is tied to the success of the nation-state, can comfortably adhere.

Learning how to adhere to this sense of a national or even continental culture, which is a political abstraction through and through, includes the crucial self-regulatory mechanism that erases from sight its political origins and nature. Culture is then said to triumph as an achievement of the human spirit, free from entanglement in the historical struggles of particular communities. The European mandarinate in the 1930s, swept, sometimes unwillingly, into that concrete history, lost its moorings in the comfortable abstractions of a general, canonic 'Kultur' and found itself adrift, without the resources to deal with the rigours of actual political struggle. European history no longer projected a space of social hope and progress; it had arrived finally, as Heidegger insisted in those years, at the abyss, at the annihilation of all values. Eliot's historic task, in poetry and prose, was to calm the resulting panic, to formulate the return of the mandarinate to the security of the ideological haven it had impulsively and prematurely abandoned. And this he did with remarkable success, a success noted in just these terms by W.H. Auden on the occasion of Eliot's sixtieth birthday in 1948.

> . . . and always,
>
> > blank day after day, the unheard-of drought, it was you
> > who, not speechless from shock but finding the right
> > > language for thirst and fear, did much to
> > prevent a panic . . .[8]   (*CSP* 275)

Auden was not alone in these sentiments. C. Day Lewis, too, came to identify Eliot as the principal consoling presence on the post-war landscape of panic, by 'supplying / Our loss with words of comfort' and by saying 'all that need be said about committedness' ('At East Coker,' in Tate, *T. S. Eliot* 115). In the changed historical situation of the 1940s, youthful commitments, once answering to the dilemma of purpose and meaning, had themselves now become the problem.

Eliot is not concerned with the world of politics as such, with the larger questions of war and peace, the socioeconomic distribution of punishments and rewards, nor with the dialectics of power. He is concerned, like Leo Strauss in America at the same time (*On Tyranny* 194–95) and in much the same terms, with defining the proper relation of the wise mandarin to politics. And that relation, his talk to the Germans tells us, must be one of detachment from the world of politics and a firm 'committedness' to higher values. It will be the particular task of *Four Quartets* to explain how this is accomplished.

From the cohesion of that brief utopia of literary periodicals in 'the years of peace', Eliot draws a significant lesson, which he passes on to the supine Germans, from his position as a representative conqueror, but a conqueror with a conscience and, who in this ticklish moment of cultural annexation, must neither gloat nor patronize, who must maintain a sensitive sympathy, and who must also offer a diagnosis and a cure. In editing the *Criterion*, he says, the 'question of a writer's political, social and religious views simply did not enter into our calculations, or into those of his foreign colleagues. What the common basis was, both at home and abroad, is not easy to define. In those days it was unnecessary to formulate it; at the present time it becomes impossible to formulate' (117). But essentially this commonality has something to do with 'a common curiosity and openness of mind to new ideas'. One could take for granted an interest in ideas for their own sake, and a delight 'in the free play of intellect' (118). The degree of free play might be a problem, of course, if the free play were to reach anarchic proportions, but the free play which Eliot recommends is contained within the appropriate institutions of society, in this case the network of literary men in Europe. In this particular fellowship as Eliot knew it, there existed an unconscious assumption which affirmed, without need of affirmative declarations, the unity of the common project:

> It was the assumption that there existed an international fraternity of men of letters, within Europe: a bond which did not replace, but was perfectly compatible with, national loyalties, religious loyalties, and differences of political philosophy. And that it was our business not to make any particular ideas prevail, as to maintain intellectual activity on the highest level. (118)

The 'fraternity' Eliot defines here is one element, and a very important one, in the whole array of the mandarinate. Within the mandarinate, this fraternity, according to Eliot, must act out in intellectual life a kind of freedom which does not compromise or belittle the obviousness or solidity of the system of power as a whole. It must stay clear of politics, in the sense of staying clear of the politics which might challenge or undermine the settled political order within which the 'fraternity' can enjoy the 'free play of intellect'.[9]

However, in reality this is not turning one's back on politics at all. This is surely the counsel of political quietism and resignation in the face of an uncertain power. The practical result of such counsel for the mandarin lies in the advice one might give a senior civil servant, namely that he 'had better not be in the habit of seeing things with his own eyes' (Sisson, *Administration* 20). One can find an enclave in which to indulge the 'free play of intellect', but it is best, in the world of power politics, to go about one's public life as a matter of institutional routine. It is the style of the loyal civil servant as wittily described by C.H. Sisson, the poet and lifelong public administrator, in his remarkable little book *The Spirit of British Administration* published by Faber & Faber in 1959. Great organizations force individuals to abdicate personal vision and to lay aside questions of value, the questions which too often lead back to the forbidden world of politics. Sisson quotes J.B. Yeats approvingly in thinking about the state of mind of the practical servant of power, '[t]he practical man cannot afford to be sincere', and then goes on to secure the point about value in administrative settings:

[The civil servant] must, not only on all questions of value but even on matters of fact, share the provisional delusions of his fellows. It is a discipline, but it is not a discipline of the truth. It requires the muscles and obedience of an acrobat rather than the patience of a philosopher. (21)

He must 'share the provisional delusions of his fellows' even if, as an intellectual or as a moralist, he understands otherwise. The always dangerous questions of value need to be disengaged from the arena of effective public power, and re-inscribed in some other language which does not engage with politics. The 'free play of intellect' needs to be thoroughly and finally privatized, in order to ensure its survival and, thus, the continuity of European culture.

It must be said that the Germans in 1946, no doubt, understood this advice very well; much of the local mandarinate had chosen the path of inner emigration in the Nazi period in any case. So it must have come as a bit of a surprise to hear Eliot, the conqueror's mandarin envoy, proposing a similar sequestration of intelligence. But, of course, they would have misheard him. Eliot was not counselling inward retreat before a murderous regime that demanded absolute conformity. He was proposing something more familiarly the response of a Tory conservative to the general conditions of risk in modernity. His was an argument for the advantages of 'affirmative culture' as defined by the Frankfurt school: that culture of the bourgeois epoch which led in the course of its own development to the segregation from everyday society of the mental and spiritual world as an independent realm of value. Its autonomy depends on its also being considered as above society. Its decisive characteristic is the assertion of a universally obligatory, eternally better, and more valuable world that must be unconditionally affirmed: a world essentially different from the factual world of the daily struggle for existence, yet realizable by every individual for him or herself 'from within' without any transformation of the paramount public world of fact (Marcuse *Negations* 95).

Eliot's form of inner emigration in a destitute time is the practical application of the lesson about freedom which members of the North Atlantic mandarinate still learn in the mandarin schools, Oxbridge, the elite institutions in America, or the higher schools in Paris. Within the privileged precincts, as long as one accepts them, there is a style called freedom, a style that might be called, in one of its characteristic moments, the 'free play of intellect'. But there are also styles of submission as well, and one of them, if the privileged enclaves are to be kept intact, requires the delicate separation of private scruples from public tasks.

Submission and the averting of one's eyes is especially the case when the mandarin must, inevitably, be involved in the morally compromising tasks of domination and control, even when the masters are styled liberals and democrats and not totalitarians. In the exercise of public service, then, say in war time, where actions very rarely achieve the loftier moral standards, the 'agenbyte of inwit' often poses a problem for the mandarin. One needs a way of closing one's eyes to the contradictions power forces on us as we serve its purposes. In a disarmingly honest moment, W.H. Auden, in 'Spain' (1937), understood exactly what was required by the master, when he spoke of the acceptance of the necessary murder in a noble cause. Blinded by the propaganda of the Spanish cause for a short time, Auden came to see finally that this collusion, unfortunately, is what the master – communist, fascist, democrat – always demands of his servants and, although it is part of our moral traditions to scruple occasionally at 'the necessary murder', the point up to which we are permitted to do so is well policed in the commanding heights (cf. Trotter 120–123).

Auden's subsequent revision and suppression of such knowledge is usually read, in Auden's favour, as personal revulsion at the immorality of such a sentiment. Moreover, Auden's editorial revisions and subsequent remarks leave the impression that it was only the extreme left (and right, one assumes) that required such submissions from adherents, that the traditional humanitarianism of the liberal would be offended by such naked purposes. The history of the Second World War and the Cold War (and Orwell's *Nineteen Eighty-Four*) should have taught us by now that the immoralities and 'necessary' murders committed in the name of the Atlantic democracies may be just as nasty as the crimes committed in the name of any of the enemy -isms. And Auden knew it too, so that his second thoughts about the fate of political morality in Spain, although noble-sounding, can just as easily be put down to Auden's desire to come in from the cold, that is, his frightened return to the traditional mandarin enclave, at whatever cost, after certain sobering encounters with the real consequences of being in serious opposition. Like Geoffrey Hill's 'Ovids' in the 'Third Reich', the mandarin needs some internal mechanism by which the pricks of conscience can be segregated from the moral numbness induced by contact with brute power.

The most pointed philosophical dissection of these states occurs in Theodor Adorno's meditation on the ways of democratic power in postwar West Germany, *The Jargon of Authenticity* (1964, trans. 1973). When read in the context of the post-war reclamation of the Germans, Adorno's sceptical analyses of the style of leadership in the Federal Republic, which soon came to conform to new administrative styles of domination, can be read also as ironic comment about North Atlantic democracies as well:

The reconciliation between the inner and outer worlds, which Hegelian philosophy still hoped for, has been postponed ad infinitum. Thus it has become unnecessary to advocate alienation, since the latter is in power anyway . . . At the same time the consciousness of the rupture changes self-consciousness into self-deception. Ideology can grasp . . . the fact that the growing powerlessness of the subject, its secularization, was at the same time a loss of world and concreteness. (72)

This separation of inner and outer makes the pricks of conscience easier to bear. And the growing powerlessness of the subject is understood ideologically as the loss of concreteness. That loss, experienced as impotence, which records the increasing political irrelevance of the ordinary human agent in contemporary history, needs to be compensated for by the invention of a kind of immaterial concreteness without consequences. It involves the invention of a freedom which rotates the weightless magnificence of meaning, but a freedom which cannot imagine itself changing the world. Eliot's broadcast to the Germans, like the more complex project of *Four Quartets*, represents a step in the normalization of this alienated consciousness as the servant of power.

Eliot's lessons to the Germans, counselling detachment from the lesser reality of politics, in the name of the higher spiritual unity of culture, also applies to the whole Atlantic mandarinate, needing to learn, after the political engagements of the 1930s, the proper, self-censoring relationship to power. The alienated intellectual working in the State Department, or Foreign Office or the Quai D'Orsay, sharing a common social position and education as, say, the editor of a prominent literary review, can take Eliot's advice about the detachment of intellectual life in the arena of culture, and apply the lesson of detachment to his or her relationship to the political master. Certainly literary intellectuals will have no trouble understanding this point in theory; the idealist traditions of the West arm us very well for making this separation, but, in the present time, even the official administrators of power must learn to separate the rich, detached play of inwardness from the sometimes morally compromising necessities of exercising power.

The spirit and its embodiment in cultural activity, Eliot suggests, is the proper realm of freedom and value. Eliot's dismissal of 'politics' as the lesser reality implies that the unavoidably necessary tasks of power require a disengagement of this inwardness, a separation that allows the mandarinate, the servants of power, to operate without the untimely interference of individual conscience. The fiction of John le Carré in the heyday of the Atlantic system after the Second World War enacts this drama of commitment and detachment superbly. Auden's Roman bureaucrat in 'The Fall of Rome' (1948) writing disconsolately, 'I do not like my work' (*CSP* 218) also captures the mood. Geoffrey Hill has also written in prose and poetry about the place of the mandarin intellectual in a system of power which defeats human conscience, 'God / is distant, difficult. / Things happen.' ('Ovid in the Third Reich,' *CP* 61). And the Arjuna passage of 'The Dry Salvages' takes on a different colouring when read in this context.[10]

The social effect of a good deal of Eliot's later work speaks to the melancholy disappointments of mandarins who have operated at some earlier time on the assumption that the inner life ought to be in some vital connection with external action, that politics is the public arena in which one enacts the common decencies of moral life. In the political claustrophobia of the war against fascism and later in the Cold War, such decencies and liberties became less and less possible.

Eliot's third German talk expands on the theme of a saving detachment by considering the more general issue of culture as a whole. The literary culture of Europe is one thing, but what are, he asks, the common features which bind Europe at all levels? Firstly, the history of Europe is characterized by many relationships back and forth across the various nationalities or ethnic groups. There has always been an interchange among diverse European communities that cannot be underestimated. To this web of associations and contacts one must insist on the centrality of Christianity as a great unifying force. Through

Christendom, Europe inherits more than religious faith: the arts, for example, and common standards of aesthetic evaluation, Roman Law, 'conceptions of private and public morality', and the continuing heritage of the crucial ancient civilizations, Greece, Rome and Israel, from which Europe traces its descent (122–23). These truisms aside, Eliot's essential message is never far off.

The essay goes on to contrast cultural unity and political unity; culture permits diversity and a multiplicity of unities, politics demands singularity and conformity. The spirit, it seems, cannot survive politics. Eliot closes with a sincere appeal to 'the men of letters of Europe': the common responsibility is 'to preserve our common culture uncontaminated by political influences' (123). He concludes with a warning that for a world which has seen such material ruin, the spirit, if so contaminated, is also in danger. This then is his message to the Germans, and, no doubt, to the domestic mandarinate as well.

One must recall in reading these essays the rhetorical situation in which they were being delivered. In 1946, Germany was prostrate, after the most ferocious assault on a country in human history. Germany was literally torn to pieces by its enemies. Divided, occupied, its major cities in ruins, its urban population barely able to feed itself and to find shelter, Germany lay mute, vulnerable and menaced. And in those early months after the war, before the arrival of the Cold War, it had also to endure the hypocrisy of the Allies who spoke of humanism, democracy, and the rule of law, but numbered the Stalinist totalitarians in the Soviet Union as allies. Germany had achieved instead of the conquest of Europe, utter alienation from the larger homeland. Eliot with a disarming but deft simplicity, only simplicity could work in this mood of despair, offered the calm and sober voice of reconciliation and of inclusion. Halfway through the first talk he asserts the importance of the poetry of France in the nineteenth century for all Europe, the poetry from Baudelaire to Valéry, and finds it best embodied in three exemplary Europeans, Yeats, Rainer Maria Rilke, and himself (112). The inclusion of Rilke is the deft touch. This and other signs of an open hand were intended to turn back the nausea, the nihilism that was not only being felt by the Germans, but by some of the more sensitive conquerors in the occupation forces.

Stephen Spender's chapter called 'Nausea' in *European Witness* (1946) speaks directly to this crisis. As a member of the occupying forces in Germany in that first summer of peace in 1945, Spender had been 'sent on a mission to find out what survived of German intellectual life'. What he found among the German intelligentsia was a profound feeling of

depression and devastation (65). The despair in the Occupied zone was
mirrored in a feeling of nausea 'from which many people in the
Occupying Armies suffer' (61). Homesickness, panic, discouragement,
impotence characterized this feeling and it soon took on more ominous
dimensions than merely the gloom one feels living among a lost, humili-
ated people. Spender's widening sense of horror is typical of the mandarin's panic when the mandarin encounters the possibility that the
settled order of things, in which, for example, one cultivates a rich interiority, in which one reads novels by Gide and remembers the cultured
voices of Parisian friends (62), is slowly crumbling before one's eyes. The
visions that follow comprise the highest degree of mandarin anxiety.

My depression was caused by the sense not just of a temporary condition
around me in Germany which could be remedied by programmes of
Reconstruction, but by the realization of a real potentiality in my environment,
as vivid as the potentialities of Nazism in 1931. This was the potentiality of the
ruin of Germany to become the ruins of the whole of Europe: of the people of
Brussels and Paris, London and New York, to become herds wandering in their
thousands across a continent, reduced to eating scraps and roots and grass. It
was the sense as I walked along the streets of Bonn with a wind blowing putres-
cent dust of ruins as stinging as peppers into my nostrils, that the whole of our
civilization was protected by such eggshell walls which could be blown down in
a day. (67–8)

The fragility of the walls that protect civilization from barbarism typifies
the view of the privileged in periods of crisis; it defines a psychological
enclave in which the mandarinate finds comfort and protection from the
herds. It does not strain one's credulity to believe that Spender's nausea
was as much a product of suddenly and unconsciously sensing his own
captivity to the power system which had produced him, a system he had
often reviled as a rebellious young man, as it was merely contemplating
the physical and moral destruction around him. But it is a captivity, in
Erich Fromm's sense, that is an 'escape from freedom'. For Atlantic intellectuals, like Spender or Auden, who as clever young men had tested the
practical value which the idea of freedom carries in the public discourse
of the West, this anxious escape from the more rigorous consequences of
a radical and concrete freedom no doubt had something of the nauseous
about it. Moreover, there was also something like Adorno's vertiginous
'loss of world and concreteness' at work here as well.

Auden's programmatic 'In Praise of Limestone' (1951) can be read,
symptomatically, in this light, as an attempt to define concreteness anew
as a problem in figuration rather than action, and to dissolve, like painful

gall stones, the last gritty psychic residues of one's abandoned commitments, to bind by tropic legerdemain what the separation of theory and
practice had allowed to drift apart.

> If it form the one landscape that we the inconstant ones
>> Are consistently homesick for, this is chiefly
> Because it dissolves in water.   (*CSP* 238)

The homesickness of 'the inconstant ones' for a destination which gives
every appearance of being real, but which actually dissolves under one's
feet, conveys the character of the protected enclave perfectly. And in the
safe corruptions of the innocuous natives, natives who are also splen-
didly innocent at the same time, we see the yearnings of the shivering
outsider trying to find his way back to 'the shady side of a square at
midday' where he knows that, even when one 'goes to the bad, the way
his mind works / Remains comprehensible'. He envies them their protected worldliness and contrasts his own nomadic wanderings on more
inhospitable landscapes.

> Their eyes have never looked into infinite space
> Through the lattice-work of a nomad's comb; born lucky,
>> Their legs have never encountered the fungi
> And insects of the jungle, the monstrous forms and lives
>> With which we have nothing, we like to hope, in common. (239)

The telling phrase is in the last line, 'we like to hope', indicating precisely
the emotional climate of the journey back to the enclave. The 'monstrous forms and lives' are not abstractions, but the menacing experiences of recent history, 'Intendant Caesars rose and / Left, slamming the
door' and, worse, the exposed places where one came to confront the
nihilisms of our time and of its seductive voices.

> 'I am the solitude that asks and promises nothing;
>> That is how I shall set you free. There is no love;
> There are only the various envies, all of them sad.' (240)

Here is the 'reality' of concrete historical existence of which Eliot would
teach his readers 'humankind' cannot bear very much. Instead the mandarin finds the magnificent enclave sheltered by power; he finally comes
to know that he needs to be protected from the 'beasts' out there, or
Spender's 'wandering herds', and the closing of the poem defines it as
accurately as one can from within the enclave, right down to the occasional flutters of anxiety (that 'please!' for example) that force their way
into the language and imagery.

I, too, am reproached, for what
And how much you know. Not to lose time, not to get caught,
    Not to be left behind, not, please! to resemble
The beasts who repeat themselves, or a thing like water
    Or stone whose conduct can be predicted, these
Are our Common Prayer, whose greatest comfort is music
    Which can be made anywhere, is invisible,
And does not smell. . . .   (Composed May 1948)

The reference to music is particularly crucial, as a revision of a nine-teenth century symbol of the highest form of aesthetic cognition, into a more worldly symbol of the safe haven itself. Inconstancy, homesickness, dissolution, the role of music, the yearning for the safety of the enclave expressed as a desire for privacy and for the 'modifications of matter' into gestures of innocence, 'made solely for pleasure', allow the mandarin to make peace with power and to discover a version of subjectivity at the very moment the 'free play of intellect' arrives to replace freedom. Naturalizing this contradiction; making a captive mandarinate accept the new dispensation, will be the task of *Four Quartets*.

It was not only that Germany revealed a grim national prospect for the Germans, but that Germany was a metaphor of a more general human ruin. And the typical mandarin reaction in the post-war period was to seek the safety of established havens with as much of one's conscience intact as possible. Eliot's later work in prose and verse taught the post-war intellectual, those who wanted to learn in any case, how to live in a state of sequestered weightlessness, defying the Newtonian gravities of actual power 'out there' in the world, by the strategy of making a magnificent inward simulacrum of power that fed one's psychological needs but did not disturb the external order of things. It was a work that helped the mandarin find a viable ideology by transforming the alienated state, the loss of concreteness, into a positive achievement of the spirit. And, in recent critical responses to Eliot's work, like Ted Hughes's *A Dancer to God: Tributes to T. S. Eliot* (1991), it is a work which still goes on, routinely, around the Eliot canon.

Eliot's work was always directed to a particular audience and not to readers in general, and certainly not to the 'mass' audience. One attempt to reach such an audience – the Anglican pageant play *The Rock* – was an embarrassment artistically, although it seems to have gone over well with the audiences to which such productions appeal and, of course, with its ecclesiatical sponsors (Ackroyd 218–19). He knew very well who it was that read his work and he understood the psychology of that kind of person thoroughly. He could not have possibly been the superb publisher he was without knowing, probably intuitively, a good deal about the readers of the kind of books Faber was publishing in the years of Eliot's tenure at Russell Square. But it was not only as a publisher that he was conscious of the psychology of his natural audience. His work is brimming with that kind of knowledge from very early in his career: the cultural 'smarts' evident in 'Aunt Helen', for example, or 'Cousin Nancy' and, of course, 'Mr Apollinax'. Above all 'Portrait of a Lady' lays bare the romantic illusions of a certain kind of bourgeois sensibility – brittle, self-conscious, deceitful, and thoroughly amoral.

Eliot never wrote in a socio-political vacuum. He may have had a sort of Mallarmean side to him (and that has been overrated in recent criticism), but it was never dominant. Eliot's writing was as thoroughly engaged with his audience as Berthold Brecht's with his. He was not a pure aesthete or a radical *symboliste*. He was a highly conscious member of Anglo-American bourgeois society in the years of its global ascendancy, and it was to that dominant group that he spoke. His views on society, religion and art, and art's function in society, develop from Victorian antecedents, especially the importance the nineteenth century placed on the leading role of a social elite – Arnold's 'lovers of culture' (204–207) – in the preservation and transmission of culture (see also Hughes, *Society* 78–82). His life-long argument – underpinned by the tradition of elitist social thinking that arrives through Charles Maurras and Vilfredo Pareto in the early twentieth century – tried to persuade the social group into which he was born what exactly constituted its best interests in terms of the structure of thought and feeling which would ensure their continued dominance in society. More specifically he spoke to the intelligentsia, making the same argument to them as Leo Strauss had. The best an intellectual, a mandarin, can expect in modern times is to find protection under the wing of the oligarchs, 'devoting a little time to giving advice to tyrants or rulers' (Strauss 206), playing, in short, Aristotle to Alexander the Great, and serving the ends of Tradition from the protected havens where it might still survive, as opposed to the demotic streets where it would fall before demagogues, or be bought by the highest bidders.

His fifty-year attack on liberal humanism and the softheaded aesthetics which it promoted never wavered for a moment. Its purpose was to maintain the continuity of European culture through the identification and nurturing of a 'natural' directive elite that would paternalistically superintend and co-ordinate civil society, and not just for the benefit of the elite, but, and this was a sincerely held belief, for all people. It would have the advantage of eliminating the anxiety of rootlessness and *anomie* among the people by reviving ancient communitarian bonds, leading to civil harmony and psychological contentment. This was what Eliot took to be the Elizabethan monarchical ideal – a strong social system guaranteed by a confident and energetic aristocracy whose ideological unity was formulated by a resilient and pervasive church, propagated by a socially integrated, courtly intelligentsia.

Of course the Elizabethan ideal itself could not be recreated in twentieth-century mass society, but Eliot felt a version of such a society structured by the principles which underlay the Elizabethan 'masterpiece' could be erected in our time. The key to this new social vision came in the shape of a properly constituted and Christian mandarin elite. It had very little, if anything, to do with the liberal notion of a meritocracy which dominated Anglo-American social thinking this century. Eliot wrote of making sure that the traditional social elite, a mix of surpassed, but still culturally vital, aristocratic elements and the economically and politically effective higher bourgeoisie could be shaped, with the right sort of ideological training, into a formidable and irresistible social formation.

The power elite he saw as exercising the kind of domination he favoured was already in existence; it was just a matter of getting their mandarins to abandon secular humanism and to adopt more rigorous habits of thoughtful obedience. It was not planning and the welfare state that would bring about social harmony, but a clearly defined structure of legitimated domination. Reason and abstract principles – the Enlightenment myth – could not provide a proper basis, only the traditional long practices of power and submission. Through a wrong turn in the evolution of European thought, these customs had lost their old legitimatory authority in the political upheavals of the nineteenth and twentieth centuries.

The actual character of the contemporary power elite which Eliot hoped might be turned to Christian purposes in *The Idea of a Christian Society* and *Notes towards the Definition of Culture* was being investigated and described concurrently in quite different terms by the American sociologist, C. Wright Mills. In *The Power Elite* (1956), Mills delineates the physiognomy of power in upper class America in Eliot's heyday, from the 1930s to the early 1950s. Although limited to midcentury America, the pattern he describes has a wider applicability. The positions the powerful occupy, he writes, permit them to transcend the everyday environments of ordinary people. When they act from their positions of command, things happen, and even their failures to act are often as full of consequence as their active decisions (3–4). But the powerful do not rule alone, Mills writes. They rule with the help of a mandarinate of advisers, consultants, spokesmen, opinion-makers, clergymen, editors, intellectuals and so forth, who are often the midwives of the power elite's higher thought and decision (4). If servants of power do not themselves claim the highest places of authority, 'they do often have the power to distract the attention of the public or afford sensations to the masses, or, more directly, to gain the ear of those who do occupy positions of direct power' (4). Some also have the power to console, and through the vast apparatus of entertainment and distraction, to accustom the powerless to the fact of their powerlessness, and, perhaps, to invent imaginary planes or states where the impotent might yet still regain the vicarious excitement of command, or, at the least, gain a sense of their own wholeness.

With respect to power, the mandarinate itself is in a most vulnerable position. It is a complex social formation which both exercises power in the name of the elite and, more acutely than most, experiences its absence. Its tragedy lies in being close to concrete freedom of action and decision, to participate in it, but, finally, to know the same impotence as the 'proles'. George Orwell's *Nineteen Eighty-Four* comprehends this point again and again; indeed the novel can be read as an elegy to the vanished freedom of the captive mandarins in the Ministries of Oceania.

The mandarinate is also the point at which the power system is most conscious of itself and of its own historic role. It is the mental space within which power most fully experiences its own reflexive states, its own moral ambivalence, its own self-definitions. The internal contradictions are therefore more fully registered in thought and feeling by the mandarinate than by anyone else in the system. Spender's nausea is, I believe, a normal response to this state of affairs.

A power elite which is essentially dedicated to the expansion and maintenance of its own power at any cost, but legitimizes its rule in the name of democratic society, or humanistic ideals, or freedom, creates a serious morale problem among the mandarins. The powerful rarely concern themselves with the contradictions of their own position, if they are even aware of them, but many of the servants do. To make the contradictions public, to embarrass the powerful, invites censure, loss of status and the punishment of exile from the principal hierarchies.

Again Winston Smith's is the appropriate paradigmatic experience.

On a lesser artistic plane, the dilemma and defeat of Rex Warner's 'Professor' in the 1938 novel of the same name also enacts a typical mandarin fantasy of wish-fulfilment, in which an idealized mandarin character is improbably raised to the chancellorship of his nation. Warner's novel dramatizes the inevitable fate of the Platonic philosopher-king in the domain of modern power politics. The Professor is cast as the hero of knowledge and wisdom, but it is left to the putschist, Colonel Grimm, broadcasting to the nation after the coup, to define the political reality which intelligence must always face: 'The Chancellor is, as we all know, a clever man. Well, I personally have not much use for that kind of cleverness, and I think that it is sound instinct which makes ordinary fellows rather distrust the intellectual' (113–14). Warner's Professor dies a noble death; he does not acquiesce to the demands of the new regime. Orwell's revision of *The Professor* ten years later in *Nineteen Eighty-Four* more accurately reveals the vulnerability and trepidations of the servants of power.

Most mandarins cannot suffer easily the loss of their status and privileges; the fate of the Auden generation, Warner included, is the case in point. Most of them found ways to return to the embrace of the elite from which they had emerged,[11] Warner as a classicist and as an apologist for privilege. Louis MacNeice is perhaps the most interesting because, as the most sensible of them, he understood more quickly than the others both the self-contradictions and the dire consequences which followed the flashy flirtations with oppositional politics and unconventional erotic styles. A reading of his sardonic memoir, *The Strings Are False*, will quickly confirm that judgement. He was also the most troubled when he found himself incorporated again into the murky moral world of the directive elites; the war came and the power structure closed off all the free zones of radicalism which the system at peace could tolerate for its brighter stars, where clever young men were for a time permitted to play at rebellion. For C. Day Lewis the way back from communism led initially through a rural repose 'fuelled, of course, by T. S. Eliot's images of religious calm' (Cunningham, *Writers* 379) and the discipline of translating Virgil during the war years. His foreword for his translation of the *Georgics* in 1940 celebrates, in Eliot's exact political register, 'the instinct of a people' expressed in 'a practical love of Nature' wherein 'we may see the depth and tenacity of our roots in earth today' (7). His vision of rural England is, of course, an essentially conservative and Tory construction (Hynes, *Auden* 389). Glorifying the agrarian ideals of a Virgil seemed, on the face of it, a startlingly conventional and tepid occupation after the robust insurgencies of *The Magnetic Mountain*.[12]

In the Atlantic period, the demands to conform have been very powerful, but the secret has been to find mental and emotional strategies by which the mandarin, and especially the intellectual, can maintain a comfortable place in the power structure without experiencing guilt or shame by having to practise or justify what Mills calls 'the higher immorality' of the power elites (see also Lukes, *Power* 55–6). Although speaking of America, Mills's description of this moral order is one that applies to the power centres of the Atlantic world in general.

Of course, there may be corrupt men in sound institutions, but when institutions are corrupting[,] many of the men who live and work in them are necessarily corrupted. In the corporate era, economic relations become impersonal – and the executive feels less personal responsibility. Within the corporate worlds of business, war-making and politics, the private conscience is attenuated – and the higher immorality is institutionalized. It is not merely a question of a corrupt administration in corporation, army, or state; it is a feature of the corporate rich, as a capitalist stratum, deeply intertwined with the politics of the military state. (343)

The immorality in short is structural. Eliot himself treads gingerly around a very similar, general point in *The Idea of a Christian Society*, the problem of Christian statesmen who find themselves frequently forced to 'perform un-Christian acts' in the proper execution of their duties. Eliot, the political realist, does not wag his finger in disapproval; he acknowledges the necessity of tactical immoralities in the province of government. He simply asserts that these un-Christian acts must never be defended on un-Christian principles (27).

What we have come to know as 'liberalism' in the post-war period equipped the entrenched mandarinate with a formal set of beliefs which helped to rationalize these dilemmas. This set of beliefs has helped to obscure for indentured mandarins the sometimes morally suspect character of their incorporation into the system of power. That is the effect of their choices, but these are systematically hidden from view. Eliot is sometimes read by left radicals and critics as having helped institutionalize this blindness. But this is not exactly the case.

By the time Eliot came to deliver 'The Literature of Politics' essay to the Conservative Union in London in April 1955 that characterization may have come true (*TCC* 136–44). But in works like *The Idea of Christian Society*, *Notes towards the Definition of Culture*, certain programmatic critical essays in the 1930s and 1940s, the essay on Kipling, and certain of the plays, such a characterization of his leading ideas is not entirely true. In that period, his work can be read, not only as an attempt to normalize mandarin loyalties, but to criticize and correct the moral laxity within the formation itself. His later work enacts the drama of these ambiguous choices, and nowhere does Eliot attenuate these ambiguities. They are debated at length and of course they have a disruptive potential, but Eliot's own loyalties are so clear, his position as one of the great Atlantic mandarins so sure, that the seriousness of his engagements is given full scope. The reason for the acceptability of his critique is that the issues are meant to be debated within the privileged domains. None of this work, even the most morally damning, *The Idea of a Christian Society* for example, is written from outside the power structure with the aim of dislodging it.[13]

Eliot's later work, then, represents the moment of conscience *within* power. In *Murder in the Cathedral*, for example, Becket's opposition is enacted within the precincts of the Cathedral. Here we are allowed to experience the exemplary tragedy of the man of conscience coming to grips with what Mills calls the higher immorality, the immorality we hear in the speeches of the Tempters and Knights, but he is allowed to come to grips with it 'in house'. The allegorical positioning of the action, Becket, his Priests, the four Knights within the Cathedral, and the people, the Chorus as feminized peasant/proles without (again the parallel with *Nineteen Eighty-Four* is striking), is significant and deliberate. And if this sequestration of the moment of conscience is true in *Murder in the Cathedral*, it is true also of the country house world of *Family Reunion*, of the walled-up interiors of *The Cocktail Party* and the final two plays as well.

CHAPTER THREE

The society of the mandarin verse play

In the 1930s Eliot increasingly turned his mind to the theatre, taking up in practice what had fascinated him as a critic for many years in his studies of Elizabethan and Stuart drama. The story of his movement towards the theatre has been told many times, both from the biographical standpoint and as an aspect of his artistic development.[1] In the second half of the Harvard lecture *Poetry and Drama*, published in 1951, he touches on the essentials of the story himself. No doubt his early interest in the dramatic monologue as verse form suggests a bent for drama. More to the point is the steady attention he paid to Renaissance drama as a critic over many decades. In fact, the drama was still capable of provoking superb examples of close reading from him long after he had turned his critical attention, later in life, to general topics of literary and cultural history. His reading of the first scene of *Hamlet* in *Poetry and Drama* must remind us of the practical critical acuities of his early criticism. But with all his experience as a critic, as a practitioner he still approached the theatre with a good deal of apprehensiveness. *Sweeney Agonistes* (composed in the mid-twenties), the two 'Coriolan' fragments of 1931, and his contributions to the Anglican pageant play, *The Rock* (1934) were his earliest excursions in dramatic writing. Another commission from the Church of England, for the Canterbury Cathedral Festival of June 1935, provided the occasion for his first sustained piece for the theatre, *Murder in the Cathedral*. The story of Eliot as dramatist, then, has been told many times.

My concern, however, is with Eliot the dramatist as cultural critic and ideologue, and with the way his writings for the theatre enact the social and cultural dilemmas of his time. In the *Criterion*, *After Strange Gods*, *The Idea of a Christian Society*, *Notes towards the Definition of Culture*, other essays and broadcasts, and in his extensive writings on education, Eliot's social criticism after 1930 grows increasingly comprehensive, touching on all the major issues which confront modern societies and cultures. However, there is one theme to which he returns again and again, a theme that has vexed many social and cultural critics throughout the century, namely, the relationship between the intelligentsia and power.[2] In this chapter I am principally concerned with the way Eliot's theatre works enact that particular dilemma in the 1930s. I want to recover what his writings for performance seem to be saying about the socio-political situation of elite political culture in that troubled decade, and, more particularly, to the way the plays diagnose the sometimes precarious, sometimes cosy relationship between power and intelligence, between the power elite and the intellectuals.

This way of putting it suggests a clear and conscious thematic intention on Eliot's part. No doubt he had conscious intentions, principally in dramatizing the relevance of Christian themes to the individual and society. My approach to the theatre works is not to rehearse a set of often-repeated commonplaces about literature and religion in Eliot's work, but to look at the dramatic works politically, to assess how they position themselves in their socio-historical context.

This critical programme raises again the old problem of all contextual criticism: how much of what can be said about the text in its political context is under the conscious control of the author, and how much is not. All contextualist criticism involves just such a bifocal critical approach. I must admit at the outset that I accept as axiomatic the practical idea that not all the thematic material that is in a work of art, nor its political meaning in the context in which it was produced and received, is under the conscious control of the artist. So that a play can have a political meaning which the author did not necessarily intend. I am aligning myself, then, with the Frankfurt School notion that, among other more explicit aims, works of art express political positions or objective social tendencies not entirely under the control of their creators (Jay, *Imagination* 177).

The *Sweeney Agonistes* fragment is a case in point. It is a very interesting formal experiment, but thematically a dead end. It combines innovative verse speech, satire, popular song, and burlesque, a mix that Auden and Isherwood were to exploit more entertainingly in the 1930s, and of which Noel Coward and Bertold Brecht were the great masters in that time. But what do I mean by 'dead end'? For one thing, the skits skirt psychological terrain that might act to leave the writer dangerously exposed; an Antonin Artaud or a Ferdinand Céline, Eliot's contemporaries on the continent, would have entered these perilous territories of the self eagerly, come what may. For Eliot such a public exposure was both temperamentally difficult and under the circumstances of his growing interest in a visible respectability, socially impossible.[3]

The play is a 'dead end' in another sense as well: it conveys Eliot's typical contempt, in *The Waste Land* period, for *l'homme moyen sensual* (Sweeney), for the 'lower orders' (Dusty, Doris, Horsfall etc.), and for the ubiquitous *métèques* and Jews of Europe and America (Klipstein, Krumpacker, Swarts) (cf. Freedman, 'Eliot's Jews' 198–206). One can take these sentiments only so far before they begin to give a disgust. With the proletarians, Eliot was only happy when he could find an occasion for expressing his Brahmin paternalism (the Marie Lloyd essay for example). In *Sweeney Agonistes* he did not feel particularly paternal; his contempt is expressed in a number of derisory turns, for example in the fortune telling episode in 'Fragment of a Prologue' (*CP* 125–127). This should remind us of the low esteem Eliot always expressed for the occult and for those who cultivated it, in the Madame Sosostris fragment in *The Waste Land*, for example, and in the drily dismissive references to astrology and the occult in 'Dry Salvages' (*CP* 212). In this respect Eliot would have very much agreed with Theodor Adorno's famous characterization of popular astrology as a philosophy for dopes.

Typically mandarin in attitude about these matters of 'popular' culture, Eliot could not take *Sweeney Agonistes* very far, because he did not seem to have a well-defined artistic purpose that required the burlesque form as an apt vehicle, nor did he have anything particularly new or interesting to say about the 'dopes' in the bottom half of society. His attitudes towards them were thoroughly Tory and predictably unsympathetic, including the association of the dangerously emancipated Sweeneys with the foulest psychotic behaviour, the secret desire, for example, to 'do a girl in / Any man has to, needs to, wants to / Once in a lifetime, do a girl in' (*CP* 134). He simply repeated, without any redeeming or original insights, the same attitudes to be found in the leader pages of the right wing press in Britain at the time (Cooper, *Voice* 27–39, 99–101). We can assume Eliot understood at least this much about the socio-political significance of his own work, even if he would not want to admit it if asked.[4]

In this respect, he was out of step with the egalitarianism of the intellectual progressives in the period between the two wars. I am thinking particularly of certain groups in society, such as the dominant liberal 'party' in the Church of England that emerged at the Lambeth Conferences of 1908, 1920 and 1930, defining a liberalism that Eliot vehemently opposed in 'Thoughts after Lambeth' (*SE* 323–24). I am also thinking of the Fabians and their successors, people like Harold Laski and Stafford Cripps, also the left-leaning intelligentsia in the civil service, the schools and the universities, the more politically conscious members of the literary world, the Auden generation, the Bloomsbury liberals, and with the middle class activists and publicists of the labour movement, intellectuals such as John Strachey. But *Sweeney Agonistes* is more than a sign of his dissent from fashion or the affirmations of others.

The working classes of Britain were well beyond Eliot's capacity to understand, though it never seemed to dawn on him that this might be so (see especially his 'Commentary', in the *Criterion* of June 1927, on the subject of community singing). And their aspirations in the middle part of the twentieth century were seen, from the commanding heights of society, as a menace that threatened to overturn not only the traditional political order, but its culture as well. Leo Strauss envisioned the masses as little more than 'millions of parrots' repeating insensibly 'the savage noise of the loudspeakers of the mass party' (195). The fear in Tory ranks was always that demos in power meant the installation of an idiot's regime; the danger lay in the fact that the dopes would either simply blunder about and demolish the natural and irreplaceable givens of society, or, more dangerously, unleash the ugly, pent-up resentment of that otiose product of egalitarianism, 'the young man carbuncular', already definitively seen through in *The Waste Land*.[5] Even a classic left-leaning liberal like Louis MacNeice grew anxious in the 1930s at the prospect of demos in power: 'It is so hard to imagine / A world where the many would have their chance without / A fall in the standard of intellectual living / And nothing left that the highbrow cared about' (*CP 1925–1948* 125). That was bad enough, but for the more thoughtful Tory intellectuals, like Eliot, the greater immediate danger lurked in the line which follows: 'Which fears must be suppressed'. The greater danger, for Eliot, lay in the suppression of those fears and the misguided defection of sections of the liberal-minded mandarinate to help demos in the theoretical and practical tasks of conquering society.

Turning, then, from the social and psychological life of the Sweeneys as the subject of drama, a life he knew next to nothing about, Eliot directed his attention to what he did know something about, the inner life and public ethos of the upper middle class from which he himself had emerged. As the most important cultural spokesman for the conservative mandarinate, Eliot, finally, gave up the simple-minded abuse of demos, left it to the Tory journalists on Fleet Street, and swung around to join the more difficult battle for the hearts and minds of the mandarinate itself.

With the two 'Coriolan' fragments, 'Triumphal March' and 'Difficulties of a Statesman', Eliot shifts his attention from the Sweeney zone to the commanding heights of society, a prominence from which subsequently he would never stray. This change of focus is anticipated by his translation of the poem by St-Jean Perse called *Anabase*. Eliot's *Anabasis* was published in 1930 and it had enough of an impact in its day to influence the young writers he was publishing at Faber & Faber. Auden's *The Orators* (1931), for example, includes a clever parody of Eliot's englishing of the Persian French.

Much interest was taken in [*Anabasis*] by poets; and it has, we believe, made its mark on English poetry, so that it will be an essential document in studying the English poetry of the present time. In the hope of introducing it to a wider public, because of its great beauty and originality, we have now reduced the price from 10s. 6d. to 5s. (From the Faber & Faber Spring List, 1937 57)

Although there is no way, at the present time, of ascertaining whether this blurb for the Spring List was written by Eliot himself (it probably was), the comments in it suggest the importance Eliot felt the poem had had on the poets of the 1930s he was publishing at Faber.

Perse's enigmatic poem rotates the mystique of power and conquest by exploring the occult epistemology of the mighty. The poem is curiously abstract and weightless; the setting is magnificently exotic, but unplaceable; and time is treated mythically as ritual and eternal recurrence. Yet the poem is also intensely physical, sensuous and soulful. It is extraordinary in its effect in that two conventional incompatibilities, the intangibly abstract and intense physical sensuousness, are made compatible, as in *Paradise Lost*. Thematically, the poem is clearly fascinated with the aloofness, grandeur, sensuousness of power: 'Omnipotent in our great military governments, with our scented girls clad in a breath of silk webs . . .' (41). It conveys the absolute confidence of the conqueror, able to exercise not only the power of life and death, but the immediacy of his mere presence as a gift: 'I have the idea of living among you' (23). The essential mysteries of power are lovingly recognized, the power of prophecy (55, 57), for example, or the efficacy of violence (53), not as a means to an end, but an end in itself, in a kind of Yeatsian ecstasy of self-completion (as in the third strophe of 'Under Ben Bulben'). And finally the poem establishes through its whole course the psychology of power, the watchful withdrawal of consciousness into itself, into a kind of dangerous narcissism of intense self-regard and external surveillance:

'The eye withdraws by a century into the provinces of the soul' (59). Eliot's two 'Coriolan' fragments try to revive, in a thinner and less august form, the Persian lyric of force, and its celebration of the mystique of power.

The first of the two fragments dramatizes the triumphal arrival of a victorious military leader from the perspective of the spectators. It is done as 'a jumbled stage-set' of scenic possibilities meant to merge into one archetypal scene of imperial triumph (Zabel, 'Point' 284). The scenic allusions include the victory parades after the Great War in London and Paris, the Fascist March on Rome in 1922, and the arrival of Coriolanus in ancient Rome. All of these figure in the making of the fragment. None of this is very well realized. The most significant aspect of the verse, as always with Eliot, is his orchestration of voices and the levels of awareness which they embody.

A first voice merely registers impressions, like a news reel; then it generalises them, by simple arithmetic. There is no idea here, let alone an ideal; nor is there any life in the verse. The organisation of mind and feeling is rudimentary. Another voice, presumably observing these observers, ironically reflects: 'The natural wakeful life of our Ego is a perceiving.' (Moody, *Poet* 165)

This other, more intellectually alert voice informs us as a dismissive comment on the credulous spectators that, at the lowest level of consciousness, we have simple gawking, the dope's epistemology in the society of the spectacle.

The arrival of modern times in the twentieth century both made greater difficulties for a political conservative and, paradoxically, made things simpler at the same time. The disembedding of personal and social experience, especially for the bottom half, from its traditional ground in an agrarian social order made for a more unruly and unsettled urban mass society, but a society, it turns out, that was also more easily manipulable. Eliot, from a note to *The Idea of a Christian Society*:

When I speak of a probable 'lower middle class society' I do not anticipate – short of some present unpredictable revolution – the rise in Britain of a lower middle class political hierarchy, though our ruling class have to cultivate, in its dealings with foreign countries, an understanding of that mentality. Britain will presumably continue to be governed by the same mercantile and financial class which, with a continual change of personnel, has been increasingly important since the fifteenth century.

Eliot, in the same passage, goes on to describe more carefully what I have called 'the Sweeney zone'.

I mean by a 'lower middle class society' one in which the standard man legislated for and catered for, the man whose passions must be manipulated, whose prejudices must be humoured, whose tastes must be gratified, will be the lower middle class man.

And after this arch dismissal, the timid-seeming disclaimer:

I am not necessarily implying that this is either a good or bad thing: that depends upon what lower middle class Man does to himself, and what is done to him. (*Idea* 77–78)

The modernity which accompanies the arrival of the market economy in early twentieth-century Atlantic culture unsettled the old agrarian order, but it did not change the fact of domination in society. It may have forced a certain sobriety on everyone, may have meant for the powerless that all that seemed solid previously had indeed melted into air, and that all that was holy in another time had been inescapably profaned, but the fact of domination did not change; the first law of power, as we all know, is holding on to power. The inventiveness of the masters was being taxed to adapt the traditional apparatuses of control to new conditions. And to that task the interstitial social formation which most characterizes the fate of intelligence in modern times, namely the 'socially unattached intelligentsia *(freischwebende Intelligenz)*' (Berger and Luckmann, *Reality* 22) was recruited to help in the management of society, not as a traditional intellectual class in Gramsci's sense, but as a mandarin supplement to the power structure.

The traditional British Tory was certainly not happy in the new society of the spectacle, of perpetual motion, of the defeat of Nature and memory at the gates of the modern city, and of the supplanting of the certitudes of the past by the new 'regimes of truth' construed by ideologues and publicists. But he could do nothing about it, except learn, as Eliot suggests in *The Idea of a Christian Society*, to manipulate the new society for his own ends. Most Tory intellectuals in the period after the Great War responded to these new conditions of modernity with irony and derision. This is the voice we hear in 'Trimphal March'.

This aloof, ironic voice which observes and mockingly mimes the munching patience of those who 'can wait with our stools and our sausages' (*CP* 139) is heard again when we come finally to the heart of the piece. The most telling moment arrives with the entrance of the victorious generalissimo. First the excited clamour of the gawkers,

                        Look
There he is now, look:

followed by the mandarin voice from the wings:

> There is no interrogation in his eyes
> Or in the hand, quiet over the horse's neck,
> And the eyes watchful, waiting, perceiving, indifferent.
> O hidden under the dove's wing, hidden in the turtle's
> 　　breast,
> Under the palmtree at noon, under the running water
> At the still point of the turning world. O hidden. (*CP* 140)

It is always a little suprising to come across 'At the still point of the turning world' in this essentially worldly context when the phrase in *Four Quartets* seems to carry so many otherworldly associations. Here, it seems to me, Eliot is trying to locate the state of mind of the governor, a mind hidden from those who wait in the streets. What the poem comprehends is not the view of the Caesar from the demotic stool; all that the masses can muster up as response to Caesar's triumph is the cry not to 'throw away that sausage'.

This other voice, however, knows the leader, knows the moods and the eyes of the Caesar, is conscious of his quietness (and what it might mean), watches the watchful eyes that perceive everything, the imperial indifference, the stillness in the midst of triumphal bustle. This is the lofty serenity of the masters in *Anabasis* and, of course, in Yeats's 'Long-Legged Fly'. At these heights we are made aware, shrewdly, that 'power is knowledge', not the other way round, which is more comforting to powerless intellectuals. If we follow the 'level of awareness' aright, then we see Caesar, not from the street, but from the wings, where the court officials and the imperial advisers stand. This is the view from those who know both the great public displays of power (and what they are for), and the struggles behind the walls of palace and ministry. In the second 'Coriolan' fragment, 'Difficulties of a Statesman', Eliot will take us behind the palace walls into the corridors of power. The mandarin voice in the first fragment anticipates those intimacies.

Whether, alternatively, in the central passage of 'Triumphal March' we are 'looking . . . through the hero's eyes' as suggested by David Moody, in a moment of 'purely poetic vision' intimating 'a transcendent order of feeling and being' (165) is rather a difficult matter to decide. But, certainly, Eliot the Christian is trying to suggest a spiritual pattern at work somewhere below consciousness which will ultimately see us through to another kind of triumph, of which this is the lesser kind. The suggestion that the poem ends with the advent of religious awareness, putting the matter of the triumphal march, finally, in a Christian pattern, hidden from sight, seems entirely plausible given Eliot's beliefs. But this is beside the point. Our attention as readers is seized and focussed by the stillness at the centre of power, and not power as a metaphysical abstraction, but concrete power, menacing, silent, embodied here in the essentially Persian figure of an imperturbable general. We ought always to take note of the origin of 'the still point' in these rather down-to-earth perceptions when we turn to *Murder in the Cathedral* and, of course, to 'Burnt Norton'.

The second Coriolan fragment, again concerns itself with the commanding heights, this time not with public triumph, but with the private anguish of the mighty. In 'Difficulties of a Statesman' we hear, via Isaiah 40:6, the distressed voice of a great public man – 'CRY what shall I cry?' – surrounded by political enemies calling for his resignation. The poem is constructed metonymically; we are meant to piece together this moment of crisis from the daily particulars of a very public life: the civil honours, the cluster of committees and public commissions, the patronage appointments, public works, peace negotiations, labour strife and so on.

Our attention on the public man gives way to the griefs of the private man with the reference to the lonely gloom of the soldiers who guard the frontiers of the empire, 'Meanwhile the guards shake the dice on the marches / And the frogs (O Mantuan) croak in the marshes' (*CP* 142). The entreaty to Virgil and to one of the more famous lines from the *Aeneid*, serves, again metonymically, to establish the calibre of the interiority we are dealing with here. Eliot, of course, is the master of this kind of shorthand characterization of people and events. Through Virgil we enter a Roman consciousness oppressed by dynastic responsibilities and expectations, a man searching the old observances ('mactations, immolations, oblations, impetrations' [142]) for solace, and having arrived at the end of his tether empty-handed, wanly calling for mother. We are in the presence of a temperament that is defined by a once vital classicism now largely defunct, and of a spirit in despair, which merges seamlessly with the mandarin despairs of our time. The verse urges us to sympathize with the statesman's inward difficulties. His crying out to his mother in the ancestral corridors modulates to a different kind of calling out for another Mother. Christian salvation in this Roman context is as yet hidden from view – 'Hidden in the stillness of the noon' (142) – though the earlier reference to Virgil already anticipates its coming. His weariness, the nightmarish solitude of the imperial hinterlands, the dynastic burdens embodied in the busts of his ancestors, work to bring the statesman to that place of complete desolation, the emotional waste land, which for Eliot is always the prelude to redemption, where he can call out in the dark, without knowing exactly for what it is he calls,

> O mother
> What shall I cry? (143)

while outside the palace walls the public voices clamour for his fall. The Sweeneys were never given this amount of patient understanding.

The Voice which is meant to answer the disconsolate cries of the statesman soars, in Roman guise, as an imperial Eagle, to 'the summit of Heaven', in Eliot's next effort for the theatre, the Anglican pageant *The Rock*. All that Eliot chose to preserve of the play are the 'Choruses' (*CP* 161–185) which contain the better writing in the piece. The rest of it is Eliot at his most patronizing (Aiken 'After "Ash Wednesday"' and Harding 'The Rock'). Apart from its avowed purpose, fundraising for church building, *The Rock* provides Eliot with a platform from which to interrogate and attack the progressive mandarinate, the liberals and reformers of society, 'who write innumerable books; being too vain and distracted for silence: seeking every one after his own elevation, and dodging his emptiness' (*CP* 173). In this fifth section Eliot also attacks the lukewarm Christians 'who sit in a house of which the use is forgotten' and compares them to snakes lazily sunning themselves. The zealous reformers of both church and society are 'like dogs, full of enterprise, sniffing and barking: they say, "This house is a nest of serpents, let us destroy it, / And have done with these abominations, the turpitudes of the Christians".'

The true Christian, on the other hand, is a builder and warrior of the faith, 'Remembering the words of Nehemiah the Prophet: "The trowel in hand, and the gun rather loose in the holster."' The image of the virile, gun-toting Christian, bricklaying and firing off pistol shots, is rather comical now, although one might recoil when we consider the time in which it was written; in the decade of the rise of fascism, guns were rather *too* loose in the holster.

What does strike one about this section of *The Rock* is the brutality of the emotions which push through it. It seems to me far more likely that the animus rifling through these lines runs far deeper in Eliot's psyche than the occasion warrants. Possibly, it derives from Eliot's American origins. The images that find their way into the verse may remember unconsciously a certain Pilgrim mythology about the colonizing of America. Here is the God-fearing Puritan settler righteously seizing the land from the original inhabitants, conscious of being 'encompassed' by snakes and dogs (the bestial imagery is typical), knowing that while some in the settlement 'must labour . . . others must hold the spears' (*CP* 173 and cf. Gordon, *New Life* 26). This is the *laager* mentality, well known to most of us in its contemporary South African form, and it is a permanent, but now submerged, feature of North American consciousness as well.

However, it is the legacy of the Enlightenment which holds Eliot's attention when he isn't rousing the faithful to the task of building churches. In section I (161, 163), at the beginning and end of section III (169, 171), again in VI (174), and finally in VII (178), Eliot attacks explicitly the scientific materialism and instrumental rationalism of the Enlightenment (see Brooks, 'Serious Poet' 109–12). He posits against it the subterranean pull of the organic community, a pattern of life 'controlled by the rhythm of blood and the day and the night and the seasons', (184) which he will expound in greater detail in *The Idea of a Christian Society* and *Notes towards the Definition of Culture* and make the earthly analogue of the 'hidden' pattern of the redeemed life in *Four Quartets*.

The Rock is a curious performance because it is so far below Eliot's usual high standard of artfulness. For one thing, his literary borrowings work mechanically, and are essentially inert, like prosthetic limbs. The attempt at an incantatory intensity by simple repetition and by additive iteration grows tiresome after a while; we tire also of the clumsy pastiche of biblical idioms and anaphoric verse forms; his pastiches of Milton ('O Light Invisible . . .') and Hopkins ('Glow-worm glowlight on a grass-blade' [183–84]) in section X strike one as strained.

His recourse to Ezra Pound in this context seems particularly opportunistic, firstly, by borrowing the idiom of Confucian concord between person, family and society, the great leitmotif of the Chinese Cantos

> If humility and purity be not in the heart, they are not in the home:
> and if they are not in the home, they are not in the City. (173)

and secondly, because of the unfortunate pastiche of the 'There died a myriad . . .' section of *Hugh Selwyn Mauberley*

> Some went from love of glory
> Some went who were restless and curious,
> Some were rapacious and lustful. (179)

The least said about this verse the better. One ought to mention also the figure of Virgil whose shadow occasionally passes over the text, especially the Virgil of the *Georgics*, in the reference, for example, to 'the pleasant countryside' (162) despoiled by daytrippers and picnickers, having lost its vital hold over the temper of a people (see Ellis, *English Eliot* 84–88 and Weiner, *English Culture* on the 'rural myth' in England 46–66). Also in the image of the 'corrupted' city, but 'corrupted' somehow by sanitation, subsidized housing and commerce (170–71), we are meant to remember, antithetically and more positively, the true urbanity of the Virgilian *urbs* which merges, at the intersection of history, with the City of God.

Eliot seems to have thought these 'Choruses' far more important in the development of his work than most of his critics. Even Lyndall Gordon, his most sympathetic reader, virtually ignores this work. Why she does is difficult to say. No doubt it could be easily massaged to fit the invisible biography of Eliot's private pilgrimage towards inward beatitude, which, she feels, redeems and absolves Eliot's actual life, with all its messy entanglements and his sometimes shockingly insensitive behaviour towards intimates and friends. *The Rock*, however, gives us an Eliot who does not entirely square with the withdrawn ascetic of Gordon's invisible life, the inner man whom a series of carefully cultivated masks kept well hidden from view. The virile dogmatist of *The Rock* is nowhere near, for example, the 'Old Buffer' caricature Eliot sometimes assumed in the 1930s, a character 'who tended to fall asleep in club armchairs (Gordon, *New Life* 25).

Gordon's account of Eliot's later life depends on seeing him as an enigma who always shielded himself, not only from the world at large, as one might expect in the case of a public celebrity, but even from his most intimate friends. Gordon insists that no one was permitted to intrude on the man's cloistered preoccupation with personal redemption and grace. Her 'real' Eliot – withdrawn, austere, ascetic, suffering, haunted – that emerges from her pages hardly seems interested at all in the world at large, what she calls 'the deceptive attainments of ordinary human love, worldly ambition, and political power, the vanities of all the fools under the sun' (26). Why he devoted so much time and effort to this foolery, lecturing the world in books, public talks, periodicals, pamphlets, and radio broadcasts about culture, society, the financial system, education, the classics of our literature, standards of morality and so forth in these later years seems, then, a bit of a mystery (cf. North 110). The bald facts of Eliot's life show him as a very public man indeed, with a decided bent for public controversy. But for all that, the public Eliot is not entirely incompatible with Gordon's inward pilgrim, although one understands that Gordon's design dictates the systematic attenuation of the vigorous controversialist and shrewd man of affairs in the interests of summoning to view the invisible saint.

The Rock very well illustrates the vigour of Eliot's wider engagements in the 1930s with the liberal-minded mandarinate, with what he saw as its cockeyed belief in the perfectibility of the Sweeneys, with its faith in instrumental reason as the foundation of human freedom, and its hope in the potentialities of planning and reform for the remaking of a moribund society.[6] And *The Rock*'s importance in Eliot's own mind is underlined by turning the pages of *Collected Poems, 1909–1962* and finding that these crude and doctrinaire verses are carefully positioned to lead directly to *Four Quartets*, rather than the artistically more significant 'Landscapes' which come before 'Choruses' in the volume, although they were written at approximately the same time.

Eliot's second theatrical commission for the Church of England[7] engages more concretely the meditation on power and the relationship of intelligence to it. *Murder in the Cathedral* was rather more successful artistically than *The Rock* and came to appeal, after its run in the Canterbury Festival in June 1935, to a wider audience than the select Christian one to which *The Rock* had been limited at Sadler's Wells the previous year. *Murder in the Cathedral* is still Eliot's most performed play, long after the others have disappeared from sight. In many ways it is his best piece for the theatre, because it is the most focussed and the most convincing.

Set in the twelfth century, *Murder in the Cathedral* avoids Eliot's usual difficulties in the making of plays. Most obviously, these include difficulties in dramatic construction, and difficulties in making socially convincing, thematically significant verse dialogue for plays set in contemporary society (cf. Eliot, *OPP* 81). Many critics and scholars agree that *Murder in the Cathedral* is organized conceptually rather than dramatically or figuratively (Ayers, 'Murder' 580, Beehler, 'Play of Signs' 335–7, Donoghue, *The Third Voice* 83). The play consists of a number of highly wrought segments which are unified by a theological (or even liturgical) idea, not by a dramatic or figurative design. This aspect of construction has been identified by a number of critics, most notably Denis Donoghue in *The Third Voice*, who nonetheless does not deny the significance and worth of the play as 'a social text'.

There is no difficulty, then, in allowing the play a high degree of meaning, but the meaning is broad and begins to operate only when the individual agents of the play have been equated with their corresponding institutions. Thus, despite the lauded 'actuality', Thomas is 'the Church', the assassins are 'society', and the play is then available as an illuminating document. The value of a play, however, is not to be equated with the degree to which it offers scope for socio-historical discourse. *Murder in the Cathedral* has too much of this kind of meaning.

(83)

Donoghue is primarily interested in plays as dramatic artefacts and, in that respect, the work is flawed, because it is 'essentially expository'. However, it is precisely the play as 'socio-historical discourse' that most interests me. Eliot's intentions here have been well explored critically; I mean the usual Christian interpretation that sees the play as a kind of 'theology as drama' (Fergusson, *Idea of a Theater* 210). Helen Gardner's first book on Eliot reads the play as the embodiment of certain Christian orthodoxies relating to martyrdom and the hidden work of grace.

Eliot himself encouraged speculation of this sort in his comments on the drama in general at the time. Gordon cites two unpublished talks in 1937 where she reports Eliot as saying 'that poetic drama could awaken the audience to a hidden pattern of reality which may supersede what is conventionally dramatic' (*New Life* 91). An audience would be receptive, he thought, so long as the narrative worked within certain realist norms as well. As a result, the hidden pattern of a more than ordinary reality would be permitted to manifest itself. Again it is not Eliot's religious intention which interests me, but the sort of ideological and cultural work which the play does in the context of the 1930s. To whom is the play addressed? What sort of social discourse is it, what social action is being dramatized, and to what purpose?

There is no doubt that Eliot had in mind a kind of spiritual allegory in dramatizing the story of a martyr (Spencer 21–22), but, in having to locate it historically, he also inevitably made a social allegory as well. And by casting the Knights as recognizably twentieth-century types he strenghtens the contemporary relevance. The merging of Roman and contemporary histories and characters encourages a similar allegorical reading of the 'Coriolan' fragments.

Murder in the Cathedral dramatizes the struggle that will occasionally break out between an entrenched power elite and the mandarinized intellectuals who serve it, cast in the form of a struggle between church and state. This is the way a traditional political science would thematize the problem, or, in another traditional formulation, as J.T. Boulton suggests, the history of ideas would take note of a struggle between Christianity and secularism (3). But these conventional accounts of the play's theme, though they delineate the evolution of institutions or the clash of ideas, do not take into account the text's political contact with its own present, the text as a communicative protocol for thinking about and acting in its own time.

The play, allegorically located within the Cathedral complex, provides a look at the inner life of a mandarinate no longer able to turn a blind eye to the 'higher immorality' (Mills 343) which governs the social and personal behaviour of the dominant oligarchy, which the Knights represent. This oligarchy operates according to a code of conduct of its own which is far more necessary to its own life and well-being than the ethical codes and habits of society in general. The play tries to square the political circle by suggesting that the general ethical and spiritual renewal of society takes precedence over the solidarity and interests of a dominant elite, even though the very elite whose dominance is being challenged is the only part of society that can enforce compliance to the general good against its own interests. We are asked to assume that the moral dissonances of the system of power have become so difficult to bear that only intransigent opposition is possible at the present time.

We are also asked to consider what form that opposition is to take. In the end we are offered Thomas as the exemplary resister. He neither enacts his opposition politically in the world dominated by the elite, nor does he formulate his resistance in the world's discourse; he finds a Christian solution, in Christian terms, to the dilemmas which offend his conscience. This solution confronts power with the authority of personal martyrdom and with the illumination we are, each of us, meant to gain by his selfless act. The power system, at the end of the day, is defied by the superb example of the saintly martyr, but is, of course, left intact. Eliot's lesson? The power of the exemplary sacrifice can renew us as individuals, and through us, renew the system. The play instructs the governors and their immediate servants of their higher responsibilities.

As a reading of the situation of the intelligentsia in the 1930s, *Murder in the Cathedral* conveys a subtextual warning to an intelligentsia in jeopardy. The solution it recommends to the problem was not one to win a wide hearing in that very political time. The play's focus on the private issue of Becket's motives for martyrdom and his discovery of the authentic discipline of submission to God's will, without vanity, works to obscure the socio-political allegory of a mandarinate pressed to conform to the dictates of power. This is the religious version of the argument about culture to the Germans in 1946. In the mid-1930s such an argument did not resonate with that part of the mandarinate which, with various degrees of zeal, had committed itself to the political transformation, even overthrow, of established power in the North Atlantic world. By the

mid-1940s the play's quietist message, in which the suffering consciousness chooses, like Becket, a form of political self-cancellation, would be
far more compelling as a result of the failure of the insurgencies and
idealisms of the 1930s.

In the play itself the characters are presented allegorically, as living on
different levels of moral refinement (Grover Smith, *Poetry and Plays* 185,
but cf. Carol Smith, *Dramatic Theory* 110). Becket is the type of the highest
spiritual and moral consciousness, acutely intellectual, embodying the
leading degree of self-consciousness to be found in the mandarin
sensibility, and acknowledged as such by his colleagues. Becket's
complexity is conveyed in many different ways, but initially with great
force in the appearance of the Tempters, who, as embodiments of
Becket's own personality and inwardness, humanize him. They locate
Becket in different times and places. The First Tempter recalls a raffish,
comradely Becket, a man of the world. He reminds Becket of his friend-
ships when he was close to the King and of 'gay Tom' who enlivened
many evenings at the very centre of power (*Plays* 18). The Second
Tempter insists on reminding him of the political Becket doing his
master's business as Chancellor, and then learning not to do it (20).

Each of the Tempters provides us with an opportunity to witness the
spectacle of Becket's weaknesses resisted and overcome. Eliot shows us
all the ways in which power always already possesses the mandarin, not
as an alien invasion of the self, but in the form of the Tempters, from
within, as the self itself. Winston Smith again is our guide in these
psychological latitudes. The mandarin subject then faces enormous difficulties in resisting both the suave blandishments of the master and,
failing that, his bareknuckle threats. The inquisitor literature of the
twentieth century, from *Darkness at Noon* to the prison writings of the
Romanian philosopher Constantine Noica, corroborate the cunning of
Becket's Tempters.

The Chorus of Women have none of these problems. They are a
typical product of Tory political philosophy. The feminized masses are
incapable of reflection, only of reflecting the common intuitive
accumulations of a traditional culture; they live lives of instinct, always
in need of firm leadership and communal security, given to panic when
they feel doubt, bovine, fecund, embodying the lowest level of consciousness imaginable. They are pushed and pulled by circumstances over
which they have no control and about which they cannot think clearly:
'Some presage of an act / Which our eyes are compelled to witness, has
forced our feet / Towards the cathedral. We are forced to bear witness'

(11). They cannot see and know for themselves, but have eyes only, which 'are compelled to witness' the coming events without knowing them; the roundabout formulation delineates Eliot's sense of the proletarian epistemology. Subject to external force, they are also sometimes in the grip of perverse compulsions as well, and, because Eliot can never seem to think of the 'lower orders' save in terms of the grossest appetites, some of them are disposed occasionally to Sweeneyish sex crimes, 'Several girls have disappeared / Unaccountably, . . .' (16). They cluster 'close by the cathedral' (11), outside the walls, because they are outside the system of power, like the washerwoman prole in *Nineteen Eighty-Four* whom Winston watches from the window and envies in the minutes before his arrest.

Eliot, of course, does not ask us to envy them. How can we? At least the prole in *Nineteen Eighty-Four* was free of the contradictions which entangle Winston. For Eliot the people must remain in thrall; they must be made to believe, and that is as much a task for the publicist as it is for the pedagogue. In order for the people to believe in the legitimacy of the church as a site of socio-ethical renewal, especially an ethical renewal of a corrupted governing class, the church must resist the Erastianism which may develop as a result of its proximity to power. The church's publicists must be careful about how the relationship of church and state is perceived.

By alienating the mass of the people from orthodox Christianity, by leading them to identify the Church with the actual hierarchy and to suspect it of being an instrument of oligarchy or class, it leaves men's minds exposed to varieties of irresponsible and irreflective enthusiasm followed by a second crop of paganism. (*Idea* 51)

Yet the church in all of Eliot's social writings is so close to the hierarchies of power, one ends up suspecting that the church's supposed independence is little more than a truth of convenience.

Murder in the Cathedral is not a work that questions the validity or legitimacy of the system of power. It takes on the issue (or perhaps non-issue) of how established power may be morally renewed in the world, and how it can be brought more fully in line with the requirements of a Christian society. It is not interested in the drama of how demos is to be emancipated. In short, Becket is not in the play in order to overthrow the system. The world of the Knights is also Becket's world; he simply accepts it as the socio-political given. The Knights in their turn act within the norms of moral consciousness of the oligarchy. These are simply the men who control society; they represent the power elite and each formulates views appropriate to this socio-political positioning. Within the social theme of the play, Becket's struggles are aimed at renewing their moral and spiritual life. His struggle with himself, and the martyrdom which he undergoes, is all the power he feels he is able to discharge in order, on the one hand, to admonish the power elite and, on the other, to authenticate his action for himself and others. The whole question of his own spiritual refinement, and the theological issues it engages, so that he can achieve martyrdom with the proper sort of inward repose, is essentially beside the point politically speaking.

It is the ethical reform of the oligarchy from within that constitutes the social theme and ideological effect of the play (cf. Stevie Smith, 'History' 170). Like the street in 'Triumphal March' or the ancestral corridor in 'Difficulties of a Statesman', the Cathedral represents one of the principal social sites of power. It is an interior space where the directive elite transacts the spiritual and ideological side of its business through the priestly mandarins in its service. It is also the interior arena where, when necessary, ideological struggles between various factions or levels of the power elite, and here, specifically, between those who exercise political power and the mandarinate's spiritual authority, are played out. The play argues that a power elite cannot long survive if it does not have contact with people like Becket, even if they must occasionally be martyred in order to rejuvenate the power structure. This is the essential message of a Christian politics.

Eliot recognizes that the moral and spiritual refinement of a Becket is absolutely necessary for society as a whole, but more properly for the governing class. As a leading spirit, the Becket-type leads an exemplary life and undergoes, in this case, an exemplary death, authenticating in death the spiritual principles for which he lived. At about this time F.R. Leavis was putting forward, in literary terms, a parallel argument about the social efficacy of poetic consciousness and its position in society as an exemplary and redemptive pattern of consciousness. The poet, he wrote in *New Bearings in English Poetry* (1932), was 'at the most conscious point of the race in his time' (19). Poetry had the power to 'communicate the actual quality of experience with a subtlety and precision unapproachable by any other means'. But, for Leavis, the goal of this 'finer awareness' is not merely literary or aesthetic enchantment, but, ultimately, the moral renovation of society, the very redemption of intelligence.

For Eliot, too, this was not only a literary matter. It was what a Christian politics was all about. His comments in 1941 about the French priest, Charles de Foucauld, who was murdered by Moslems in North

Africa in 1916, confirm this point. Eliot had read René Bazin's biography of de Foucauld in the early 1920s. The holiness of the man's life in the North African desert was exemplary. 'His aim,' Eliot writes, 'was not primarily to convert by teaching, but to *live* the Christian life, alone among the natives' ('Towards a Christian Britain' 116). He concludes that it is '*through* such men as de Foucauld that the reborn Christian consciousness comes' (117, my emphasis). Eliot's sense of the necessity of martyrdom teaches more than a spiritual lesson; the martyr-figure delineates a pattern of more general relevance. Historically, this medieval form of respect owed to suffering and sacrifice (cf. Davidson, 'Saint's Play' 153 *passim*), owed the saint or martyr, the radicals of the exemplary spiritual life, has been shifted, in a secular time, onto the shoulders of the artist by the arrival of bourgeois society. Such forms of feeling; desire for authenticity, unity of theory and practice, the metaphysical hunger to align the self with the 'genuine' natural or supernatural order of things, and the acceptance of sacrifice, of suffering for one's art, have now come to be increasingly associated with the emotional temper of the artist. These constitute the social meanings of artistic consciousness and the life that embodies it; the rage for the contemporary literary biography feeds the same socio-spiritual hungers which made the saint's life and the books of martyrs standard fare in the Middle Ages.

The tortured artist-genius, from Chatterton to Sylvia Plath, positioned epistemologically, like the martyr, outside everyday society, assumes a new position in the bourgeois order of things. She becomes the explorer of consciousness and of the extremes of human experience and knowledge. A new kind of spirituality falls on the shoulders of the secular saint. The uneasy relationship which bourgeois society has maintained with these psychic scouts has been endured simply because it has been felt that such adventuresomeness in the artist vivifies society, renews and validates it. Feudal society used the church and its various institutional and ideological extensions as the protected social enclave for such spirits within aristocratic culture. Art in the bourgeois era marks off a new kind of interior space where the aesthetic denotes the new name for an old spiritual adventure and appoints new artistic and psychological languages, uncontaminated by orthodox Christianity, in which to act it out.

Eliot is making a claim here for the incorporation of the spiritual struggle which Becket undergoes, or some similar form of it, as an absolutely indispensable, and saving, aspect of all oligarchic epistemology. In *The Family Reunion* and *The Cocktail Party* he will dilate this idea in terms of contemporary society. In *The Idea of a Christian Society* he will

indulge in a utopian exercise in which the 'Beckets' will not only be recognized, but nurtured and protected, as the Community of Christians.
The Knights in *Murder in the Cathedral* cannot see this yet, although the
play accepts without question their right to exercise power. They are
simply blind to the importance of the spiritual or psychic explorer. The
play works to make the audience understand why Becket's suffering is
necessary for the good of the elite, although, in the typical metonymic
logic of the governors, it is also for the good of all (Burke *Philosophy* 96).

Eliot stages the debate that resounds within the precincts of power. A
leading mandarin suffers a fit of conscience as he finds himself entangled in a corrupted polity; he suffers also from a sense of his own sinful-
ness and a desire to atone, but his moral scruples run dead against the
paramount reality which the power elite, in the form of the Knights,
endorses and which it shares with the audience in the theatre. That is
why the Knights are able to turn and so familiarly address the audience
after the murder. This martyr enjoys immense prestige among the lower
mandarinate, the Priests in this case, (14–15) and the 'people' – i.e. the
Chorus of Women – who pay him respect to the point of discipleship.

The challenge to the established political order has the effect of bringing out the usual contradictions of social and political life, a tearing away
of the ideological veil which obscures the 'higher immorality' of the elite
from general view, an action which maddens the powerful into parox-
ysms of abuse.

> THE THREE KNIGHTS . . .
> You are the Archbishop who was made by the King; whom he set
>   in your place to carry out his command.
> You are his servant, his tool, and his jack,
> You wore his favours on your back,
> You had your honours all from his hand; from him you had the
>   power, the seal and the ring.
> This is the man who was the tradesman's son: the backstairs brat
>   who was born in Cheapside;
> This is the creature that crawled upon the King; swollen with
>   blood and swollen with pride.
> Creeping out of the London dirt,
> Crawling up like a louse on your shirt,
> The man who cheated, swindled, lied; broke his oath and betrayed
>   his King.   (38)

This speech and the dialogue that follows between the Knights and Becket
make quite clear the sort of relation which the powerful always want to

maintain with their mandarins. We made you, and so we shall break you, if necessary. The point of bringing up Becket's lowly origins is to underline how he has been constructed by power into its own vile little 'creature'. And the sting of that is not lost on Becket when he himself mentions Cheapside again a little later in the same scene. Against this stripping bare of the mandarin's position to reveal that he is precisely a nothing socially and politically, the mandarin as 'renegade' (47) puts forward a higher morality. By this means the moral rebel obstructs the easy workings of power, a power typically untroubled by any serious moral scruples. Yet the only outward expression of this resistance to power which the play offers us is martyrdom, self-sacrifice. The focus is here on personal purification in an exemplary fashion. The example does not urge others to visible and concrete political action, but makes reform entirely inward and private.

The whole action of the play, dramatizing an internal dispute within the elite social formation, is imparted, perhaps surprisingly because it is the elite itself which is being criticized, entirely from the perspective of the elite. The people as social actors – again always outside looking in – are seen as ineffectual, numbed spectators, unable to understand or reason, but needing the dramatic spectacle of the martyrdom in order to absorb through their nerves the importance of what is happening. The lesson which they learn, at one level, might be seen as the primitive lesson of tribal redemption through blood sacrifice; the Chorus of Women are finally consoled by the propriety of the sacrifice within the metaphorical framework of seasonal rebirth and of resignation to fates which they cannot understand. At another level, the play simply puts on a splendid tragic ritual for the people and for the lesser mandarins, firstly as a threat, and, then later to occupy them with spectacle (but cf. Samuelson, 'Sword' 73–75). The Stalinist show trial of the 1930s is an example of the genre drawn from life.

The Priests/mandarins want to understand the sacrifice as the exemplary authentication of the social whole embodied in the triumph of the church (transposed to another context we might think of it as the triumph of the vanguard Party): '. . . the Church is stronger for this action, / Triumphant in adversity. It is fortified / By persecution: supreme, so long as men will die for it' (52). What Becket learns is that only the fool thinks, 'He can turn the wheel on which he turns' (19), a knowledge offered to the intelligentsia from a religious point of view, but which has significant political meanings as well. The only way is the way of submission, to open oneself, so that suffering and martyrdom become an occasion for the divine pattern to show itself.

Chorus, Tempters, Priests counsel deferment, delay, even physical resistance. Why? Because in this telling there is no programme for confronting power, no intellectual space is defined from which to theorize the prime movers of the social wheel. The result, according to Stevie Smith, is terror ('History' 173). The only way Becket can reach the stillness of the turning wheel is to yield to the mover, the one point that he cannot occupy himself as a self. He affirms the arrival of 'the figure of God's purpose' (43) as a result of a letting go of the self, for becoming the medium through which that purpose manifests itself in the world as action, 'It is not I, Becket from Cheapside, . . .' (41) who acts. But it does involve a kind of action, of course, not only a matter of inward transformation, 'Unbar the doors! throw open the doors,' he calls out to the Priests, who, still entangled in the world as defined by power, rush to turn the 'house of prayer . . . into a fortress' (45). Becket is well past this kind of futility, 'We are not to triumph by fighting, by stratagem, or by resistance, / Not to fight with beasts as men' (46).

The system of power, as a result, remains intact. Becket's 'action' has all its weight elsewhere, and at best, in the here and now, it is experienced as 'a sudden painful joy' (43), as a resonance, and a possibility of change, but not as a strategy for supplanting worldly authority. Certainly, the play conveys a theological point about Christian martyrdom, but, politically, it defies gravity. It also implies that the powerful will always need spirits like Becket in order to reaffirm their own moral legitimacy, but paradoxically in the very moment when the elite is most visibly illegitimate. The play also conveys, perhaps even in spite of itself, a clear-sighted analysis of the actual relations between a mandarinized intelligentsia and the powers to which it is bound in history, notwithstanding what 'power' it may also possess, may think it possesses, from 'heaven'.

In this respect, then, the play also conveys an ominous warning to the intelligentsia of the 1930s. The behaviour and speeches of the Knights at the end of the play are clearly part of a socio-political allegory that is unmistakeable. At the end, the Knights, sounding like government spokesmen, address the audience in proper rhetorical attire, all of them admiringly unctuous about the man they have just killed, flattering the audience with their candour, pointing out the nature of the dispute and the necessity of keeping good 'order' in society and preserving 'the welfare of the State' (50) in an unhappy time. They reflect paramount reality in all its settled, unquestionable obviousness. Richard Brito, coming forward as he does with the authority of a 'distinguished family' behind him, argues very well, to 'hard-headed, sensible people' that Becket was simply an aberration, a man suffering from some sort of 'mania', which manifested itself as a monstrous 'egotism' that could only be fed by obsessive self-display, indeed a mania so intense that it invited its own annihilation, so that the sacrifice of the martyr is little more than a kind of 'Suicide while of Unsound Mind' (51). A thousand political 'suicides' in contemporary political history and not only in the totalitarian regimes of right and left, have been submerged by the same reasoning process. And in case the people do not teach themselves to believe it, there is always the system of surveillance, detention and discipline which Reginald Fitz Urse, the First Knight, alludes to in his closing remarks: '. . . I suggest that you now disperse quietly to your homes. Please be careful not to loiter in groups at street corners, and do nothing that might provoke any public outbreak' (52).

On one level Eliot's aim in the play is clear enough, if we simply revolve it in orthodox Christian terms. As socio-political allegory in the 1930s, however, it is quite another thing and there is a good deal in it which Eliot does not consciously intend. We are left with the feeling that the argument of the Knights about Becket is essentially specious and immoral, although the action of the play does not question their political right to exercise authority and to put the argument forward. By Becket's acquiescence and the sense of the inevitableness of the Knights's authority, the play dramatizes a central paradox of social life and delineates a way of speciously resolving it. Dissent from the immoralities and corruptions of the powerful is most authentic and real when it is least effective in changing matters. In the end, for the non-Christian dissenter, for the secular humanist intellectuals and mandarins of the 1930s whom the isms of the day had seduced into other, oppositional professions and into possible plans of action, Eliot's silence on the exercise of material power sounds ominously like a warning.

Yes, it is Becket who holds our admiring attention if we are Christians and accept the established disposition of things, but if we do not accept, and are interested in resisting or changing or even overthrowing a system of power that is unjust or corrupted, the play confronts us, in spite of itself, with an illustration of how we can expect to be treated; that the Knights are given the final word about the fate of resistance speaks directly to the heart of what seems to be Eliot's subtextual message to the intelligentsia. In the end we do not believe the Knights on the matter of Becket's motives and psychology, because the play has shown us why we should not; however, we just might believe, in fact we always *do* believe, the official version of events in the matter of less exalted and less attractive personalities, and especially so if we see ourselves as good, hardheaded, sensible people.

The Family Reunion moves towards these dilemmas from another direction. The contemporary country house setting concentrates our attention in a smaller, but recognizable, social geography of England. I agree with Albert Wertheim when he says of the British 'homecoming' play in general (and *The Family Reunion* is his model,) that the family and the house are representative of society ('Homecoming' 154), but not in the way he means it. The Monchesney manorial house does not represent society in some general sense, but it is a microcosm of a particular class. Wishwood parallels Canterbury Cathedral as a traditional location for the elaboration of social power. The Monchesney clan are not particularly powerful in any active political sense, indeed they are offered to us as a family, essentially in social retirement and decline, living off the inherited capital of the past. The scion has been away for a decade, the younger brothers, John and Arthur, are comic figures who never appear: one is stupid, the other reckless, both of them are stock characters drawn from English social comedy. There are others: the matriarch, Amy, a variety of well-meaning but baffled dependants and other retainers, the loyal gentleman's man and chauffeur, the good physician who ministers to the body of the family, the cartoon policeman, and the weak or absent patriarch. But the play is more than the sum of its character-types.

The powerful female presence in the play, the virago Agatha, the self-sacrificing Mary, are intended to balance the knight errant who is destined to focus in his own psyche the psychological, emotional and spiritual crisis of a whole class. The two women also provide an occasion for discipleship, even though there are tremors here of Eliot's usual 'horror of women' and his 'predisposition to see women as creatures of sexual sin who dare men to consort with them and so receive their ineradicable taint' (Gordon, *New Life* 83). But Harry is the only one who, like Becket, affirms the existence of a level of spiritual reality which, when one has eyes to see it, finally defines the character of one's whole being. The privileged, sequestered lives of the family, on the other hand, even if several of them are dim-witted, pedestrian and parasitic, are treated as a matter of immovable fact. There is no suggestion of a specifically social criticism here. If they are criticized at all, it is as failed individuals, rather than as the typical products of class society.

The urgent psychological pressures which Harry feels, throw into high relief the personal limitations of his aunts and uncles. For them

Wishwood represents a static unchanging world of satisfied needs and easy command (*Plays* 77). Harry does not share this confidence. After he has been astonished by Amy's observation that nothing has changed at Wishwood, Harry must listen to the obtuse Gerald when he recommends a drive in the country and the acquisition of 'a couple of new hunters'. Charles follows with inconsequential advice on stocking the wine cellar and Ivy airily encourages the rustication of the gardener. And the kitchen too, Violet adds, needs attention now that the aging cook 'is too old to know what she is doing' (64–65). We are certainly not being asked to believe that this set is at the active centre of power in England. But they are associated with a yet viable aristocratic class and carry, therefore, a certain social authority that we are asked to believe still means something in a class-divided society. The argument for taking such people seriously, as members of the dominant class, is developed explicitly in *Notes towards the Definition of Culture* (42–44), but it has been there in Eliot's social criticism all through the 1930s.[8]

The model character of this fragment of the social formation, it turns out, is now dead. Harry's father, Agatha tells Harry, might have represented the true type of the refined gentleman who could have chosen a life in rural retirement, although in this 'damned house' (115) the pattern was never realized.

> Your father might have lived – or so I see him –
> An exceptionally cultivated country squire,
> Reading, sketching, playing on the flute,
> Something of an oddity to his country neighbours,
> But not neglecting his public duties. (103)

There is nothing particularly remarkable about all of this. The family portrait here has been drawn from an eighteenth-century model of the traditional squirearchy. Squire Allworthy in *Tom Jones* and Mr. Knightley in *Emma* are ancestors of the type of Harry's father. But it is little more than an abstraction; a schematic diagram of an English family seat drawn to accommodate the theme.

Eliot understood a good deal about English life at this level of society, but he was not really of it. Wishwood is in England certainly, but it could, with some deft changes of decor, gesture and accent, be located in Brahmin New England just as easily. Indeed Harry's spiritual-moral dilemmas seem somewhat awkwardly positioned or uncharacteristic of the English temperament in the social context of the play. I would not say the play is unconvincing, just a little out of focus, not quite what an

English writer would have made of these materials. But an American, with a deep affection for England, but still tied psychologically to the powerful Puritanism of his native region (Kirk 139), might very well produce such a play. The spirit of the action and the theme is essentially the New England Puritan fascination with evil and derangement. One might see this as very much a New England play, curiously feeding back into the British upper class context some of the obsessive psychological energy of the American mind. The curious thing about American religious feeling is that it rarely impresses one with its spiritual content or its holiness, but it always astonishes by its psychological force. The central trio – Harry, Agatha, Mary – may well hear the music of paradise on the other side of purgatory but pitched high, in the key of hysteria.

The family metaphor is very important in other ways as well. For one thing, it provides a formal source for the play. The Aeschylian dynamics of the cursed family in *The Orestia* are suggested and juggled, but do not carry much conviction in Eliot's rendering. There is no real dialogue with Aeschylus here; it is a matter of convenient scaffolding (but cf. Belli, *Greek Myths* 54, Carpentier, 'Orestes' 17–18 and MacVean, 'Argos' 128). The family metaphor is important for another reason mentioned in much of the commentary on the play, but rarely explored. This is the view which Gordon, for example, buries in a parenthesis, that the Monchesney clan epitomizes the whole human family (*New Life* 88). This seems to me a rather large and importantly preposterous observation and it is one often repeated.

It is a grotesque joke to think of the Monchesneys as symbolizing the whole 'human family'. They are quite clearly a family drawn strictly to the scale of a dominant social elite. Stepping back for a moment and reading the play as a social document, we might note that the Monchesneys, realistically speaking, represent a minor fragment of the oligarchical network of families, business firms, transnational bureaucracies etc. which dominate and draw together the North Atlantic world. This does not mean that what the play conveys, therefore, has no relevance to a whole society. It does, but it does so in an entirely different way than is usually supposed by a reflex liberalism.

The members of the manorial family do not need to stand for all of us, because they are the only social fraction, in Eliot's scheme, epistemologically positioned to undergo, potentially, the peak experiences which define, from above, the character of a whole society. Harry from his inherited position in the commanding heights is best equipped by temperament, education, authority *and* by divine election to 'represent' us all. This sense of being chosen by God, in the Calvinist tradition of American Puritanism, provides the one intangible element in the career profile of the potential saint. It is the one cicatrice in an otherwise seam-less social surface, which allows Harry to cross the frontier into a world of spirit which is 'inexplicable' (114) to ordinary mortals. These are repre-sented by the other family members in the play and, on the other side of the social divide, by the servants and the Chorus, a rather dim-witted, Sweeney-like bunch who do not like their routines disturbed and who suffer the usual epistemological cramps.

> We do not like to look out of the same window, and see quite a
>   different landscape.
> . . .
> We understand the ordinary business of living,
> We know how to work the machine,
> We can usually avoid accidents,
> We are insured against fire,
> Against larceny and illness,
> Against defective plumbing,
> But not against the act of God.   (120)

Within the magic circle of the manorial family it is possible to glimpse the divine pattern; such a vision is not necessarily accorded all of the members of the family, but they are all touched by it. Evelyn Waugh juggles similar ideas in *Brideshead Revisited*.

Those few in the manor who come to higher consciousness do not, in fact cannot, stand for all humanity in some sort of easy symbolic equiva-lence. The superior spirits redeem the time of chronometers and, thus, redeem the established order of things (cf. *Idea* 42–3). Their exemplary experiences and their knowledge, Eliot argues, ought to define society, not the quotidian activities of the dopes, activities to which the liberal mandarinate was busily devoting its intellectual energies in the 1930s (see Auden's 'A Communist to Others' or Day Lewis's *The Magnetic Mountain*, for example). In the play, the Chorus explicitly stands down from the leading historical agency which Marxist thought had assigned to prole-tarian consciousness. The privileged epistemology, the play tells us, finds its greatest amplitude in the commanding heights, not in the lower depths.

It is Harry, the Lord Monchesney, who sees and embodies most clearly the intersection of the visible and the invisible. Agatha and Mary are lifted up by Harry's words and passion to the point where they are capable of understanding Harry's pilgrimage, as their final speeches show. Downing, the chauffeur, by long and loyal contact with the master, also comes to 'understand' and accept Harry's election, and can even see the Eumenides, although he calls them ghosts; it seems that, in Eliot's rendering of the social world, chauffeurs do not read Aeschylus. But Downing's understanding of Harry's significance is very much to the point. All members of society, Eliot seems to be saying through the kindly chauffeur, can be redeemed by contact with the leading spirit, the spiritual voyager, but only if they do not ask too many questions and only if they still their own Sweeneyish hungers (cf. *Idea* 34). Even the befuddled Charles admits at the end that he might come to understand Harry's project, and, for a moment, the fog lifts (121). But the Chorus, as always, persists in perplexity.

> We do not know what we are doing;
> And even, when you think of it,
> We do not know much about thinking.
> . . .
> And what is being done to us?
> And what are we, and what are we doing?
> To each and all of these questions
> There is no conceivable answer.
> We have suffered far more than a personal loss —
> We have lost our way in the dark. (120–21)

Certainly Eliot's contempt for the lower orders is attenuated here, but not by much. In the context of both the serious and the fashionable leftism of the 1930s such a portrait of 'the people' challenges that Marxist notion of the making of consciousness as a product of class struggle, with the proletariat as the social formation of greatest epistemological privilege.

The bankrupt political traditionalism of the past, which no longer satisfied the leftist mandarinate in those years, required some new factors as part of its ideological retooling as a renascent conservatism. Eliot's Christianity is hardly a 'new factor'. It was never intended to be so. What was required was not some particular refinement of a traditional conservatism, but a transformation of the socio-historical context, some new set of historical circumstances – in fact, something like 'a society . . . so desperate' (*Idea* 23) – that would exhaust the false hopes of the radical activists of the 1930s. And, in addition, the moment required the mandarinate's growing disillusionment with the liberal programme for society in the interwar years. Eliot felt confident that the mandarins would eventually come to see that liberalism, while preparing the way for its own negation (*Idea* 16), could not satisfy the deepest aspirations and needs of the human being.

The 1940s provided precisely the socio-historical situation which could render Eliot's agenda relevant. The rise of fascism, the Munich crisis, the Soviet-Nazi pact, the war itself, the Holocaust, the moral nihilism of power politics, the display of an unprecedented level of world-historical terror at Hiroshima and Nagasaki, brought the rebellious, liberal, socially conscious mandarinate of the 1920s and 1930s to heel in the 1940s. And, in these changed circumstances, Eliot's programme for the individual and society seemed finally to make sense. It is in *Four Quartets* that the reclamation of the wandering mandarinate reaches its highest and most telling potency. And as Ronald Bush, David Moody, Helen Gardner and Grover Smith have amply demonstrated *The Family Reunion* anticipates again and again the far more subtle maze of Eliot's masterpiece. In the 1940s, the war crisis, the hunger for order and reassurance among the mandarins, and the parasymbolist fabrication of an aestheticized mysticism in *Four Quartets* finally achieve a perfect consonance. As a result, the rapid canonization of the poem and the elevation of Eliot to the status of the age's sage becomes inevitable.

In the period of *The Family Reunion*, however, this was not so clear; Eliot's analysis of the situation and the implied solutions enacted at Wishwood seemed little more than the earnest redundancies of a passionate, but irrelevant, Quixote. The problem lies in the fact that Wishwood is a protected enclave, set off from 'the world', served loyally by the domestic help, but aware also that there are social and political dangers out there beyond the sheltered haven. Arthur's Bertie Woosterish car accident in Ebury Street reported in the newspaper at the end of Scene 1, Part II (100) provokes Gerald into blurting out that this is the sort of thing which 'the Communists make capital of' (100). We are meant to understand about Gerald's limitations that he has not noticed his own pun. And this sense of the impropriety of exposing the family to the gaze of outsiders excites the torpid Charles to peevish comment: 'In my time, these affairs were kept out of the papers; / But nowadays, there's no such thing as privacy'. These people and this house constitute a traditional form of the domestic culture of power in England. And although Gerald and Charles are British comic types, this does not change the social positioning of the action. The manorial house is a private place where one does not have to close the blinds and where the help are 'our servants who belong here' (63).[9]

We can assume that the Knights in *Murder in the Cathedral* will know the family world of *The Family Reunion* very well indeed, because it is also their world. The brutal political business in the Cathedral is transacted by men who come from families as distinguished as the Monchesneys, and the sort of private repose they, in their turn, will find in their own domestic havens is made visible in the later play. Wishwood is not singular; it is the type and pattern of a myriad privacies all over England in which the settled oligarchy finds domestic ease. The decor of such privacies has been very lovingly delineated by Mark Girouard.

Harry, as the inheriting son, educated in the proper ways of power, and armed with superior intelligence, could have entered the wider public world of affairs, the Knights's world, without any impediments. But he chose not to. We are meant to be surprised by this unconventional turn of events in the conventional life-narrative implied by the social positioning. Perhaps we are meant to be surprised as well by Becket's defection from the enjoyment of worldly power, although his position as Archbishop acts to attenuate our surprise; after all, in his resistance to profane power he is only satisfying the demands of his spiritual office. We ought to be surprised if he doesn't fulfil the dictates of his sacred calling. But Harry is another matter.

His defection from assuming the management of the family seat seems, at first, irresponsible; he refers to it modestly at one point as 'bad manners' (117). We soon come to realize that Harry's actions are not a shirking of his duty at all, but responses to higher responsibilities. For one thing, there is the question of his feelings of guilt about his dead wife, lost at sea some years before. He seems to confess (66) that he has murdered her, although the others choose to believe he means it metaphorically, that he 'pushed her over' in a manner of speaking, an interpretation of the deed which Downing, Harry's chauffeur, seems to corroborate, which means that Harry's 'conscience can be clear' (67). Harry retorts that his malady goes 'a good deal deeper / Than what people call their conscience' and involves a kind of metaphysical dread, 'a cancer / That eats away the self' (67). That cancer is not a disease of his own mind but a disease of the world in which he has to live. Whether this is also the world in which the others have to live is not immediately apparent. Because he insists that he is awake to a reality to which the others have no access (except for Agatha and Mary, who seem by instinct to have arrived at the threshold of understanding) we are left to piece together Harry's world from the gnomic comments he exchanges, first with Mary in Scene 2 of Part I, and, later, with Agatha in scene 2, Part II. Most commentators agree that Harry's consciousness has worked its way through guilt and remorse, through the corruption of the world, symbolized in the Aeschylian curse on Wishwood, to a vision of the hidden pattern in the everyday which vouchsafes the presence of the divine, and which provides him with the protocols for salvation.

Harry comes to realize that if he faces the depravity in himself and his family (who epitomize the whole human family), he can play a part in a pattern of redemption . . . The dead wife represents his polluted soul; Mary a rather perfunctory temptation. The country house, with its decayed family, is a naturalistic front for what is in essence a morality play in which figures move in set patterns, as they try to . . . free the house from the curse of its decline.

(Gordon, *New Life* 88, 90)

Ronald Bush, exploring the verbal links between the play and 'Burnt Norton', agrees with Gordon on the essential outlines of Harry's metaphysical dilemmas (190–192), which are ultimately rooted in Eliot's personal quest for redemption. Grover Smith also finds the theme of redemption central to the action of the play (208). Harry must return home in order to know himself. He must confront the memories of his childhood in order to purge himself of past guilts and traumas (Wertheim, 'Homecoming' 151).

The situation of personal guilt releases consciousness for a more profound journey on which very few of us can go. Harry's will be a lonely exploration. Like Becket, he is launched on a pilgrimage which can only lead to some form of transfiguration, either through martyrdom or asceticism. Harry becomes a superb spiritual voyager and visionary. The avenging Eumenides who haunt him through the first part of the play turn out to be beneficent guides who will eventually lead him through the inferno of a depraved world into destiny's last word.

For an audience impressed by Harry's heroics of consciousness, *The Family Reunion* is a play of great power and suggestiveness. At the risk of sounding awfully pedestrian in the embrace of so much exultant mysteriousness, I find it interesting nonetheless that the Harry who is off to confront the reality humankind cannot bear very much of, 'Somewhere on the other side of despair', and who will turn his back on his inheritance for the atonement inscribed in desert, thirst and deprivation, in heat and ice, caring over the fates of humble people (111) will do all this with chauffeur in tow, and with a forwarding address 'care of the bank in London' (117). Not even Charles de Foucauld, who is quite clearly the model here, was so well serviced by privilege. But I do not want to trivialize the serious issues which Eliot's audiences saw in the drama in 1939 and during its revivals in the 1940s and 1950s. However, at this point we do glimpse a serious contradiction in Eliot's twin focuses in the play, Harry's individual pilgrimage and the nature of the Wishwood world. It never seems to occur to Eliot that the protected enclave itself, and its epistemological inheritance, might need to be shaken off entirely in order for Harry's journey to matter. But Eliot cannot deny or reject the Wishwoods of England. The world that Wishwood represents is the fundamental building block of his social vision and of his social programme, namely, the maintenance of a traditional elite as the epistemological high ground of society, embodying its directive force.

Harry is a kind of culture hero for the sort of audience one might have found in the Westminster Theatre in March of 1939 when the play opened. But there was not enough of that sort of audience around to sustain the play for more than five weeks in the months before war. Martin Browne put the short run down to general distraction caused by the tension in international affairs. The political crisis in central Europe had taken a new turn towards war in the spring. Hitler annexed Bohemia and Moravia and the agreement concluded at Munich in November 1938, which had distressed so many thoughtful people, including Eliot, was now shown to be an Axis charade performed for the benefit of the British and French appeasers. Browne believed that the play required a great deal of attentiveness and audiences in the spring of that year had their minds elsewhere. In the 1946 revival of the play the reviews were far more sympathetic to Eliot's aims (see for example Keown, "At the Play" 434) and Browne notes that audiences were far more receptive to the play after they had experienced 'the nightmares of the 1940s' ('From *The Rock*' 63). He concludes from this that Eliot was acutely prescient and that history, so to speak, needed a half decade to catch up with his vision.

Harry is an intellectual/spiritual hero like Becket, who comes to speak some of Eliot's finest poetry, as do Mary and Agatha, but, unlike *Murder in the Cathedral*, the play is little more than a dramatic cantata, what Desmond MacCarthy called at the time of the first production 'a drama of inner life' ('Some Notes' 455), statically ritualistic rather than dramatic. The plot is minimal; the dramatic structure a claustrophobic pastiche of Aeschylus; the arias long and sonorous. In a different register Auden and Isherwood's *The Ascent of F6* deals, more entertainingly, but no less gnomically, with the same kind of culture hero. Michael Ransom is drawn from the then celebrated but enigmatic character of T.E. Lawrence. I do not think that Lawrence is a model for Harry, though they come from the same region of the psyche's geography. Indeed the obsession in the 1930s with the extraordinary introvert mysteriously endowed with redemptive power, an individual shaped by privation, isolation and danger, but, more importantly, by intense inner struggle with the self and all its flaws, has often been commented upon (Graves and Hodge *Long Weekend* 218; Hynes *Auden* 189–92; Cunningham *Thirties* 173–76). The typical narrative always features the journey to mountain top, or desert, or other frontier region or place of exile, where the soul, undistracted by the routines of everyday life, is released in its solitude to face its own demons. Through such a struggle it is cleansed of its sins, motives are purified, and the person is then released to acquit the work of redemption. The ur-text, of course, is Christ's time in the desert (McCarthy, 'Eliot's *Murder*' 7). Stanley Spencer's series of paintings in 1939 called 'Christ in the Wilderness' offers a visual commentary on the significance of this pattern in the period.

Harry is cast in this mould. His is a compelling kind of rebellion against the upper middle class obtuseness in Wishwood, and its easy materialism. But it is not a rebellion which hopes to displace the Wishwood inheritance, precisely in the same way that Becket's rebellion is not positioned to displace worldly authority. Indeed one might say that both plays affirm power, even in the moment of seeming to reject it. Wishwood may be 'cursed' and in decline for the dramatic purpose of maintaining an Aeschylian scaffolding, but Wishwood will remain secure and intact. Two women, tuned to Harry's obsessions, come to understand and encourage the audaciousness of Harry's quest and take Wishwood in trust during Harry's exile.

The nature of the quest, what Harry is really after, seems oddly irrelevant to the social meaning of the play. No one knows where Harry is going and why and what he hopes to accomplish there. This is due to Eliot's own ambivalence. In the 1939 production Eliot had to tell the actor Michael Redgrave, in order to establish a more concrete set of motivations, that Harry was off to take a job in London's East End working among the poor (Gordon, *New Life* 92). Of course, it is significant that the 'sop' Eliot threw to Redgrave was one that would have appealed to a socially and politically conscious age, even if the meaning of Eliot's advice was highly ambiguous, intending, one presumes, to convey both his exasperation at Redgrave's literal mindedness and his disdain for the fashionable, political bleeding hearts.

Harry, we are asked to acknowledge, is one of those supreme temperaments through which the divine makes itself known in the world. Harry is Becket rescued from the political entanglements of the earlier play. A society can have a number of such personalities whose transfigurations through personal sacrifice are essential social factors in the continuing psychic and moral health of that society. Without them the whole world becomes a kind of Wishwood, full of well-meaning, harmless duffers who will not turn back the encroaching idiocy of life, but inadvertently hurry it along. The Harrys and the Beckets, members and servants of the elite, redeem intelligence, superiority and power by the temerity and principle of their faring forward into the unexplored.

In *The Family Reunion*, a spiritual process is enacted as a moment of crisis and conflict within the manorial family in the same way that the death of Becket dramatizes conflicting senses of personal responsibility within the whole oligarchy itself. Such enactments are universal or make universalist claims when viewed from the vantage of the elite formation itself; elites always interpret their own experiences as representative of society as a whole. A healthy, wise society, Eliot suggests, sustains the Harrys and the Beckets as indispensable spirits and gives them the means by which they can pursue their destinies. With this end in view, *The Idea of a Christian Society* (1939) provides a schema of society, an idea of society, in which the Beckets and the Harrys, and the Celias from *The Cocktail Party*, can find the proper sort of social nurturing from which to undertake their redemptive inner voyages, the function of which, Eliot believed, was to redeem us all.

When commentators like J.R. Harrison, Roger Kojecky and William Chace have explicated Eliot's social criticism, the emphasis has been placed on the Christian roots of his social vision. In their work, Eliot is located in the tradition of Catholic conservatism in Europe that emerges in the nineteenth century, principally, in France, as a mode of resistance to the dominance of Enlightenment socio-political ideas propagated as the intellectual legacy of the French Revolution and romanticism. This is no doubt true. Eliot, however, never put his conservatism forward as a systematic political philosophy. At best he conveyed his sociopolitical orientation as a series of modest-seeming hints and suggestions about the possible making of a traditional Tory and Christian programme for society. Eliot, after the nastiness of *After Strange Gods*, became rather more careful in the kind of target he would present in the public controversies of the 1930s and 1940s.

The post-*Strange Gods* persona of the distanced observer of society is one of Eliot's most convincing impersonations. The hardheaded and 'inquisitorial' ideologue (Daniells, 'Christian Drama' 20) re-invents himself as an essentially honest, but possibly ineffectual, political amateur who gazes sadly, but knowingly, on the panorama before him and about which, he realizes, he can say little of permanent value, except perhaps by way of offering modest clarifications and untanglings of a few confused terms and ideas, and, even more modestly, asserting that the little he can say must be necessarily provisional and tentative, except, of course, for the incontestable principles on which the little he can say, of an immediate and topical nature, must necessarily rest. This coy prose persona was developed in the 1930s after a false start with *After Strange Gods* where the very subtitle 'A Primer of Modern Heresy', and the bellicose prose style, projects with pugnacious arrogance the assumption that the author is in possession of incontestable doctrines which earn him the right to call others dangerous fools and heretics.

The orthodoxy and the firmness with which his beliefs were held never changed of course, but the decor of the presentation did. The sour taste which *After Strange Gods* produced on its publication (Aiken, 'After Ash-Wednesday' 161–5) resolved Eliot, for one thing, never to reprint the work and, more importantly, to adopt a more civil prose mask in the future. One of the problems of Eliot scholarship and criticism is its obsession with Eliot the poet and critic. We are used to occupying ourselves with Eliot's literary personas, but have yet to come to grips, in any serious way, with the mask of the prose controversialist and ideologue. And yet in the 1930s it was in prose commentary on society, public morals and culture to which Eliot principally devoted himself. And increasingly it was this Eliot that came to the fore, as the poet of *The Waste Land* and *Ash-Wednesday* became more indistinct.

Eliot's social criticism engages with the contemporary world more concretely than the explicators of his *ideas* have supposed. His prose works on society and culture, written with that most disarming of Eliot's personas, the modest commentator of society with no interest in the hurly-burly of the moment but focused on the elucidation of difficult terms and concepts, tackle concretely and urgently the important Establishment task of keeping the wandering intelligentsia in tow. In *After Strange Gods*, for example, he defines intelligence by the contrast it makes with the 'dopes':

The number of people in possession of any criteria for discriminating between good and evil is very small; the number of half-alive, high or low, good or bad, is considerable. (61)

This repeats sentiments that had already been made explicit in the *Criterion* (e.g. April 1929: 378). On the shoulders of 'the few' Eliot laid the usual heavy burden of reponsibilities, responsibilities that are typically social, cultural, pedagogical, but also, crucially, spiritual, even to the most pointed renunicatory ends:

It will not do merely to call for better individuals; the asceticism must first, certainly, be practised by the few and it must be definite enough to be explained to, and ultimately imposed upon, the many. (*Criterion* January 1931: 314)

Asceticism, and the forms of renunciation and detachment which it entails, gave to Eliot's account of the relation of intelligence to society its own particular character. It would be in *Four Quartets* that this theme would achieve its fullest formulation. But in the 1930s the dilemmas of 'the few', both with respect to the powerful and to 'the many', are rehearsed, again and again, in his prose. The plays offered enactments and illustrations of what he meant.

The *Idea of a Christian Society* is particularly relevant to the dramatic works I have been discussing because, in addition to being contemporary with them, it proposes a social solution to the difficulties which the Beckets and the Harrys present to society. The book's lasting importance comes from the contribution it makes not only to the question of the social function of the martyr, saint and ascetic, but of the social function of the avant garde artist and intellectual, who still live out exemplary spiritual and creative experiences, though not in orthodox Christian terms.

In recent years, a number of cultural historians have begun the work of constructing a theory of the avant garde (Poggioli, Burger and Herwitz, to name only a few). Eliot's contribution to this conversation in *The Idea of a Christian Society*, however, is very rarely acknowledged, principally because of the Christian dimension of his thought. Eliot's book proposes a way of assimilating all those in society who are spiritually and intellectually active, whether they are formally Christians or not. The 'Spirit descends in different ways,' he writes, regardless of labels (*Idea* 42). And this is an important point. Eliot is at pains to insist on the relative openness of his primary unit of intellectual control, the Community of Christians. It cannot be a formal and closed 'caste' of the type described by Coleridge a hundred years before and called the 'clerisy'. Eliot's Community is 'composed of both clergy and laity, of the more conscious, more spiritually and intellectually developed of both'.

It will be their identity of belief and aspiration, their background of a common system of education and a common culture, which will enable them to influence and be influenced by each other, and collectively to form the conscious mind and conscience of the nation.

... there will always be individuals who, with great creative gifts of value to mankind, and the sensibility which such gifts imply, will yet remain blind, indifferent, or even hostile [to Christianity]. That must not disqualify them from exercising the talents they have been given. (42–43)

Eliot's care in keeping the door ajar even for those who are hostile to Christianity is crucial. The reason for 'institutionalizing' all those of conspicuous spiritual and intellectual attainments has a double aspect: firstly, to recognize the unique importance of the Beckets and the Harrys to society as an apparatus for the moral refinement of the governors (see especially *Idea* 47–8) and, and secondly to defuse, by co-optation, the creative power of this elite that, potentially, may be directed to opposing the established order. In this second form, the Community functions socially as the primary assimilative apparatus, and it does this through the vital, ideologically sensitive institutions, the church, education, the media and the higher cultural institutions which stage manage a society's formal cultural inheritance.

Bourgeois society, essentially suspicious of intellectual elites, has tended to isolate and marginalize those whose spiritual, creative and intellectual activities did not conform to the narrow expectations of bourgeois liberalism and its rationalist outflows. Eliot proposes to reverse this process, so that instead of being rejected, the avant garde is brought into the protected enclaves of the governors.

For Eliot, the church will remain the paramount social institution, the primary ideological state apparatus, even though it does not coincide entirely either with the power elite or with the Community of Christians. The church, he writes, in 'matters of dogma, matters of faith and morals, will speak as the final authority within the nation'. But this will not necessarily always ensure social peace; at times, he argues, the church may have to resist the State 'in rebuking derelictions in policy, or in defending itself against encroachments of the temporal power . . .' (47).

In the other direction, the ecclesiasts may even find themselves under attack from the Community of Christians. This criticism may, at times, be necessary as a corrective in the behaviour of the church hierarchy. Whatever the case, the intellectual and creative elements of society will operate within the established power structure, not outside it, as potential centres of opposition and rebellion. Eliot's sense of these matters was schooled no doubt by his lifelong interest in anthropology, and especially the matter of policing behaviour and belief within archaic societies. He would have understood Claude Lévi-Strauss, in *Tristes tropiques*, on the matter of the two alimentary paths adopted by ancient societies for neutralizing individuals possessing dangerously disruptive powers, either by absorption, through the practice of cannibalism, or by *anthropemy* (from the Greek *emein*, to vomit), that is, by recourse to exile. Eliot is definitely speaking of an absorptive society, in which those possessing dangerous powers are neutralized by inclusion. But inclusion means essentially the creation of a society with two kinds of social being defined epistemologically.

It would be a society in which the natural end of man – virtue and well-being in community – is acknowledged for all, and the supernatural end – beatitude – for those who have eyes to see it. (*Idea* 34)

Becket and Harry have the eyes to see it, and so society should, well, actually must find a place for them, so that their journeys towards 'beatitude' can be protected. Celia in *The Cocktail Party* also has eyes to see it. And, further, this play of the late 1940s takes up from *The Idea of a Christian Society* the difficult question of protecting – in the figure of the Guardians – the superior spirits in their necessary pursuit of grace. But *The Cocktail Party* is a play of the late 1940s and it, and the two plays which followed in the 1950s, find themselves in changed conditions from those which obtained in the 1930s.

The ten years between 1939 and 1948 were momentous ones and writing for the theatre was not what was required from the pre-eminent man of letters in the Atlantic world. The times required other kinds of work from Eliot; 'war jobs' is what he called them looking back twenty years later (Hall 60). 'War jobs' included many tasks, from firewatching in Russell Square to finding jobs for Christian friends[10] to broadcasting, editing anthologies and, most importantly, composing *Four Quartets*.

However, the composition and reception of a great lyric poem was not so easy a task for a man who in the 1930s had become increasingly associated with a dogmatic Christianity and with firmly conservative social and political principles. He had, further, engaged vigorously in promoting and defending these principles in public speeches, in print and on the radio, and he never shrank from attacking the ideas of others, without giving or expecting any quarter. By 1939, he was visible in England as a poet, certainly, but one who now rarely wrote poetry, he was also a coterie playwright of unfashionably dogmatic and, sometimes, confusing theatre pieces, and he was a public controversialist of decided and often offensive views.

In 1930, Eliot's *Ash-Wednesday* posed the question: how must an ironist write in order not to be read ironically? In 1940, Eliot's *Four Quartets* was faced with a somewhat similar dilemma. How was an aesthetic artefact of surpassing lyricism and great formal beauty to be read when composed by a dogmatist, a man who had spent ten years speaking bluntly on the issues of the day, on questions of religion, society and politics? In other words, what could a confirmed ideologue, immersed in the concrete history of a decade, write in order to be taken seriously as the author of a poem which aims to transcend those lesser engagements? This was as much a problem again of public perception of the poet and the work as it was a matter of the intrinsic qualities of the work itself. The first step, then, was to rescue the poetry from the author's own reputation and, in this task, the role of academic literary criticism played a decisive role. *Four Quartets* entered the world as the text of an ideologue and by the time of Eliot's Nobel Prize in 1948 had been transformed into the work of a sage.

CHAPTER FOUR

Representing Four Quartets: *the canonizers at work*

Eliot's authority in the period between 1939 and 1950 can be summarized in one word – 'commanding' (Mulhern, '*Scrutiny*' 211 and cf. Davie, *Companions* 79). The war decade culminated in an honourary degree from Harvard in 1947, the Order of Merit in January of 1948, the Nobel Prize in November of the same year, a volume of essays of tribute edited by two young admirers, Tambimuttu and Richard March, in September, other tributes, and to cap it off, a hit play on Broadway in 1949 and, again, in the West End in early 1950. *The Cocktail Party* was a play that anyone who was anyone *had* to see even if most people in the audience were not sure what exactly the play meant.

Eliot was also in demand socially and, when he wanted to, he wore his celebrity easily. At a private celebration hosted by the literary mandarin Cyril Connolly on Eliot's return from Stockholm in 1948 the poet, uninhibitedly, sang 'Under the bamboo tree' from *Sweeney Agonistes*, much to everyone's delight (Ackroyd 290). For the then very fashionable Connolly, in the pages of *Horizon*, and in Palinurus's 'word cycle' *The Unquiet Grave* (1945), Eliot represented incontestable sagacity (96, 106, 107) and is always evoked as the 'master' (96). Connolly in those years saw himself as a bridge between the older generation of the established modernist masters and the younger avant garde. Eliot's 'monumental reputation' (Ackroyd 291) made him the central figure in what was left of the older generation and Connolly (and others) cultivated him with careful energy.

Whether Connolly or the *Poetry London* circle, or the re-liberalized Stephen Spender or the *Scrutiny* party, to name only a handful of those who looked to Eliot for leadership, actually championed values and standards gleaned from the master is still an open question. In fact, it can be argued that Eliot's actual socio-political and cultural views were already *passé*. And there were plenty of observers who not only could see that, but were able to point it out, as E.M. Forster did in his good-humoured dismissal of the cultural politics of *Notes towards the Definition of Culture* in *The Listener* in 1948. But negative comments about Eliot's ideas and values did not seem to matter much when set against his enormous prestige. The master's position in those years is best summarized by two contemporary statements. First, D. W. Harding in 1943: 'for me it ranks among the major good fortunes of our time that so superb a poet is writing' ('Conclusion' 219) and, second, Eliot's good friend and flatmate John Hayward, who wrote that

No English writer living is more revered by his admirers or, it may be added, more respected by his critics. None, in his writing, has done more to create the climate of thought and sensibility which has conditioned the form and content of English literature in the past quarter century. (*Prose Literature* 35)

On these estimates at least, Eliot's authority was complete. But what did it consist of? How was it constructed?

First of all, Eliot's original entry into the world of letters as a 'man of 1914' meant that he connected the fearless explorers of that earlier generation, many now dead (Woolf, Joyce, Lawrence) or in disgrace (Lewis, Pound) with the contemporary world.[1] And it was as an 'Exploring man' himself that Eliot was still remembered by C. Day Lewis in 1966 in his elegy, 'At East Coker' (Tate, *T. S. Eliot* 114), after the master's death. The fact that he had participated in those earlier avant garde adventures in the making of a heroic modernist spirit provided Eliot with an artistic pedigree of great weight and consequence.

It had been Eliot's sagacity in seeing past the bohemianism of those early years that helped erect the second pillar of Eliot's authority in the 1940s. Eliot may have been a creative artist in a period when the power elites who dominate bourgeois society were growing more suspicious of the socio-political reliability of the artist, but Eliot was the one artistic revolutionary who seized the opportunity of his fame to quickly find a place for himself in the social mainstream and to take a version of 'modernism' with him into bourgeois society. He was able to do this because, for a creative man, especially a creative man blooded in the *Blast* wars, he had also acquired the proper sort of credibility. He had been, since the mid-1920s (after his apprenticeship at Lloyds Bank), a businessman of some shrewdness and effectiveness. His original position at Faber & Gwyer had been secured not entirely because he was a young poet who might be used by the new firm to spot the hot young talent of his generation, but partly, as Frank Morley is at pains to explain, because he had spent eight years as a banker (62). He had already proven to the

Rothermere family (in the matter of the funding of the original *Criterion*) and to the new directors of Faber & Gwyer that he was a thoroughly reliable young man who, on the evidence of his actual behaviour, seemed to want nothing more than a place in society. He was not going to rock any boats that counted, even though he had made a reputation for himself as a revolutionary in art (see I.A. Richards's very revealing comments in this connection in 'On TSE' 4–5).

At Lloyds Bank, Eliot's work record was exemplary (Winton, *Lloyds Bank* 155; Richards, 'On TSE' 5) and from his own few comments about that experience he was always very proud of his eight years in the City. The various attempts by his bohemian friends to procure a subsidy for him so that he might concentrate on his literary work were always firmly rebuffed by Eliot. He preferred the security and position which the Bank gave him to the shakiness of bohemian bonhomie and the charity of often fickle patrons (Ackroyd 101, 166; *Letters* 276, 279–80). The upper middle class, to which Eliot was born, had already, by the mid and late nineteenth century, seen through the romantic bohemias of the European capitals and Eliot in the 1920s was not going to be trapped in the same nomadic life as Lawrence or Pound.

Eliot's career as a City man has usually been seen as a persona or mask in the making of 'the invisible poet', with the poetics of impersonality as its theoretical underpinning (see especially Kenner in his *Invisible Poet* and *The Pound Era*). Eliot's City dress and behaviour, first in his bank job, and later in his position with Faber, have been emplotted in the Eliot narrative as endearing masks worn by the poet in a clever masquerade which he carried off all his life. The masquerade's crowning glory can be seen, in this version of the life, in the film clip of the Eliots vacationing in Nassau after their wedding in the 1950s. Eliot, now running to corpulent, smiles in the sun, the picture of a successful and prosperous company director, with a devoted wife at his side. Why literary historians and critics have persisted after all these years in believing that the City bank clerk who rises to a directorship in a major London publishing firm, and ends a long successful business life smiling for the newsreel camera in the Caribbean is a masquerade, a persona, a kind of clever make-believe, remains a mystery.

The persistent attenuation of these quite undeniable facts about Eliot's behaviour in the critical literature tells us more about the scholars and critics who have perpetuated, admiringly, the little myth of Eliot's business life as a form of make-believe, than it does about Eliot himself. Like most well-born, well-educated and cultivated American men of his generation, he took a great deal of pride in his accomplishments, as a Harvard and Oxford man, as a banker, as an acquaintance of aristocrats and other social leaders, and, most pleasingly, as a very well-placed man in a society normally closed to outsiders. He had demonstrated in his life that he did not need to marginalize himself socially and politically by occupying some shady bohemia in order to write astonishingly modern and avant garde poetry.

Here the contrast with Ezra Pound – the flamboyant literary gypsy – is very telling. Pound dearly wanted to be listened to on public affairs all through his life. After 1935 Eliot had already won such a position of respected authority. What Pound never fully realized was that right reason alone, good common sense about politics, economics and culture (even if he had had these things to offer), is not enough. His own wayward bohemianism entirely undercut everything he had to say to the world at large. Even Eliot in 1920 was already insulating himself from Pound's perverse genius for getting on people's nerves (Ackroyd, 101). It probably seems very strange to us now to think that Pound actually thought that his writings could have some influence over the politicians and statesmen of his time. The naivety is breathtaking. As his isolation grew more visible, his tone grew more shrill, and as it grew more shrill, his behaviour took on more bizarre colours, until finally he crossed the boundary, according to the American authorities at least, into criminal insanity and treason.

For Eliot, on the other hand, the profession of letters came to be subordinated in time to the requirements of a nicely crafted career in business. If this is difficult for us to accept, it certainly was not difficult for Eliot's business colleagues in the company. Frank Morley notes that Eliot was not primarily functioning as a 'literary adviser' at Faber & Gwyer. He was not like Edward Garnett at Cape, where the proprietor, Cape himself, was always fretting about the bottom line, while his 'adviser' was out lunching 'at the Mount Blanc in Gerrard Street' discovering 'another bloody genius' (Cape, quoted in Morley, 'Publisher' 63). This was not Eliot's function in Russell Square.

Eliot wasn't an outside expert. He was in the firm as a man of business, as one of the inner council, making business decisions. And to the business he displayed complete loyalty. (Morley, 63)

The business side of Eliot can be glimpsed in other ways as well, for example, in the advertising blurb for the issue of his *Collected Poems* in 1936.

To our occasional nagging [to issue a new *Collected Poems*], Mr. Eliot has invari-
ably replied that if he did not have to read so many manuscripts he would have
more time for writing poetry. To which our reply has always been that after all
we make it possible for him to keep body and soul together, and he ought to take
the rough with the smooth. (from the Faber & Faber Spring List, 1936)

The bantering tone of these quips about Eliot's work life lifts the curtain
of privacy for a moment to reveal a man comfortably accommodated to
the business world. Normally, the supposed masquerade of Eliot's work
life – the aging clubman in bowler hat and rolled umbrella catching the
Piccadilly Line at Gloucester Road for Russell Square while assiduously
pencilling in the crossword in *The Times* – is seen as a deliberately con-
cocted public persona that masks the inner agonies of his art. It is the
extraordinary authority of the art, in this telling of the man, which
licenses the mask as protective colouring, as merely the witty impersona-
tion of a company director. Indeed, for watchful mandarins, secretly
impressed with worldly power, it is probably the other way around: the
authority of his art is at least partly purchased by the exemplary
accomplishment of the career.

A third dimension of Eliot's authority in the 1940s was his position as
the man who shaped a second generation of modernists at Faber &
Faber through an aggressive publishing programme, seizing the business
opportunity which Eliot's own celebrity in the 1920s and 1930s provided.
It was the exploitation of this opportunity that made Faber & Faber the
most important publishing house in London in mid-century. The Faber
& Faber modernism that arrived in the 1930s in the work of the 'political'
writers of the Auden generation is a profoundly interesting episode in
the sociology of literary reception and the making of reputations. Eliot's
endorsement of their youthful work began a circle which was completed
when these Faber writers, having come round at last after their youthful
(and largely frivolous) flirtations with radical politics and radical psy-
chologies, ended up defending and advancing the cultural politics of the
master.

The importance of Eliot's position as a publisher should not be underestimated. The Faber & Faber publishing strategy in the 1930s was
absolutely brilliant from a business point of view and for its impact on
the cultural politics of the time. The fact that there was a publishing
strategy is, of course, indisputable. It would have been, first of all, simply
good business practice. The success of the Faber company in establishing itself as the leading publisher of modern writing in Britain in the
twentieth century is one of the great *business* stories of our time, a story,

sad to say, that has not yet been told.[2] That a publishing plan was in place
has been corroborated by Geoffrey Faber's own words to Nancy Cunard
in a letter of 11 January 1939. In this unpublished letter Faber justifies his,
and Eliot's, refusal to publish Cunard's translation of the Cuban poet
Nicolas Guillen's *Espana* by referring to the fact that the company had
made it a deliberate policy to make modern poetry 'saleable'. He tells
her that he and Eliot have a very clear sense of what ought to be kept out
of their list. When they have occasionally not done this, he writes, they
have lived to regret it. He praises her translation and acknowledges its
affinities with Auden's 'Spain', published a year earlier, but declines her
request by saying that it would be too much of a 'sideturning' from their
'carefully planned route' (letter in Humanities Research Centre, Austin,
Texas). The fact that a 'carefully planned route' in marketing modernist
poetry, in marketing modernist culture, existed at Faber, obviously Eliot's
major strategic contribution to the enterprise, should be of no suprise to
anyone today. It is still amazing to find, however, scholars and critics who
are astounded to learn that cultural artefacts do not just mysteriously
happen, but are enmeshed in the same market economy that produces
and distributes desklamps and paper clips.

A survey of the publications of Faber & Faber in the 1930s and 1940s,
drawn from the company's quarterly lists, suggests the general principle
by which Eliot and Faber tried 'to cultivate the art of making modern
poetry saleable'. Of course, only a thorough exploration of the Faber &
Faber archives, the company's lists, minutes of editorial meetings,
reader's reports, correspondence with authors, the sorts of manuscripts
rejected by the editorial board, and other like documents will give a clear
picture of how this exceedingly important cultural institution went
about the business of constructing a successful version of modernity in
the North Atlantic world.

The publishing programme was aimed at presenting 'modernism'
not only as a movement in the arts, but as a phenomenon of more
general relevance. What I mean by this is that in addition to the publishing of well-known and now familiar figures of modernist literary
culture – Eliot himself, Pound, Joyce, David Jones, the Auden generation including George Barker, Djuna Barnes and many others – figures
who now constitute one of the major canonic currents of modernism,
Eliot and Faber expanded the list horizontally to include books which
illustrate the extensive penetration of modernist culture in society in
general. The distinguished publications on modernist visual culture and
its sources in the 1930s and 1940s, for example, included the remarkable

series of books by Adrian Stokes, *Inside Out, Colour and Form, Rough and Smooth*, and those strange masterpieces *The Quattro Cento* and *The Stones of Rimini* that so beautifully and obliquely illuminate Pound's *Cantos*. R.H. Wilenski's *The Modern Movement in Art* was designed to appeal to a more popular audience. Originally published in 1927 to exploit the emerging mass market for culture, it went into many reprints and cheaper reissues right up to the 1960s. P. Morton Shand's translation of Walter Gropius's *The New Architecture and the Bauhaus* was a major addition to the Autumn 1935 list:

Walter Gropius, the greatest pioneer of the new movement in architecture and the founder of the Weimar Bauhaus, pleads in this arresting little book that what the past did for wood and brick and stone, the present shall do for steel amd concrete and glass. (83)

This blurb also includes the remarks of the then young John Betjeman, extracted from his review in the *New Statesman*. It is rather a coup to have got the words of the already militant wood-brick-and-stone man in the promotional material for an apostle of steel, concrete, and glass.

Adrian Stokes, again, on *Russian Ballets*, Eric Gill on *Work and Leisure*, Rudolf Arnheim on *Radio*, and the distinguished list of books on the arts of the moving image, from Paul Rotha's classic *Documentary Film* (with a preface by John Grierson) to Raymond Spottiswoode's *A Grammar of the Film*, reveal that the Faber strategy for defining *and* marketing the modern in the 1930s extended across the whole of culture, including, even, the revolution in all those aspects of daily life which everyone typically takes for granted, the design and decoration of domestic spaces. Raymond McGrath's *Twentieth-Century Houses* (1935) is the kind of publication which makes the Faber programme very clear. The book

. . . describes the progress made in the planning, construction, equipment and decoration of the house. It describes the causes and character of the revolution in design, a revolution more profound than any which has occurred in the other arts. The scientific, the economic, the sociological and the geographical influences at work are examined in relation to the house and those who live in it. (Spring List, 1935, 54)

The book examines everything from McGrath's own decorations in Broadcasting House for the BBC in the 1930s to the design of aeroplane furniture for the South African subsidiary of Imperial Airways.

Finally, no mention of Faber & Faber and the visual arts can ignore Herbert Read, who contributed a series of books that spanned the high and low ends of the visual art scene of modernity. *Art Now, The Meaning of*

Art, Education through Art, and the classic *Art and Industry* not only reveal the Faber agenda, but illustrate the deliberateness of the strategy. From the blurb, which Eliot no doubt wrote (Eliot had known Read since 1917 and it is inconceivable that he would have left this matter to a minion), the linking of high culture with the world of the masses and popular culture is made quite explicitly. Indeed this is the point of *Art and Industry*.

> In *Art Now* (published in 1933 and now in its second edition) Herbert Read explained and justified those modern developments of the art of painting, which have so much bewildered the ordinary man of recent years.
>
> In *Art and Industry* he shows us how the same artistic spirit has begun to affect the design of objects which are in everyday use. This is both an easier and a more difficult task than that which he set himself in the former book. It is easier, because everybody has begun to be familiar with the look of 'modern' houses, furniture, decorations and so forth. It is harder, because art at work has to satisfy several masters – the abstract principles of design, the requirements of use or comfort, and the conditions of machine production. Mr. Read's book is perhaps the first (at any rate in English) to approach the very interesting and complex questions created by these different claims, in a systematic way; and to relate them to the general problem of artistic and industrial education.
>
> Visitors to the Winter Exhibition of Industrial Art at the Royal Academy will find their understanding of the exhibits enormously increased by a reading of *Art and Industry.*
>
> The book is very liberally illustrated, and the publishers have spared no effort to make it, in itself, a model of the very best modern machine production. (Spring List, 1935, 54)

The marketing of the book is brilliantly carried off, from the initial engagement of the attention of Read's earlier readers to the sense of the unavoidable presence of modernist culture everywhere in modern life, and from the remarks about the materially germane exhibition at the Royal Academy to the closing comment about the book as itself an apt illustration of its own theses.

I think that even this glance at the way the Faber company construed modernity reveals the general goal of their programme. The pervasiveness and inescapability of the modernist revolution in everyday life, the popular arts, mass culture, and, of course, at the tonier end of the scale, in the dissemination of cultural artefacts for the highest of brows suggests modernism's general relevance to society. In this way the artefacts of high modernist culture, the poetry of an Eliot, or a Pound, the fiction of Barnes, the experimentalism of a Joyce, for example, are seen as the tip of the iceberg of modernism. A great deal of the modernism of everyday life is submerged in society and has, no doubt, become so pervasive, or so the programme wants the consumer to believe, that social life is no longer conceivable without it.

The brilliance of this strategy would not have been lost on anyone on the London publishing scene at the time. Of course, this very interesting story, the chronicle of Eliot as an inspired strategist in the marketing of cultural artefacts in modern Britain, has yet to be told. In the 1930s and 1940s, those intellectuals and writers who were there well understood Eliot's authority in these, more commercial, matters. Although anyone close enough to Eliot in *The Waste Land* period to have seen his masterful commercial deployment of the poem (Rainey, 'Price of Modernism' 91 *passim*) would not have been surprised by his later Faber successes.

All of these successes together, however, could not outreach the single most important reason for his authority in those years. Eliot's eminence in the 1940s was most solidly sustained, even with all his personal accomplishments, by something beyond his control, the evolution of the historical situation itself. It was a situation that had reached bottom with the war and had taken down with it the concluding aspirations of the younger generation. The false dawn of the political solution of 1930 gave way to the 'final solution' of 1939, and the unspeakable calculus to come in the next decade. 'The clever hopes . . . / Of a low dishonest decade' succumbed to the dark (Auden, *EA* 245). The numbing sense of being empty-handed and speechless in the crisis, precipitated by the out-break of the war, brought back to Eliot an audience which the headily reformist and secularist 1930s had taken away. 'The windiest militant trash,' Auden scornfully recalled in 'September 1, 1939' (*EA* 246) led, at the end of the day, not to the Just City, but to 'barren pastures' and, more notably, to 'the deserts of the heart' (*EA* 243). Over such landscapes Eliot's consoling voice called back the lost.

In the 1940s, Eliot's poetry and prose ministered to an intelligentsia shaken by total war and to the destitution of the human (and humanist) spirit caused by it. The reconstruction of an affirmative subjectivity in the culture of the North Atlantic mandarinate in this epoch of nihilism becomes Eliot's paramount war task; Eliot, having learned, according to Empson, 'the style of the master', in the 1930s, begins to acquire the style of the sage. He not only speaks *to* the literary, bureaucratic and academic mandarinate of the Atlantic world in this critical junction of its history, but he begins to speak *for* it as well. And panicky mandarins, no longer knowing what to say or do, simply begin to listen. There is no reason to believe that Eliot did not apply to his own work, in this extraordinary moment of silence, the advice he had given Hugh Sykes Davies in the

1930s about writing for the *Criterion*: 'People like', he said, with his eye squarely on the readers, 'just to be told what to think' (in Tate, *T. S. Eliot* 359).

Of course it was not Eliot alone who helped the mandarinate recover its confidence after its encounter with nihilism, but his was certainly the most authoritative voice to which people who wanted 'just to be told what to think' listened. There were others of course. In the shattered world of European scholarship, for example, Ernst Robert Curtius, in *European Literature and the Latin Middle Ages* (1948), and Erich Auerbach in *Mimesis* (1944), revive not only the integrative concept of European Latinity, but also the thread of European subjectivity and the verbal culture which is its external sign from Homer to the present day. More controversially, Pound's *Pisan Cantos* re-mapped personal and cultural memory in order to re-invent, against the fragmentation and dispersal of an older inwardness, a more durable subjectivity that transcended the ruptures of war, ruptures concretely conveyed by the absence of Cantos 72 and 73 from the sequence for several decades. David Jones' *The Anathemata* (1952) and Hugh MacDiarmid's *In Memoriam James Joyce* (1954), both works largely composed in the 1940s, attempted to salvage from the ruins the strong continuities of a devastated civilization. And, finally, both Martin Heidegger's 'What are poets for?' and Theodor Adorno's *Minima Moralia*, two texts I will return to later, approached the same dilemmas from radically different directions in the German context.

Sustained, then, by Eliot's eminence, *Four Quartets* broke the silence. And a mandarin readership, carefully cultivated for more than a decade, listened. The process by which *Four Quartets* came to be canonized has been recalled by no less an authority than Dr Jean Sutherland Boggs, the Harvard art historian and director of the National Gallery in Ottawa, a Canadian mandarin of the highest order, who recalled quite clearly the prestige the *Quartets* enjoyed at the University of Toronto when she was beginning as a student there in the Forties. It was read out in her English classes with the reverence usually reserved for scripture, and it was read in the unspoken context of a kind of scripture that especially ministered to the shattered spirit of the higher bourgeoisie (CBC, radio interview, 29 April 1988). It was a text that was seen as providing important directions in the journey back from the horror of total war, 25 million dead in Europe, totalitarian and genocidal politics, the terrors brought by the new weapons of mass destruction, and finally, in the British context, the demoralization among the traditional directive elites in the aftermath of the Labour Party victory in the General Election of 1945. But before the poem's structure of thought and feeling could be inscribed more gener-ally in the common intuitive life of an influential social formation, it had to be rescued from its first critics and reviewers. They had not yet caught up with the fact that the Eliot of the late poetry, *Notes Towards the Definition of Culture*, and his late plays now had an historical moment to which his work could speak without apology.

The earliest critical responses to *Four Quartets*, especially in those years when the last three were appearing in the *New English Weekly*, were quite clearly polemical, thinly veiled ideological critiques, both hostile and sympathetic, of religious beliefs and political principles with which Eliot had become associated in the previous two decades. Eliot's religious pro-fessions in the *Ash-Wednesday* period, which had seemed the private obsessions of an increasingly irrelevant and quixotic consciousness in 1930, began to take on more sinister overtones in the claustrophobic atmosphere of a society in the grips of total war. Thus, George Orwell in *Poetry London* (1942) saw in them the final flowering of 'a reactionary or austro-fascist tendency' which had 'always been apparent in [Eliot's] work, especially in his prose writings'. This, for Orwell, resulted in a 'gloomy Petainism to which [Eliot] now appears to have given himself' (Grant, *Critical Heritage* 486–87). The implied accusation of treacherous defeatism (for that is precisely what the name Petain denoted in the 1940s) finds a more muted currency also in the *TLS* review of 'East Coker' from 14 Sept. 1940:

['East Coker'] is a confession of a lost heart and a lost art. These are sad times, but we are not without hope that Mr. Eliot will recover both . . . (472)

That Eliot is seen to be a 'lost heart', indeed to have 'lost heart' in these 'sad times' has a tartness of local reference, now somewhat obscured by time, when we remember that this *TLS* review appeared exactly a week after the first big German air raid on London on 7 September 1940.

F.R. Leavis found these insinuations immediately offensive:

Mr. Eliot needs no defending, nor do I flatter myself that I am the defender he would choose if he needed one. But as a matter of decency there ought to be some protest against the review of 'East Coker' that appears in your issue of yes-terday . . . What is not permissible in a serious critical journal is to write in contemptuous condescension of the greatest living English poet (what other poet have we now Yeats is gone?) and exhibit a complacent ignorance of the nature of his genius and of the nature of the technique in which that genius is manifested . . . The present seems to me a peculiarly unhappy time for such an exhibition in *The Times Literary Supplement*: our riches of spirit are surely not as superabundant that we can countenance it. (21 September 1940, 483)

A week later Ralph Instone, who gives his place of residence as 'In the Field', in provocative contrast to Leavis's relative comfort at 'Downing College, Cambridge' the week before, dismissively observes that Leavis's arguments, such as they are, are worm-eaten by logical fallacies (28 September 1940, 500). Instone goes on to say that what is required is a plausible defense of 'Mr. Eliot's presuppositions', by which is meant his social and political values, with the implication that once we know what they are, we will have seen right through the poet to the conservative ideologue, perhaps even to the budding *petainiste*. As for the poet, Instone wittily observes, 'we shall continue to enjoy his incidental music and to raise our eyebrows at the *leitmotif*'.

By the time of the *TLS* Christmas Book Section, the master's authority can be seen to have begun exerting its considerable influence on the poem's first readers. Conceding that 'East Coker' is 'a grim poem certainly and overcharged, it may seem to many, with a bleakly negative despair', it nevertheless reveals an 'impressive' integrity at work (7 December 1940, xxiii). The effect of Eliot's 'commanding' position in English cultural life is made manifest here against voices that still clung to an older view of the master, the view which saw his work simply in ideological terms, and the man himself as something of a slippery character.

Eliot also had his ideological defenders. In glossing 'Do not let me hear / Of the wisdom of old men, but rather of their folly', again from 'East Coker', James Johnson Sweeney expostulated in 1941:

In reality they, the old men, are nothing more than infinitesimal details of the Divine pattern. And their notion of their importance as individuals, their dread of losing their imagined spiritual autonomy – their fear 'of belonging to another, or to others, or to God' is only another heritage of the Renaissance individualist approach. At best it is merely the wisdom of the children of this world in their generation – a short term wisdom. For if we face facts frankly we will realize that

> The only wisdom we can hope to acquire
> Is the wisdom of humility: humility is endless.

This is especially clear today when we consider the emptiness of the material civilization we have so long adulated. (Grant, *Critical Heritage* 427–28)

Sweeney is still speaking the language Eliot himself helped coin in *For Lancelot Andrewes*, *After Strange Gods*, and during his editorship of the *Criterion*. His defence bristles with the code-words and notional idiom of the neo-conservatism that appeared as the important ideological force in a Christian literary revival in the 1940s, of which *Four Quartets* was then seen as forming a principal part. It is worth noting also that Faber & Faber promoted this 'revival' through an aggressive publishing and publicity program.

The revival's ideological centres were situated, fairly securely, in certain academic circles in non-cosmopolitan America (*The Southern Review* and Vanderbilt University, for example), several publishing houses (Faber & Faber, Sheed & Ward, SCM Press), and a few academic and ecclesiastical seats in Britain.[3] And if there is any doubt that Eliot himself was actively engaged in promoting it materially (beyond his obvious involvement in publishing Christian apologetics), activities such as pulling strings for the placement of like-minded Christian intellectuals in positions of influence, and some unpublished letters from Eliot to John Betjeman might underline the point. When the war began, Eliot wrote several times to the younger poet, then working in the Ministry of Information, recommending 'a list of men' who are to be 'kept alive' in wartime 'for the important work to be done after this war is over (whatever the result) . . .' (18 September 1939, Special Collections, University of Victoria). The afterthought in parenthesis is perhaps the *petainiste* note heard by Orwell in 'East Coker'.

Eliot's own polemical engagements and his religious activities in the political climate of the 1930s all too often invited unthinking hostility as well as the corrosive embrace of those who appropriated Eliot's quite severe, even ascetic, religious principles for their own purposes. R.W. Flint's 'reconsideration' of *Four Quartets* in 1948 is little more than gushing approval of the work, a singular success, he seems to say for 'our side', erupting occasionally in snarls and gibes at a variety of ideological enemies, real and imagined, ranging from the 'secular existentialism' (108) of Sartre and Camus, then making its first tour of the middle brow periodicals of the North Atlantic world, to the Marxists, styled 'the poor benighted Hegelians' (115) to whose edification, it seems, 'Dry Salvages' parts II and III are particulary appropriate.

Eliot's attitude to the efforts of men like Flint on his behalf is not part of the public record. One suspects he was not particularly happy seeing his work used in this way. But, then again, to a large extent he brought this situation on himself. The responsibility he felt as an eminent man of letters, as an editor of a leading periodical and of a major publishing firm, and the responsibility he felt as an active Christian led him into a wide-ranging involvement with ideologues of various hues, the friendly, the hostile, and the just plain obtuse. Such involvement is never without its price.

In the 1940s, as the war situation and its aftermath grew more malig-
nant, attacks and defences had grown sharper and more ill-tempered,
even abusive, than they had ever been in the two previous decades. The
famous incident at the inaugural poetry reading of the Institute of
Contemporary Art in 1949, when Emmanuel Litvinoff read his powerful, if crude, attack on Eliot's anti-Semitism, a poem addressed directly
'To T. S. Eliot', with Eliot himself in attendance, revealed a continuing
core of hostility at the time of his greatest public visibility (Abse, *A Poet*
131–32). Indeed, even the mild-mannered E.M. Forster could not resist a
mild-mannered slap at his former Bloomsbury acquaintance in the
course of a *Listener* review of *Notes Towards the Definition of Culture*:

It would seem that, when Mr. Eliot is wishing to instruct, his prose remains
lucid, considerate and assured . . . When, on the other hand, he is writing for
people who may answer him back, he becomes wary and loads his sentences
with qualifications and precautions which make them heavy. (253)

In America, at about the same time, Eliot's role in Ezra Pound's
Bollingen Prize resulted in the old and heavy allegations – sympathy for
fascism, anti-Semitism, anti-democratic elitism – being the common
currency of news weeklies and semi-literary magazines.[4] The immediate
historical context inevitably weighs down the work of the experienced
controversialist.

Four Quartets was first received in this polemical climate and read as a
weighty contribution to those controversies. But *Four Quartets* was not
destined to drown in a debate from which Eliot had already escaped by
the mid-30s. The poem had readers who heard something more in it
than a 'flowering' of earlier socio-political tendencies. The poem was
timely, not because it prepared the road for *petainiste* values or derided yet
again the Renaissance individualist approach, but because it seemed to
suggest that in a moment of cultural despair and fragmentation there
existed a more fundamental level of experience by which the shattered
unities of a traditional inwardness could be rescued and reformed.

By sweeping away the contingent, imposed polemical constraints,
both those constraints originating in Eliot's own explicit allegiances and
those which opposed them, these readers became intensely aware of
'unmediated' experience as the groundwork of the *Quartets*, experience
unencumbered by history. They believed themselves able to produce
clear sensitive accounts of the poetry as poetry beyond the gravitational
pull of superficial socio-political allegiances, whatever they might be.
This sense of having gone beyond immediate historical contexts in order

to lay bare the essentials of human nature and of a living reality distinguishes an important theme in the making of a new inwardness after World War Two.

It is in this context that *Four Quartets* had its profoundest historical effect on the intelligentsia. The poem, of course, pursued radical intellectual and aesthetic purposes. It needed, for one thing, to openly acknowledge the validity and appropriateness of the experience of nihilism in a destitute time. It could not pay lip service to feelings of despair and devastation; the poem had to seem to mean them, after all this was an intelligentsia which had seen through everything already (Prichard) and would not allow itself to be patronized. The poem needed to address readers who had been trained, even by Eliot himself in his early years, to savour ambiguity, irony and the deliciousness of the knowingly obscure, an intelligentsia that could not trust itself any more to believe the simple teachings of a naive faith, especially if that faith were expressed in the blunt words of the dogmatist. To win through to the proper measures of Christian assent, quite possibly a simple matter for simple folk, the path had to lead back through the mazes of modernity to the moments of origin when 'long ago the accusations had begun' (Auden, 'In Memory of Sigmund Freud', *CSP* 167). But the poem, first, had to be set free of the gravitational pull of the polemics of the time.

Not surprisingly, it was F.R. Leavis in 1943 who, pursuing certain shrewd remarks by his fellow 'Scrutineer' D. W. Harding, suggested that the poem's authority lay beyond the attractions or revulsions to thought of any 'given intellectual and doctrinal frame':

The genius, that of a great poet, manifests itself in a profound and acute apprehension of the difficulties of his age. Those difficulties are such that they certainly cannot be met by any simple reimposition of traditional frames. Eliot is known as professing Anglo-Catholicism and classicism; but his poetry is remarkable for the extraordinary resource, penetration, and stamina with which it makes its explorations in the concrete actualities of experience below the conceptual currency; into the life that must be the *raison d'être* of any frame – while there is life at all. With all its positive aspiration and movement, it is at the same time essentially a work of radical analysis and revision, endlessly insistent in its care not to confuse the frame with a living reality, and heroic in its refusal to accept. (*Education* 103)

Leavis's judgement demonstrates both a refreshing attentiveness to the poem and a dismissal of those readers who saw in the *Quartets* a difficult poem making simple doctrinal points in elusive language. Leavis responded positively to the poem's 'immediacy' of experience as 'the equivalent in poetry of a philosophical work – to do by strictly poetical means the business of epistemological and metaphysical inquiry' (94). D. W. Harding had anticipated this line of critical thought after the first publication of 'Burnt Norton' in the 1936 *Collected Poems*.

The total effect of Eliot's 'procédé', as Leavis calls it, results in a certain quality of 'unseizableness', (95) or what we might have called ambiguity some years ago and today might call polyvalence or polysemy or indeterminacy, though Leavis's word carries, perhaps, the particular flavour of his encounter with the poem. His analysis of the opening of 'Burnt Norton' describes the pressures and shifts of thought and feeling in the movement of the verse, catching 'the specific indeterminate status of the experience' (95). He sees this as fundamentally a process of defamiliarization, 'the complex effect of a de-realizing of the routine commonsense world together with the evoking of a reality that lies hidden among the unrealities into which life in time, closely questioned, paradoxes itself . . .' (96)

The verbal slippage at

> . . . But to what purpose
> Disturbing the dust on a bowl of rose-leaves
> I do not know . . .

and the precipitation of anxiety on the suggestion of further erosion, once the stays are pulled, figured even in the lineation, that gives the word 'disturbing' its faintly menacing note, is marvellously conveyed by Leavis as 'a sudden drop to another plane, to a distancing comment, [that] brings out by contrast the immediacy of what goes before, while at the same time contributing directly to the sensuous presentness of the whole – ' (96). The 'sensuous presentness of the whole' is achieved by the spatializing action of the 'sudden drop', the result of a progressive widening of the discourse to encompass and seal that part of it which seems philosophical, a dilation inaugurated at 'Footfalls echo . . .' leading, finally, to the poem's first inclusive icon – the garden – 'our first world'. In these echoes, vertigoes, intermittences, hesitations, as the lecturer's voice fades, 'reality', the sign of inclusiveness, is sought as an 'absolute reference', that confronts 'the spirit', Leavis writes, 'with the necessity of supreme decision, ultimate choices, and so give[s] a meaning to life'. (97)

In 1946, Raymond Preston seized Leavis's main point and extended it over a closer analysis of all four quartets than had been attempted hitherto. As does Leavis, Preston also sites the 'poetic' substance of the sequence in the centrality of immediate experience to the poet's 'thought':

Eliot has squeezed out of experience and meditation a concentrate which appears in one light as philosophical or theological thought; but it is thought which is inseparable from keenness of perception and feeling, thought which hardly for one instant leaves perception and feeling behind. (*Four Quartets Rehearsed* 64)

Although Preston, throughout, insists on these unities, asserting that 'you cannot isolate the "poetry" any more than you can isolate the "philosophy" ', it is clear that 'the direct shock of the sudden vision (cf. also 31), the delicacy and poise and compelling precision of the language, the realization of present and historic and primitive experience, of the experience of the saint and the experience of the sinner', give to the poetry its authority and power (64). The accuracy and pellucidity of the language, Preston suggests, delivers convincingly the whole 'presence' of certain experiences, an affective verisimilitude that is remarkable as a laying bare of the poet's subjective states, free of any framing ideology, or, to put it another way, not so much free, as so decisively realized that the frame cannot distort them.

To this work of reclamation by Harding, Leavis and Preston, we should include the work of Helen Gardner whose *The Art of T. S. Eliot* (1950) establishes more thoroughly many of the same points. Hers was the decisive blow in the process of re-positioning the poem. That *Four Quartets* is her principal point of interest is very clear from the structure of her book. She brackets a survey of Eliot's earlier work with several opening and closing chapters on *Four Quartets*. Recognizing that a good deal of the early commentary on the poem, up to 1948, has been made with some narrow polemical purpose in mind, she brings us to an 'approach to the meaning' (158–186) by linking the doctrinal dimension, what she calls the moral sense of each of the four poems, to both the literal level of meaning, the particular and concrete experiences from which the poems evolve (the significant lyricism of time and place), and the mystical meanings to which the iconography points in the making of an essentially visionary art.

In this latter mode, she links Eliot to a rich tradition in English poetry, the one which runs from Langland, through Vaughan, Traherne, Smart, Blake and Wordsworth. But he differs from these poetic precursors by one very important and defining difference, namely his greater understanding of his own role, not as visionary or prophet, but as 'a poet, a great "maker" '.

When we read *Four Quartets* we are left finally not with the thought of 'the transitory Being who beheld this vision', nor with the thought of the vision itself, but with the poem, beautiful, satisfying, self-contained, self-organized, complete. (185)

Her insistence on Eliot's artistic achievement as not only rising above dogma, but surpassing also the serious philosophical business which Leavis and Preston felt the poem transacted, is an ingenious stroke. Yes, certainly the kind of lyrical evocation of immediate experience, a lyricism so intense it is even able to do the work of rebuilding metaphysical foundations, according to Leavis, is an important, even decisive factor, in prising the poem free from the oppressive disputes of the day. But for the purposes of recommending the poem to a mandarinate which has a matured and pervasive modernism as part of its training and culture, resulting in a well-tuned alertness and sensitivity to the aesthetic and to the aesthetics of the autonomous artwork in particular, *Four Quartets* must ultimately be put forward, not only as significant 'thought', but as the rarest 'art' as well.

In the closing sentences of Gardner's book, the aestheticizing and affirmative tendencies of modernism are now fully realized. Gardner is responsive enough to the modernist project as defined by Eliot, and implemented by Faber & Faber, and sensitive enough to the prerequisites for assent in a mandarinate trying to escape from 'the dangerous tide of history', that her opening and closing emphasis on the poem's ineffable artistry is absolutely right. And even more so, her identification of the poem's artistry with the poem's sound world, with the poem's 'music' (chapter 2) is also decisive. Apart from the often-noted fact that such an identification reminds us of one of the originary dicta of nineteenth century symbolism, known best in English through the work of Walter Pater and James Whistler, Gardner's use of music as an analogy for the poem's artistry also underlines the special place which music will come to play in the making of North Atlantic culture, particularly in the period of the Cold War.

That Eliot himself was in agreement with this presentation and assessment of his achievement cannot be doubted. Indeed, there is every reason to suspect that Eliot was very interested in having Gardner 'encouraged' to write such a book. The expansion of the article Gardner published in the Summer of 1942 on 'The Recent Poetry of T. S. Eliot' in John Lehmann's periodical *New Writing and Daylight*, which was the initial formulation of the book's ideas, was urged by no less an Eliot confidant than John Hayward himself, to whom, in her Preface, Gardner says she owes her 'greatest debt'. It was Hayward, she writes, 'who first suggested I should write this book' and who, it turns out, helped her during its composition 'in both large and small matters', not the least of which was the ferrying of the master's thoughts on the matter of the poem's import.

But even putting that direct evidence of Eliot's interest aside, Eliot would have been interested in such an account of his work in any case: it delivered his masterpiece, in the very terms Eliot himself would have most preferred, from the bustle and huff of partisan opinion.

Certainly the work of Leavis, Gardner and Preston, as criticism, is more satisfying in a general sense than the stifling comments of Orwell, the anonymous *TLS* reviewer, Sweeney, Flint and others. And because of their closer attention to Eliot's actual language, formal imagination and thought, rather than zeroing in on his reputation and 'presuppositions', they convey convincingly the point and texture of their own encounters with the text. Their experience of the poem itself functions not only as an exemplary exercise in reading and feeling, but as a paradigm of affirmative deliverance as well, and exemplifies the only safe route open to an unnerved intelligentsia crammed on all sides by dangerous and unpredictable social and political necessities. Their accounts certainly sound more accurate than those of the ideologues. But are they? Leavis, for one, after the passage of thirty years or so came to reconsider his earlier judgements about the sequence. In 1975, in *The Living Principle*, he realized that the poems are not in fact as interested in experience as he once thought, but recommend a rejection of experience in time and even betray a fear of life, a theme that may be implicit in Eliot's writing from the beginning. Helen Gardner, by now Dame Helen, never reversed her earlier views on the poem's worth and was rewarded by the Eliot estate with the handsome task of narrating the story of the poem's composition (1978).

I think it is fruitless to pursue the question of how tellingly accurate the critical responses of the latter group of critics was in the 1940s. Their accuracy cannot be measured by some final appeal to the actual meaning of the poem. If their work is accurate at all, it is accurate to the historical situation in which the poem was originally received. Their main function was in construing a critical language that readied *Four Quartets* for the work it was destined to do in the 1940s and 50s. Their emphasis, for example, on the poem's non-ideological character and its position as a supreme artwork was a necessary preparation of the poem for its assimilation into the common intuitive life of the mandarinate, its natural audience. The poem certainly addresses itself to the 'difficulties' of the age, as Leavis asserts, but these are not essentially metaphysical, although it is part of the effect that they appear so.

The 'difficulties' are much more concrete and limited. Quiescent mandarins, for example, typically like to believe about themselves that they are deaf to the voices of party and faction, of one 'interest' as against another, that they attend to higher ends amid the distracting tumult. So Eliot's words on 'faction' in 'Little Gidding', by seeming to transcend history, to make weightless the burdens of history, ministered to readers for whom the full nightmare had culminated in the wreckage of Europe and of European culture.

> We cannot revive old factions
> We cannot restore old policies
> Or follow an antique drum.
> These men, and those who opposed them
> And those whom they opposed
> Accept the constitution of silence
> And are folded in a single party.   (*CP* 220)

I realize that the 'constitution of silence' and 'single party' to which Eliot refers here use the language of politics to convey ironically the notion that all factions are resolved into one pattern, the single party of death, which is Eliot's peerless response to the militant partisan. But it is not the persisting militant that Eliot has in mind. The state of mind he is most interested in reaching is that of the lapsed or uncertain militant. What is comforting here, however, for an increasingly querulous mandarinate in the 1940s, is not the superbly turned aphorism that all political divisions are resolved in death, but that there is no recourse to political action in the public domain that will resolve these dilemmas, so that resignation to the existing order of things is 'our' only saving strategy in a destitute time.

And there were other aspects of the poem that ministered to the subjective needs of a shaky mandarinate as well. The confessional style working the subject towards a difficult humility – 'So here I am, in the middle way, having had twenty years' – also opens an important new avenue of feeling; as does the rejection of a certain facile verbalism, the poison of the intellectual – 'The poetry does not matter'; or the tentative, even weightless, re-connection of the present crisis with the past through the 'common genius' of the English tongue – 'On a summer midnight, you can hear the music'; or a reassertion through quotation and allusion of the continuing relevance of the literary tradition – 'O dark dark dark' – and even the unobtrusive generosity of spirit in quoting from a poet – Milton – whom one has publicly derided in the past (and will again, more subtly, in the future); or, in an age growing more sophisticated about psychology, an heroic stripping bare of all personal artifice, that is, of personality – 'And you see behind every face the mental emptiness deepen', in favour of some more elemental level of experience – 'The river is within us, the sea is all about us'; or the lofty dismissiveness of the usual, popular pastimes, of the usual 'drugs, and features of the press', the Olympian perspective taking in not only 'the shores of Asia', but also 'the Edgware Road' in the same line. This last of particular interest to a mandarinate that had come to understand in their blood the concrete connection between Asia and NW2 and was now confronting for the first time, at the end of Empire, the fact that what remained of that connection was 'the wind that sweeps the gloomy hills of London, / Hampstead and Clerkenwell, Campden and Putney', and so on. The spectral affinities among explicit theme, appropriate style and tone, and Eliot's superb intuitive grasp of the psychological state of unnerved readers occur in the grey zone between conscious wariness and unconscious assent. The poem's 'art' and its 'unseizableness' allay the suspicion of those who no longer want to be duped by cant. Calmed, they are able to precipitate more easily inward, unspoken assent.

The more serious criticism of *Four Quartets* in the 1940s uncovered a poem that could enunciate not only the notional idiom of a particular audience in a particular historical context, but also adopt its range of authoritative speech tones. This idiom was not invented by Eliot, nor did he simply reflect back to a particular social formation its language and thought. Eliot has put into his own words, often beautiful and striking words, the discourse of an identifiable social group, the way in which that social group could begin to re-imagine its relationship to the real, to history, and, most significantly, its relationship to power after the disasters of political radicalism and war. At that moment in time it was important for the mandarinate to embrace the weightless magnificence of a philosophically pure and musical experience free of the burdens and risks of history. It is in this sense primarily that *Four Quartets* fed back into the social formation from which it emerged a coherent text of subjectivity and in that dialectical tension the poem came to interpellate a new subject and thus helped to set the stage for a new evolution of dominant ideology in the North Atlantic world. Its prestige among the mandarins derived from what might be called the mutual recognition of text and reader.

We have here then an interesting lesson in one of the functions of criticism. Gardner and the others I have mentioned helped rescue the poem from its forced and unnatural labour in the debates of ideologues, debates Eliot had mastered and surpassed in the previous decade. They positioned the poem so that the mutual recognition of text and reader could occur in its most productive form and their success in that enterprise, whether they accurately described the meaning of the poem or not, endures to this day. Critics, it turns out, are not only the handmaids or caretakers of composition, but the servants of its consumption.

CHAPTER FIVE

Four Quartets: *the poem proper*

In some emergency we may have to pretend that we are not frightened, in order to prevent a panic.

T. S. Eliot, *A Sermon Preached in Magdalene College*, Cambridge,
1948.

I. BURNT CHILDREN

The 'interpretation' I would like to offer of *Four Quartets* positions the text
as a social and political document in the historical context of its reception. I want to recover, as far as it is possible, those meanings the artefact
carried over to its mandarin readers in the midst of the crisis of Europe
at the end of the war. The first stage in delineating the poem's 'meaning'
in this way has been the subject matter of the previous chapter. The critical repositioning of the poem as an autonomous aesthetic artefact and
as pure subjectivity permitted those readers, weighed down by the
dangers, pressures, and devastations of total war and its aftermath, to
satisfy metaphysical hungers that Adorno, referring to an earlier crisis,
called 'the ontological need' (*Negative Dialectics* 61) in modernity, and,
from that, to make out a saving renunciatory detachment. In one sense
the poem acknowledged the belated arrival, twenty-five years later, of all
of Europe to the intellectual and moral ruin of Germany and Central
Europe in 1918. The spiritual chaos of that earlier crisis of defeat gave to
Martin Heidegger's *Being and Time* its particular point and savour in the
1920s.[1] Heidegger's book defined its own task as the relentless and unsen-
timental unveiling of 'the ontological' that had become thoroughly
obscured by philosophical traditions obsessed with the ontic. It was a cry
of faith in a new 'depth' ontology, that was intensely poetic, self-
assertively unblinkered, ironic, but, above all, consolatory. It had the
capacity to console the German intelligentsia by condemning to the
sphere of the everyday (and, thus, to inauthenticity) all that was the

immediate cause of anxiety and distress in Germany in the 1920s – the collapse of Wilhelmine moralism, the hyper-inflation, the political charades at Weimar, and the arrival of mass culture. It systematized the emergent epistemology of the artistic bohemias of the nineteenth-century capitals, and helped produce the avant gardes of the twentieth. For the 'honest' thinker, *Being and Time* held out a more heroic fate by thrusting small woes aside, no matter how significant they seemed, to let a more radical Anxiety do its proper work, namely to bring Dasein back to itself, 'back from its absorption in the world' (233).

More importantly *Being and Time*, like *Four Quartets* later, disclosed by implication the path by which alienated intellectuals and mandarins could come to accept a place in society, that is, accept society's protection and even its esteem, while simultaneously holding to a severe inward renunciation of and contempt for the social world. Theodor Adorno's *The Jargon of Authenticity* unambiguously dissects the *Lebensphilosophie* that came to function as a stratagem for intellectual survival in the moral ruins of a defeated Germany. He shows its expansion, after the second defeat, into a desperate political and administrative language game, especially among the German mandarins, for routinely concealing the refigured physiognomies of domination after the debacle. The clean break between inner and outer worlds, between subjectivity and the coercive agendas, hidden and otherwise, that 'manage' the everyday Self, drives 'the subject . . . back into his cave'. There he consoles himself with inwardness and the illusory belief that 'the force from which he flees . . . has no power over him' (71). What was implicit in modernism's autonomist aesthetics slides silently over the boundaries into society and politics.[2] As long as one's fundamental beliefs, or truth itself, or art, were essentially autonomous and complete in themselves, then society did not *really* matter, except as a source of danger (but see Burger, *Avant-Garde* 35–46). Learning how to live with this contradiction, learning how to be *in* society, but not *of* it, has been one of the historic 'achievements' of High Modernism.

Apart from what *Four Quartets* has to say about the various religious and aesthetic themes with which it engages, the poem's social and political function has been to point out one of the ways a vulnerable mandarinate might survive the compulsions of history, might reconcile freedom and necessity in dangerous times. The mandarinate have learned to participate in the public sphere as convincing actors and, thus, preserve a privileged social position close to power, while at the same time cultivating a kind of inward freedom which does not visibly interfere with the ritual behaviour of the public actor. It was in the 1930s that the mechanisms for living with such a paradox were worked out by the European intelligentsia (more urgently in Berlin and Moscow) regardless of the isms in power.

Eliot's precise delineation of the bowlerhatted company director twinned invisibly with the tormented poet, remains one of the master models for the period. Indeed its authority as a model for living in society still persists, and explains how the author of the following lines,

> I am neither internee nor informer;
> An inner emigre, grown long-haired
> And thoughtful; a wood-kerne
> Escaped from the massacre,
> Taking protective colouring
> From bole and bark . . . (Heaney, 'Exposure' 72–73)

living through his own dangerous times, might recognize in Eliot the necessary protocols of self-protection in the postwar societies of surveillance and revenge. 'In principle everyone, however powerful, is an object. Even the profession of general no longer offers adequate protection' (Adorno, *Minima Moralia* 37–38).

In Eliot's model, we are encouraged to renounce the public sphere inwardly, cultivating a kind of ironic distance from it, acquiring an understanding with ourselves and with the trusted colleagues who share our predicament, but we are no longer encouraged to publicly forsake society altogether, as in the bohemias of old. This inner freedom, purchased by the continuous, uncritical public exhibition of outward loyalty and abasement to those who exercise power, becomes the sardonic little secret of the mandarins. Orwell's resounding nay to this blithe bisection is famous: 'The fallacy is to believe that under a dictatorial government you can be free *inside*' (*CEJL* III 133). Even if what Orwell believes is true, it is a truth that is simply 'inoperative' at this time. The operative 'truth' to which pliant mandarins succumbed in those years was to have found themselves 'in the most shameful and degrading of all situations, that of competing supplicants', and 'thus virtually compelled to show each other their most repulsive sides' (Adorno, *Minima Moralia* 28) while believing they were free 'inside'. The path towards social re-integration was blocked, however, by a crucial legacy of modernism, its cultural elitism. To find this state of hierarchical division intolerable and to act on it in the public sphere, especially in any overtly political form, is simply to smother oneself, according to Heidegger, in the 'everyday publicness of the "they", which brings tranquillized self-assurance' (233) and, therefore, inauthenticity. This is partially the message, also, of *Four Quartets* to the North Atlantic mandarinate. But it is not all; the new post-war world order required something more. As Jeffrey Perl notes, Eliot himself learned to '[adjust] to the logic of the situation' in the post-war period and it became necessary to accept certain 'developments in life', like, for example, the discovery that it was something the victors called democracy which had triumphed in the bloodbath. Whether this 'dis-covery' was little more than lip service for tactical purposes, or, as Perl prefers, Eliot's genuine recognition 'that democratic values fit closely with his philosophical position' after all (120), is a matter we cannot resolve. Nonetheless, it was a timely 'discovery' in 1945. But whether true or false for Eliot, the psychological paradigm it conveyed to his readers was as convenient, under the circumstances, for the sincere, as it was for all the rest.

Personal and professional survival in dangerous times was one matter, but it was complicated by another problem, the problem of nihilism. For the class of mandarins generally, and for the intelligentsia specifically, the end of the Second World War did not mean, except in the most sim-plistic terms, the victory of one side over another, the victory of democ-racy over totalitarianism, it meant something more profound than the verbal acrobatics of the propagandists. Adorno put it in a momentous phrase: 'What is being enacted now ought to bear the title: "After Doomsday"' (*Minima Moralia* 54). It resembled what the experience of Germany's ruin had meant for Heidegger twenty-five years earlier, the general defeat of all sides, and, philosophically, the final defeat of all humanist illusions about 'Man'. The literary modernism of the 1920s shared in the tasks of weighing up the damage of that earlier calamity; it was Heidegger who gave it its philosophical voice, Eliot who gave it strik-ing poetic expression.

But what do I mean by 'nihilism' in the context of the 1940s? I do not mean a purely philosophical abstraction, such as is found in the view that nihilism is simply an extreme form of scepticism, by which one might maintain that nothing in the world has a real existence. The term casts a wider net of reference than this. It describes a psychological condition as much as it denotes a philosophical concept. In other words, it identifies a datum in feeling, namely the feeling that we are trapped in an absurd existence without values and meaning.[3] The celebrity, for example, of Camus's *Le Mythe de Sisyphe* (1942) in the decade after the war suggests how widely the public experience of nihilism extended, at least among intellectuals, cultural workers and mandarins. Stephen Spender's characterization of Orwell's *Nineteen Eighty-Four* as finally communicating a quality of 'metaphysical claustrophobia' describes more specifically the mood I have in mind (*Creative Element* 133). From this, a radical sense of dread follows which leads to the most shocking recognition of all, that this blighted 'existence without values' might possibly penetrate to the deepest levels of individual existence, that 'there is nothing deep inside each of us, no common human nature, no built-in human solidarity, to use as a moral reference point' (Rorty, *Contingency* 177). This emptiness at the human core seems to explain how human beings are capable of descending into the undreamt of infernos of cruelty and barbarity which characterize European history in midcentury. Eliot did not believe in such extreme nihilism; his Christianity would not allow him to, but his sense of the human prospect conceded that Europe had reached a spiritual nadir akin to nihilism in the war years, from which it needed to be rescued (cf. Perl, *Skepticism* 118). This radical despair was the logical outcome, for Eliot, of a century and half of liberalism.

Emilio Cecchi recalls a conversation with Eliot in London in 1947 that dwelt on the problem of nihilism in Europe in those years and the inescapable duty of the artist to speak the truth, even if it meant facing hostile criticisms. Mention is made of Paul Valéry's truth-telling in his 'majestic' 'Ebauche d'un Serpent' which had recently appeared and been 'charged with gratuitous and decadent nihilism'. They agree that this is nonsense; Valéry is saying no more or less about the human prospect than can be found in The Book of Job or in certain choruses of Sophocles. Their conversation turns to a discussion of 'an extraordinary little book' published in Paris just after the war, called *L'univers concentrationnaire* by David Rousset which both men had recently read. The volume recalls the Frenchmen's experiences as a prisoner in several Nazi concentration camps during the war years. Cecchi refers to the book as 'probably the profoundest testimony regarding Buchenwald, Neuengamme, Helmstedt and so on; a book not written as a story of a frightful description, like so many others written with pens dipped in colours of decay'. Eliot's reaction to this book, as reported by Cecchi, is most interesting.

And Eliot wondered whether the gates of such hells, in the spiritual and material order, can readily be considered to be closed for ever. Or whether mankind, now capable of reaching such extremes of frightfulness, has a weaker resistance to new and infernal suggestions; whether the wheel of bloodshed can stop at last or will follow its murderous course. These things were said lightly so as in some way to mitigate their frightfulness. But I felt that with the man I was speaking to, as with myself, the dread was almost stronger than the hope. (in March and Tambimuttu, *Eliot – A Symposium* 75–76)

This memory of Eliot's views accords with Stephen Spender's memory of an earlier conversation with Eliot, where the older man spoke of the future of 'our civilization' as Spender puts it: 'Internecine warfare . . . People killing one another in the streets . . .' (in Tate, *T. S. Eliot* 49 and cf. Wilson, *Europe* 141). Having crossed a kind of ethical boundary, 'mankind' could not now forget the murderous knowledge that lay on the other side of the frontier. Conrad's *The Heart of Darkness* had already imagined the arrival of the psychopathology of the 'final solution'; and Eliot in the early 1920s had followed Conrad into the surrounding darkness when he was composing *The Waste Land* and 'The Hollow Men'. But it was in 1948 that the full enormity of what Conrad had imagined in the 1890s dawned on Eliot in his brief melancholy footnote to Conrad in *Notes towards the Definition of Culture* (41n).

Henri Fluchère, in his memories of Eliot in the 1940s, remembers the work of the earlier Eliot, and touches on the same psychological ethos of dread and hope. He too refers to Rousset's influential little book.

The Waste Land of T. S. Eliot, with its dried out stretches of sterile ground, its drumming threats of thunder, and its death by water or fire; his *Hollow Men*, whose empty heads and hearts one could hope to refill with human thoughts and emotions, come short of the horrors spread out over '*l'univers concentrationnaire*', and look like a mild purgatory as compared to the dehumanized hell into which we have been hurled. What else can we do, but affront such misery, and, courageously, try to establish new assets over the ruins of an absurd world. (in March and Tambimuttu, *Eliot – A Symposium* 145)

In these accounts Europe comes to resemble ground zero in the final obliteration of the soul, with the concentration camp as the epicentre of the explosion. The blast scorches everyone. And as the noted pacifist Carl Heath asserted, in a Quaker pamphlet from 1947, Europe was not in need of 'reconstruction', the cant word of the engineers and the planners, but of 'redemption' (3).

Spender's *European Witness*, discussed in chapter 2, touched on the nature of the experience I am trying to describe. Contemporaries corroborate Spender's anxieties. Herbert Read recorded in his wartime essay 'Art in an Electric Atmosphere' the experience of 'picking his way among the ruins' in London on the morning of 17 April 1941, the day after one of the great Luftwaffe raids. He trekked from the City to the West End and passed many devastated buildings and institutions.

But the ruins, I reflected, were not merely so much rubble and twisted steel. The endless and intricate structures of a civilization were falling down. It was not merely the jewellers' and furriers' shops, the workmen's tenements and the warehouses which I passed: it was also the Bank of England and the Royal Academy, the Church of England and the *Times*. These institutions, too, were among the ruins, and if they survived at all, they would have to be rebuilt in a new style. And to be quite honest, many less conservative institutions were looking a bit shaken in that morning air – the Labour Party and the frustrated rump of the Communist Party, for example. And all the bright young art societies, so hopeful and experimental before the war – what had become of them? Indeed, it seemed in this lurid April light that all our institutions, institutes, associations and federations had become so many empty forms, structures with their windows blown out, their walls cracked, their reports and memoranda a heap of sodden ashes. (75)

For Read this scene of devastation, disheartening in the extreme, becomes paradoxically an occasion for optimism in the future. 'We shall rebuild', he writes, but only if we do not go back to the bad old ways. The promise in the future lies in discarding 'the notions of victory and defeat, [and] if through common suffering we are driven to humility and goodwill, then reason may prevail in human affairs and we shall build up from the ruins a society free from the grotesque and irrational institutions of finance, snobbery and greed' (79). From these new conditions, if they come about, a new kind of art will arise as a spontaneous expression of the spiritual life of the new society.

I suppose it is rather facile, from the perspective of half a century, to be surprised at such an astonishing ingenuousness from so sophisticated and worldly a man. But is it too much to ask of a mandarin of Read's intelligence, experience and sagacity, some greater measure of realism? Certainly the ordinary people of England might be excused such sentimentalities considering their powerlessness. But even waves of Luftwaffe nightbombers could not blast away 'the grotesque and irrational institutions of finance, snobbery and greed', *that* easily. Setting his pieties about the future aside, I'm not sure Read would actually have been astonished to learn that 'the new society', he says he hoped would come in the aftermath of the disaster, was already thoroughly compromised by VE Day. How else can one square the rosy optimism of the victor's publicists about the future of 'the world we fought for' with the effortless self-betrayal of the Allies's own much-trumpeted moral superiority in the war?

From the moment that operatives for American intelligence approached Klaus Barbie and many other Gestapo and SS officials in the summer of 1945 to recruit them to a new service, notwithstanding their horrific crimes, Read's 'new society' was doomed (cf. also Spender, *Witness* 53–55 and Stern, *Hidden Damage* 343–44). It took a middle level agent in those post-war intelligence services, interviewed many years later by Marcel Ophuls for the film *Hotel Terminus*, to put his finger more accurately on the moral pulse of that aftermath when he admitted the world looked awfully grey, ethically speaking, in the light of the power politics of the time, despite the moronic moralism of the propagandists. Harold Nicolson, the worldly mandarin from another era, surveying the 'mass insanity' from Sissinghurst, perceived very clearly the damage done by 'the great hurricane of hysteria' (*Comments* 80): 'The worst effect of total war is that it destroys the moral sensibility even of those who entered it with the finest motives' (98). Perhaps Read's optimism was simply a kind of necessary moral restraining device in order not to have to imagine the yet more dismal abyss from which he judiciously averted his eyes that April morning.

Read may have been temperamentally or ideologically incapable of seeing past his own optimistic slogans, but in the situation which all of Europe faced he did manage to avoid the facile cynicism of a Cyril Connolly for whom the carnage represented little more than an occasion for preening:

The great marquee of European civilization, in whose yellow light we all grew up, and read or wrote or loved or travelled, has fallen down; the side-ropes are frayed, the centre-pole is broken, the chairs and tables are all in pieces, the tea-urns empty, the roses are withered on their stands, and the prize marrows; the grass is dead. (Connolly, *Ideas and Places* 29)

One wonders how amused the wounded and maimed, or the wrecked souls emerging from Sobibor in 1945, would have been to learn that their fates were comically entangled with the overturned lawn furniture at the last garden party in Europe. It was easy for a secure mandarin like Connolly to play at despair, but his angst-chic only makes sense if the real thing were widespread enough to make its simulation believable.

There was no need for shamming in Germany in those years; the abyss was as visible to the new conquerors who could see it, as it was to the defeated. Eliot's careful pronouncements to the Germans in his postwar broadcasts must be read in the context of the spiritual damage to which he knew he was ministering. And on the very lip of that abyss, in the silence that fell over Germany at the end, in what Rousset called a 'world like a dead star loaded with corpses' (*World Apart* 109), the little group at Freiburg that listened attentively to Heidegger's 'Wozu Dichter?' in December 1946 must have been melancholy enough: 'The world's night is spreading its darkness. The era is defined by the god's failure to arrive' (*Poetry, Language, Thought* 91). The time has grown so grimly destitute that even the default of God could no longer be discerned as a default, he told his auditors. The word for abyss – *Abgrund* – meant originally the ground, or that which is undermost, the soil, in which things root and on which they stand.

> The age for which the ground fails to come, hangs in the abyss. Assuming that a turn still remains open for this destitute time at all, it can come some day only if the world turns about fundamentally – and that now means, unequivocally: if it turns away from the abyss. In the age of the world's night, the abyss of the world must be experienced and endured. But for this it is necessary that there be those who reach into the abyss. (92)

For Heidegger this reaching into the abyss – Eliot's 'the place of disaffection' – is the task of the poet in a destitute time. But the experience of the abyss itself is not limited to poets alone. It is everyone's experience (Wilson, *Europe* 135); it is everyone's melancholy, and at issue is the question of one's relationship to or attitude towards the experience of nihilism. Most people can find refuge in tradition, or, if that has also been foreclosed, as it had for the folk cultures of the new masses, the simple formulas and programmatic optimisms of the propagandists and publicists will probably have to do.

Even contemporary philosophy fails in the face of the abyss, Adorno wrote in exile in the same aftermath. Ever since its 'conversion into method', philosophy, or the inquiry into the good – *to kalon* – has fallen into 'intellectual neglect . . . sententious whimsy and finally oblivion', because 'life has become the sphere of private existence and now of mere consumption' (*Minima Moralia* 15). Recalling this epochal defection, Adorno begins his own post-war reflections 'from Damaged Life' with a despondent meditation on the life of thought as the cultivation of a melancholy science. 'Nevertheless', Adorno writes, 'a consciousness that wishes to withstand the unspeakable finds itself again and again thrown back on the attempt to understand, if it is not to succumb subjectively to the madness that prevails objectively' (103). And that, in a nutshell, spelled out the intellectual agenda of the war years.

The German theologian Helmut Thielicke, in his 'preface to the American Edition' of *Der Nihilismus*, recalls the conditions, immediately after the German capitulation, in which the lectures on which the book is based were given. He remembers the jammed lecture halls at the

University of Tübingen filled with ragged figures, former officers in remnants of their uniforms with their badges and regimental patches ripped off, refugees from the East, and survivors of the prison camps. All of them, Thielicke notes, were hungry, and, as the lectures were delivered in unheated rooms, the lecturer stood at the lectern in his overcoat and the students took notes with numbed hands.

Before us sat a generation of youth which had been shrewdly and cruelly misled by the holders of power. And now they faced a world of rubble and ruins; not only their homes, but also their idealism, their faith, their concepts of value were shattered. But the vacuum in their hearts cried out to be filled. At the same time these young people were profoundly skeptical. Whatever we professors said they turned it about in their minds ten times before they would accept it: these burnt children dreaded the fire, because it might contain the coals of fresh seductions. (*Nihilism* 11)

It was precisely this hunger, and not only among Germans, as a result of the epochal failures of secularism, the political isms of the 1930s, and the liberal conception of the individual, which Eliot had foreseen, and counted on, in the closing paragraphs of 'Thoughts After Lambeth' in 1931. Of course, he could not have predicted the extent of the devastation brought on by war. The enormities committed in peace and war, in what the historian Christopher Dawson called in 1947 'the nightmares of the hive' (*Here* 9), surpassed any one person's capacity to imagine the worst.

Eliot also would have understood the scepticism and wariness of Thielicke's 'burnt children' and he had learned how to respond to their hungers. His own dilemmas in the personal changes announced by the publication of *Ash-Wednesday* fifteen years earlier had already not only taught him about the necessity, in certain moments of crisis, for candour, but also its proper music, a candour that could reach into the abyss and make itself heard, not as one more passing seduction, but as the final vocabulary of the soul itself.

His close friend and collaborator J.H. Oldham had told a BBC audience in 1944, the gist of which he had commmunicated to Eliot personally in a letter during the Munich crisis in 1938 (*Idea* 85–86), that 'Mankind stands face to face with the ultimate question of human existence'. The question, Oldham said, had been posed speculatively by Nietzsche as the possibility of embracing 'a complete nihilism', and from it had come 'a moral chaos' ('Christian Humanism' 16), not as a clever sally in a philosophy seminar, but as the concrete conditions of life in the ruins. In a parallel development, the philosopher Keiji Nishitani, like

Thielicke in Germany, also felt compelled by the collapse of traditional Japanese society to address the question of nihilism in a series of lectures to small groups of bedraggled students in Kyoto in the wreckage of postwar Japan. These talks became the notable book *Nihirizumu* (1949), translated in 1990 as *The Self-Overcoming of Nihilism*. He traced the importance of Nietzsche in the history of European nihilism and his influence in Japan. The book also tentatively establishes a link between European nihilism and the Zen Buddhist concept of 'emptiness'. He affirmed also, for his traumatized auditors, the radical importance of nihilism in their time, when

... our historical life has lost its ground as objective spirit, that the value system which supports this life has broken down, and that the entirety of social and historical life has loosened itself from its foundations. Nihilism is a sign of the collapse of the social order externally and spiritual decay internally – and as such signifies a time of great upheaval. Viewed in this way, one might say that it is a general phenomenon that occurs from time to time in the course of history. The mood of post-war Japan would be one such instance. (3)

Nishitani's assessment of the mood of post-war Japan applies just as well to post-war Europe. Nietzsche's answer to such an impasse, experienced *avant la lettre*, involved the cultivation of that lofty detachment from society which is implied in a sharp aside in The Gay Science: 'It is even part of my good fortune not to be a house-owner.' Adorno's response, in the midst of the crisis of the 1940s, recognizes the justice of Nietzsche's remark, but also the fact that it now falls short. 'Today we should have to add: it is part of morality not to be at home in one's own home' (*Minima Moralia* 39).

Thielicke, finding himself inescapably amid the ruins, remembered the state of mind of the 'homeless' who turned to him for instruction.

Standing there before these men, whose expectancy came at one like a breath of warm air, it was impossible to deliver a refined, detached academic lecture. Here one could not be content to give instruction; here there was an intellectual and spiritual hunger that needed to be satisfied; here there were wounds that needed to be bound up. It was a situation that called for tender consolation and firm, forthright direction. (12)

Eliot's audience was not so vividly or physically in attendance, but it was precisely to the satisfaction of the same hungers, to the binding up of similar wounds, to the tasks of consolation, firmness, and direction that *Four Quartets* was aimed. And what did Thielicke's students, Eliot's readers, and Oldham's radio listeners need consolation for? Oldham saw the problem in social terms as the necessary subversion of the humanist meta-narratives of Progress and of the progressive perfectibility of 'Man':

I will not make too much of two devastating wars in a single generation, though it seems very superficial to dismiss them lightly as minor set-backs in the continuous upward advance of mankind. I am thinking rather of the deep disintegration of society out of which they came. (Oldham 18)

It is difficult not to notice, in Oldham's irony, the quiet satisfaction of a conservative happy to have lived to hear history's cruel verdict on the liberal-humanist conception of 'mankind'.

Thielicke formulated the issue in terms of nihilism as the corrosive element in human destiny, the final objectification of the human.

He cannot escape the creeping process of self-disintegration, which is all too euphemistically called the history of the human mind, the process which one day will expose the sounding brass of the philosophies and the tinkling cymbals of poetry and religion and with a tragic inevitability bring to light the fact that the whole history of the human mind is nothing but a journey through a field of corpses, that it consists only of graves garlanded with ideologies, but that beneath this camouflage is nothing but dung and dead bones, and that therefore we are gazing at nothing but Nothingness. (29)

And Eliot? More simply still,

> . . . human kind
> Cannot bear very much reality. (BN I 190)

But also in his closing paragraphs in *The Idea of a Christian Society*, Eliot's very personal admission, quite rare in his work, that a single political event in 1938 – specifically the Munich crisis – 'brought a profounder realisation of a general plight' to consciousness. It was not a 'political' realization or a 'disagreement with policy,' it was something more pervasive and dreadful.

The feeling which was new and unexpected was a feeling of humiliation, which seemed to demand an act of personal contrition, of humility, repentance and amendment; what had happened was something in which one was deeply implicated and responsible. It was not, I repeat, a criticism of the government, but a doubt of the validity of a civilisation. (64)

The very rarity of such open moments of candour, *in propria persona*, must give these words an authority which Eliot's more typical strategies of deflected confession work to obscure. He was 'deeply shaken' by these events and the desire for an act of contrition, of fashioning a saving humility in the presence of this stain, might provide us with a way of reading some of the purposes that lie at the origin of 'East Coker', completed and published in the *New English Weekly*, 21 March 1940, four months after the appearance of *The Idea of a Christian Society* in late October 1939.

For Eliot the dilemma which was more generally evident to all by 1945 had been glimpsed much earlier even than Munich, most profoundly in *The Waste Land* period, but again, from a new perspective in the early 1930s. Although arguments have often been made that there was a philosophical or metaphysical dimension to the ambience of radical dread and revulsion in Eliot's early work, this is not borne out by Eliot himself. Certainly there is the issue of religious belief and doubt as Lyndall Gordon has shown, especially in *Eliot's Early Years*. But, as she has also amply demonstrated, there was in the early years a strong undercurrent, or predisposition, towards certainty about matters of Christian faith and commitment. Of course, having taken that inward step in the mid-1920s, *and* made it unambiguously public, Eliot had a firm ground from which he could launch his life-long critique of liberal culture, both generally and in all the specific places in which it had led to the weakening of the values and institutions of the traditional ethos, a weakening that, he felt, had led directly to political authoritarianism of the Nazi kind (*Idea* 15–16). In this respect, it was absolutely necessary, as a first step back, to make use of disillusion as a precondition for seeing the emptiness at the heart of all liberal-humanist discourse. It was precisely 'uncynical disillusion' which fortified F.H. Bradley during the period of the rising tide of liberalism in the nineteenth century and which helped him resist it (*FLA* 60–61).

The state of uncynical disillusion leads inevitably to the sense that the Christian, in destitute times, must be patient, must learn to bide his or her time, so that the full scope of the 'general plight' might disclose itself sufficiently to all. But especially to the mandarinate. Eliot's sense that the hour will come when 'society has become so desperate' (*Idea* 23) that it will finally turn helplessly to Christ, constituted the often unspoken political *dictum sapienti* of a good deal of Eliot's social criticism, of the essay on Machiavelli in *For Lancelot Andrews* for instance, or *After Strange Gods* as a whole, and 'Thoughts After Lambeth'. This was also a motif in his commentaries in the *Criterion* all through the 1930s. It was also picked up by other writers, not surprisingly ones very close to Eliot. Alec Vidler, the ecclesiatical historian, argued in *Secular Despair and Christian Faith* (1941) for 'the need for despair' as the obligatory process of clearing away the rubbish of liberal humanism as the precondition for any revival of meaningful personal and, therefore, social existence (23–24). Eliot will put it more succinctly: 'to be restored, our sickness must grow worse' (EC IV 202). It is the sense which Eliot shares with Heidegger that 'the abyss of the world must be experienced and endured' that provides one of the principal constitutive conditions of reading *Four Quartets* in the 1940s.

This is a poem that greets its readers, both in an admonitory spirit and consolingly, on their way back from the ruins of a shattered world. Denis Donoghue has come closest to recognizing this particular rhetorical positioning of the poem with respect to its readers in the 1940s.

Eliot's problem in *Four Quartets* is a strategic one; how to evacuate practically all the areas in which his readers live. A proposal of this kind is tolerated only in wartime . . . and perhaps he wanted to use the idiom of war in order to enforce a deeper discrimination of peace-time commitments. The critique is religious, dogmatic, and Christian. Eliot's hope is to clear a space, or if necessary to take over a bombed-out area, and there to build a new life of the spirit . . . (*Universe* 260)

The poem proposes a new subjectivity for its mandarin readers, a sub-jectivity that, in addition to all its positive aspirations, also poses no polit-ical threat to the Western power elites, who were made doubly vigilant by their experience of dissident movements in the 1930s and the new challenge of an armed, hostile, and aggressive empire in the East, a new enemy perceived to be working through countless fifth columnists, academics, fellow travellers, atomic spies, and other traitors in the North Atlantic world. This serviceable subjectivity assumes the ascetic 'redemption of time' as its general theme. But the poem goes on to imply, as forcefully as the delicacies of the situation permit, that, to quote Donoghue again, 'the human scale of action is puny beyond or beneath redemption' and in need of 'cleansing, surgery, and "voiding"'' and that 'the voiding of all human allegiances' implies 'that they are in any event meretricious' (261).

I think Donoghue errs in believing that the next step in the strategic envelopment of the reader is to take the reader swiftly from worldly renunciation to an affirmation of the divine. Eliot understood his readers better than that. Secular, humanist intellectuals could not be brought to God that easily. They could only be brought along to some-thing they would instinctively resist, by first being set on a path of least resistance. The irresistible path was the path of art. Undoubtedly, aes-thetic consciousness is deployed in the poem as a theme (e.g. BN V), but it is also there, in the extraordinary artfulness of the poem itself, as a beguiling demonstration of aesthetic power. Later, in order to make room for the 'real' work of divine grace, the poem-as-superlative-artefact steps back from itself, simply and unpretentiously, and asserts the need to recognize the limits of that power and, finally, to renounce it. That most of Eliot's mandarin readers did not follow him out beyond the reach of art towards God points finally to the crucial historical paradox of *Four Quartets*, its peculiar failure in the very midst of its immediate success. It is a failure the sting of which only Eliot would have really understood.

Rather than following Eliot out past the boundaries of art, the poem's readers seemed quite happy to sojourn in the safe harbour of the poem's artfulness. The almost thirty years of modernism, so brilliantly promoted by Eliot at Faber & Faber, no doubt helped to provide the proper sort of aesthetic context in the building of 'a new life of the spirit' in wartime, but it was not quite what Eliot had in mind. The new subjectivity which *Four Quartets* was read as enacting, stems, in just these ways, from the poetics of modernism and its timeliness in offering to frightened artists and intellectuals in the 'witch hunting' 1940s and 1950s an *aesthetic* refuge from the societies of surveillance-in-depth which emerge after the war. This comes to represent ironically the social and political destination of the poetics of aesthetic autonomy in a general sense, not as the completion of some original artistic aim or teleology, but as a result of the hazards of history.

Such a poetics aims to cancel for ever art's capacity to help bring about social change, its capacity to make something happen. In the 1930s, art had for a time been recast as a weapon in the war for political change and social justice. The effectiveness of avant garde art in winning for a brief moment the attention of the masses in the 1930s was a lesson that the power elites learned very quickly and this momentary loss of control over the media apparatuses in mass society was not to be repeated after the war.[4] With the failure of the programmes for change and with the descent of Europe into the fiery barbarism of war and, then, further down, into the icy barbarisms of an armed peace, the conception of art as possibly politically potent had to disappear, that is, if one wanted to continue as an artist with any kind of public presence in the capitals of the North Atlantic world. The best mode of conduct for intellectuals on tiptoe was to cultivate a rich private life, but not to attach any political weight to it at all. Adorno, in *Minima Moralia*, describes the parallel process among indentured scientists and technologists increasingly recruited during and after the war to organize the new wave of modernization for the power elites of the Atlantic world (124). In this process, Los Alamos in New Mexico proved to be the testing ground, not only of new weapons of mass destruction, but the testing ground of a startling new ethics of complicity. The career of W.H. Auden delineates an important artistic paradigm of the same process.

After 1939, as Auden began his sobering exercises in self-censorship by editorial revision and cancellation of his own work, he used the occasion of the death of Yeats to reposition himself as a subject in history and to make his peace with the Atlantic oligarchs: 'Poetry makes nothing happen: it survives / In the valley of its making . . .' (*CSP* 142). Auden's elegy struggles to drown out the subterranean sigh of relief as the poet, shaken by history, admits he has climbed down for good from the speaker's platform. He deploys instead the persona of the worldly confidant who knows the score, with a tone of smiling resignation in the comradely society of the mandarin enclave. The poem's very fluency, however, traces anxiety's path out into the world which the speaker knows has no place for art that does not offer itself as essentially ineffectual, in the ways that matter to a watchful and suspicious oligarchy.

In order to settle the point, Auden, a few months later, tackles the suicide in America of the leftist revolutionary writer Ernst Toller. There the process of coming in from the cold of opposition completes itself through the strategy of undermining Toller's moral and political affirmations by psychologizing him, by suggesting unconscious motivations and complexes over which Toller had no control. Political commitments that challenge power merely become symptons of psychological disorders to which poor Toller succumbed. In this respect Toller's death is 'made safe for democracy' by being treated entirely as Toller's personal affair, not as an act that might also convey potent and uncomfortable political meanings during a period when Toller, the former revolutionary in exile, was being investigated, hounded is the right word, by the American authorities.

> What was it, Ernst, that your shadow unwittingly said?
> Did the small child see something horrid in the woodshed
> Long ago?. . .   (*CSP* 143)

The inadvertent condescension here is astounding. The tender, paternal note in the use of Toller's first name works to diminish the old revolutionary 'war-horse' while trying to pay him homage. But Auden's unease is audible in every syllable. At best Toller may be 'an example to the young', but the worldly and knowing speaker in the poem, passing

himself off as a former comrade-in-arms, having now grown up, understands that 'Ernst' didn't really mean it.

> We are lived by powers we pretend to understand:

> They arrange our loves; it is they who direct at the end
>   The enemy bullet, the sickness, or even our hand.

> It is their to-morrow hangs over the earth of the living
>   And all that we wish for our friends: but existence is believing

> We know for whom we mourn and who is grieving.   (144)

The 'powers' that the poem tells us 'live' Toller are one thing, essentially
psychological and personal; but 'the powers' that 'live' the poem's
speaker are quite another. The powers that have pressed him to these
judgements are political through and through. The politics of Toller's
life are dismissed equally with the politics of his suicide. The voice of the
poem with its enactment of adult compassion and comradely tenderness
speaks, nevertheless, what the reader is asked to accept without question
as a difficult, and inescapable, realism. The reader is meant to experience the tolling bell of realism as a calling back to the embrace of society.
In some ways it is also, like *Murder in the Cathedral*, a warning and a threat.

The spectacle of Atlantic leftist intellectuals and artists trying to find
their way back into society, psychologically, had its poignant, embarras-
ing, and farcical aspects as well. Auden and Spender are the famous
cases; C. Day Lewis less famous, but no less anguished about his own
situation. His interest in Virgil in the 1940s represents a kind of emotional hospitalization, a sequestered rehabilitation among the classics
after the delirium of the newsreels. In 'Word Over All', the signature
poem of this penitential period of political revision, the central emblems
of the crisis are the figures of the 'drowning imagination' and a shadowy
character he calls 'the sea-waif', who, having lived from 'surge to surge',
can no longer 'chart / Current and reef aright' (*CP 1954* 220). Day Lewis
imagining himself as a 'sea-waif' verges on the maudlin of course, not to
mention the inadvertently comical. Having lost his bearings, the poet
adopts again the old notion of aesthetic autonomy, 'word over all', which
returns now, not as modernist innovation, but, more desperately, as one
of the new compass points of the displaced soul.

The characterization of art as separated from the world, a world that
was increasingly seen as transitory and faded, appealed to an intelligentsia grown increasingly frustrated and disillusioned with society and
with political engagement, especially so in the years of the Civil War in
Spain, when the difficulties and dangers of the real world of politics

touched everyone. The public dramas of political action, typically mixtures of adolescent fantasy and adolescent power worship masquerading as realism, came to seem ever more complicated ruses for self-destruction.

Evelyn Waugh more or less accurately described the muddle of the middle class dabbler in communist politics in the 1930s: the so-called Left intellectual or fellow-traveller always began his engagement in a humanitarian spirit which obscured the underlying immaturity. The world's intransigence ground away at the idealism until the shaky foundations stood revealed. Dismayed, the intellectual woke up one day to find that he had unwittingly and 'finally surrender[ed] himself [to] the cold, dark pit of politics' (quoted in Carpenter, *Brideshead* 320). And for many it was a very cold and dark pit indeed. Orwell for one offered his wounded *Homage to Catalonia* as a hiker's guide to the geography of betrayal in the 1930s. Louis MacNeice, his magnificently sardonic, sorrowful elegy, *The Strings Are False*.

It was from the pit, a particular and historically concrete manifestation of Heidegger's 'abyss', that Eliot's *Four Quartets* attempted its deliverance of a middle class mandarinate that had had its fill of the shadow world of politics by the late 1930s. Eliot's approach to his readers communicated to them that he was one of those who had 'experienced and endured' the abyss of the world, that he was one of 'those who [*could*] reach into the abyss'. As the author of *The Waste Land* he had already earned the authority to speak on these matters in this way. As the author of *Ash-Wednesday*, however, he had seemed to slip back towards conventional religious avowals; these might satisfy spiritual needs of his own, but they seemed, from the perspective of a secular age, quixotic and irrelevant.

In 1936, in the third section of 'Burnt Norton', he spoke again from the abyss (93–129). This was a way of re-establishing his credentials. Yes, there was the little matter of what had seemed in 1930 to be the all-too-easy call of a renewal of Christian faith hanging over his words, but by the 1930s such professions no longer seemed so disappointingly bourgeois and banal to increasingly dispirited and frightened sections of the mandarinate. In a society waking up to ideological surveillance as a permanent and pervasive condition, those whose psychological comforts, not to mention occasionally their jobs and perks, had been placed in jeopardy during the shouting years listened in silence to the beguiling voice in 'Burnt Norton'. The quiet, donnish opening – 'Time present and time past / Are both perhaps present . . .' and so on – calms us and takes us tonally into one of the safest havens of the intelligence, the seminar room and lecture hall. It predisposes us to listen, if we recognize the dialect of this tribe. And Eliot's conventional religious beliefs, which had seemed an insurmountable obstacle at one time, in the changing psychological climate, were suavely accommodated to a new shape. Maurice Bowra in a characteristic reappraisal in the 1930s:

Eliot hit me very hard inside, but I resisted it, because I could not quite believe that everything was so drab as he said, and I resisted the Christian part. But now I see that he was on the whole right, and that the Christian part is in fact hardly Christian at all, but really a plea for the inner life. (quoted in Carpenter, *Brideshead* 92–3)

or the American poet Louise Bogan in a review of *Four Quartets* in 1943:

Eliot here stands at a distant remove from the 'aged eagle' role in which he presented himself, with considerable affectation, in 'Ash Wednesday' thirteen years ago. He has learned lessons in patience and sympathy, a firm base for renewed poetic strength. (72)

What had been a sticking point in 1930 seemed less so after 1936, when 'Burnt Norton' was first read as the final poem in the *Collected Poems* of that year.[5] The fact that a Christian revival was also well under way by 1936, with a good deal of intellectual and promotional support in the Faber publishing programme, did not hurt either. Under these changed conditions, Eliot's Christian orthodoxy almost entirely disappeared as a problem in the darkest days of the war crisis, when Eliot composed the three extensions of 'Burnt Norton'.

What the whole poem offered, in short, was an edifying account of existence that asserted a theo-ontological foundation in the face of a nihilism that had come to seem the final destination of history, the 'Hotel Terminus', so to speak, of the European soul. And it did so in a poetics and style which disclosed the way in which isolated and marginalized intellectuals in particular might find their way back to social and political incorporation. The poem marked the path former dissidents might take to make peace with the very societies they had said they hoped to overthrow, and in the process they quietly deserted those former noisy selves with which they had hoped to overthrow them.

This was the central dilemma for many intellectuals in every society in Europe. Only the inveterate and the foolhardy continued openly down the political road. The rise of the totalitarianisms, the economic crisis, Spain, the intemperate political rhetoric of extremists, the rising curve of violence and the indifference to it, the growing sense that a new

European war could not be avoided, and the changing nature of personal life and of personal relations,[6] all contributed to a gradual turning, for large sections of the Atlantic mandarinate, towards society, its established power structures, and its traditional sources of cultural authority.

More particularly for artists and intellectuals, and for the mandarinate in general, this meant a turning towards those authoritative figures who might offer safe haven in psychological and political terms. Certainly Harold Nicolson sensed that this was Eliot's 'saintly' and 'selfless' task, rescuing a generation from 'apathy or cynicism' ('Echo' 34–35). Eliot's consoling words had very much the same effect as the Professor's on his students in the 1938 novel of the same name by Rex Warner. The students, made anxious by political turmoil, listen attentively to the sage: 'The Professor stopped and noticed that some of the students had been calmed by his words. Their faces wore an expression almost of gratitude. He had not aroused their energy but allayed their fears' (15). It is part of Warner's design in discrediting liberal humanism during his communist years that, at the end of the novel, the Professor, the epitome of liberal humanist optimisim, is revealed to be naive and ineffectual. Warner seems to be saying that the Professor ought to have spent rather more time rousing student energy to oppose fascism, than timidly allaying their anxieties. But that, like Spender's similar message in *Forward from Liberalism*, was the partisan bluster of the mid-1930s speaking; by 1948, Warner, like Day Lewis, had abandoned the political bravado of the earlier decade and immersed himself quietly in the ancient classics. The public communist withdrew into the haven of classical scholarship, which, in the words of the critic N.H. Reeve, led finally to 'his eventual enlistment as a more trustworthy Establishment figure' (1), and led him also, we might add (because Eliot would have approved), to becoming a public apologist for the traditions of the English public school.[7] It was rather a feeble finale for the man, who for a time in the 1930s, in addition to his revolutionary politics, was thought to be 'an English Kafka' (Reeve 16). In these sheepish reversals, a whole generation learned how to read *Four Quartets*.

II. REHEARSING RENUNCIATION

Four Quartets was published as a complete work for the first time in 1944. The separate poems had began to appear in 1936 with the publication of 'Burnt Norton' in the new collection of Eliot's poems in that year. After a five year gap, 'East Coker', 'Dry Salvages', and 'Little Gidding' followed in succession, one a year from 1940 to 1942. The last three poems are strictly speaking 'war' poems. They were composed during the war and, the last two especially, during the darkest days of the war. 'Burnt Norton' stands out because it was composed in 1935, partially from materials not included in *Murder in the Cathedral*.

One might expect that the difference between the first and the last three might be more severely visible than the differences among the final three. In fact if one is looking for differences among the separate poems they are not hard to find. 'Little Gidding' is as different in mood from 'Dry Salvages' as it is from 'Burnt Norton'. Certain formal considera- tions – the five-part development, the alternation of lyric modes, the recurrence of image and phrase motifs, the classical refinement of the speaking voice – give the sequence a discernible homogeneity, as opposed say to *The Waste Land* with its interplay of lyric voices, prophetic incantation, and popular speech. The voice of *Four Quartets*, on the other hand, finds its specific gravity in a kind of classic poise. I know that the sentence I have just written simply begs the question of the poem's 'voice'. I chose to use that very fuzzy word 'classic' in order to make a deliberate reference to Eliot's important essay 'What is a Classic?' deliv- ered, first, as the Presidential Address to the Virgil Society in 1944, the very year that *Four Quartets* first appeared as a single sequence in England.

In this essay, Eliot defines, or at least offers a number of attributes of, what one might mean by calling a work of art 'classic'. Maturity of mind, maturity of manners, and maturity of language are the three principal dimensions of his definition. These maturities require a corre- sponding maturity in his audience, in his 'age' as Eliot puts it. In commu- nicating to his 'age', the master must contract a style, a 'common style', which brings to maximum fulfilment all the language's resources in the task of communicative comprehensiveness and universality. This thumbnail sketch of the essay does not exhaust its meaning. It is worth taking a moment to examine what lies behind his description a little more closely.

The first thing to note about the essay is how much it deliberately con- forms to Eliot's own prescriptions about the characteristics of the classic work. The essay itself, in other words, is the best example on offer of what a classic work feels like, or ought to feel like. And it embodies, silently, the one aspect of the classic which is most difficult to put into so many words, its inner composure and stillness. Nowhere is this more evident than in Eliot's one reference to a specific passage in a particular 'classic' text, Virgil's *Aeneid*. The episode to which he refers occurs in book VI and involves the encounter of Aeneas and the shade of Dido in the underworld. The possibility for ordinary melodrama is resisted by Virgil and Eliot calls the meeting 'one of the most poignant' and 'one of the most civilized passages in poetry' (*OPP* 62). It is not simply that the passage tells us about the attitude of Dido to Aeneas – she cannot forgive the man who rejected her in book IV – but more importantly what the passage 'tells us about the attitude of Aeneas'. Dido may not forgive him, but the fact that Aeneas does not forgive himself confirms the civilizing difference for Eliot. And this in spite of the justificatory fact 'that all that [Aeneas] has done has been in compliance with destiny, or in consequence of the machinations of gods who are themselves, we feel, only instruments of a greater inscrutable power' (62). This instance of civilized manners on Aeneas' part attests to the presence of Virgil's own civilized consciousness and conscience, of a level of civilization that is not narrowed by 'purely local or tribal code[s] of manners' (63).

What makes Eliot's comments about this episode in the *Aeneid* so very interesting is the comparable level of civilization for which Eliot himself strives here (cf Reeves, *Virgilian* 108, 158–62). The encounter is a curious passage to isolate in Virgil's epic, and must have seemed so to the audience of classicists, who listened to the original lecture in 1944. But how revealing the passage is as we read it today with a fuller awareness of Eliot's biography, especially with our knowledge of the morally disturbing episodes with his own first wife in the 1930s and 1940s as background. His rejection of her, her emotional disintegration, her confinement and seclusion, his sense of guilt at her fate, and his need for atonement, all of these events glimmer in the background as he quietly illuminates the encounter of Aeneas and Dido in the underworld. What he says about Aeneas' conscience, that 'Dido's behaviour appears almost as a projection' of it, that Aeneas would yieldingly *expect* Dido to snub him and thus, we are left to infer, permit her, by her own action, to vindicate her earlier humiliation and degradation, well accords with what we now know to have exercised Eliot's own troubled conscience over a long period of time. In this respect Eliot tests his own civilization in manners, consciousness and conscience against Virgil's own. Eliot speaks masterfully on a public theme and, simultaneously, confronts a private demon without the loss of lucidity and control, and, most tellingly, with an unusual sympathy that steers clear of sentimentality. Of course his immediate audience would not have understood the tension in the passage under discussion, unless they were intimate with the details of

Eliot's life. Nonetheless, it is, for Eliot himself, a crucial moment in the essay as he privately sets himself a task loaded with personal difficulties and masters them without one false note. It is this inner composure which for Eliot authenticates specifically and privately his general ideas about the classic work. He sets before us, whether we know it or not, and with some poignancy, a superb example of a matchless maturity. He also reveals to his listeners and readers in 1944 his capacity for seeing past the heartless grandeur of a great public work – what he calls its 'absolute zero of frigidity' (54) – to the unexpected intimacies of the heart.

Eliot's rhetorical tactic here is subtle, and highly effective. His defence of classicism is clear, forthright and predictable, but his choice of this moment of conscience and intimacy in Virgil as the exemplary moment of the classic temper is intended to suprise us. And I think it does. Its aim is quite clear. Eliot subverts that contemporary prejudice against classic conceptions of art which abhors their heartlessness and their distance from the intimacies of 'real life'. It is in the most intimate moments of individual existence, very private and personal ones, that the true temper of the classic sensibility is not only glimpsed, but consolidated. Its superiority to any other theory of art lies in just this capacity to penetrate to the emotional core of existence, yet to maintain an exemplary poise that saves us from the feckless wallow of an undisciplined emotionalism. The steely aesthetics of early modernism ('good art must have no inside' Wyndham Lewis says in *Tarr*) still stands somewhere behind this formulation, but Eliot's refinement of the position suggests both a maturing of an adolescent radicalism and a more shrewd assessment of a reader's comfort zone in the matter of persuasion and assent. The inner composure of Aeneas (and Eliot himself), in short, embraces the saving inner resource of the classic temper.[8]

The problem of facing up to the nihilism of a destitute time lay not so much in the inevitable revelation of the emptiness of traditional European culture, and the unravelling of its authority and practical usefulness for everyday life, but in the way, Eliot argued, certain tendencies in the nineteenth century had come to dislodge the traditional classic resources of the 'mind of Europe' as the constitutive paradigm of European subjectivity. Through that displacement, they acted to weaken the European spirit, leading it first to despair and then rendering it incapable of confronting the contemporary abyss. The twin legacies of liberal-humanism and romanticism, Eliot's old enemies, were principally at fault. The entirely misguided faith in the progressive goodness of the individual human being and the equally false faith in a civil society based on abstract principles pressed a self-blinded Europe on the dark journey towards nihilism. But these 'strange gods' had now run their course and confronted the destitution of the 1940s with empty hands. Eliot's views on these matters are very well known, both in his own work and in the paraphrases of his many commentators.[9]

What is interesting in recalling them is to see how the conservative cultural history which Eliot championed in the 1930s and 1940s presumed a particular subjective position for his mandarin readers as a function of the decay of the liberal-humanist culture to which these readers had been trained, a culture which, in the collapse of Europe, had left them spiritually supine. My aim is to reconstruct the structure of thought and feeling he intuited in the readers of *Four Quartets* in the 1940s in order to disclose the poem's approach to those very readers whose inherited reserve of liberal-humanist cultural capital had been exhausted by contemporary history. In this way, one can bring to light the poem's rhetoric in the context of a particular historical situation, a rhetoric which assumes a specific subject position for its readers. I believe that Eliot's experience as a publisher had more than adequately trained him to think in terms of the mindset of a class of readers. Certainly as a publisher he was interested in the kind and quality of the work he committed the Faber company to invest its capital in, but he was just as interested in seeing a return on that investment and that meant, in the days before opinion polls, market surveys and the surgical precision of geomarket analysis, developing that intuitive sixth sense about what a group of readers might buy.

One ought to add immediately here that the principal rhetorical stratagem of the poem is to maintain that it is not rhetorical, that its zone of profoundest effect lies somewhere beyond 'the pathology of rhetoric' (see Bush, *Character* 17–31 on Eliot's horror of 'rhetoric'). Only those readers willing to follow Eliot out past the gates of calculation would be rewarded with the poem's balm. The poem's success in finally conveying this 'truth' of its own concealed designs, or lack of them, forcefully argued by the group of contemporary critics discussed in the previous chapter, suggests that Eliot's intuitions about the majority of his mandarin readers, and their needs, was, as always, bang on.

If we turn to R. H. Coats's 'An Anchor for the Soul: a Study of Mr. Eliot's Later Verse' in *The Hibbert Journal* in January 1946, we can see how spontaneously readers took up the subject positions for which Eliot's poem silently prepared them.

. . . yet Mr. Eliot is a true poet, with a message for our time. We are living in an epoch of bewilderment and unrest. In art, science, politics, philosophy and religion. We are like a ship overtaken by a hurricane and drifting on a lee shore. It is not a time to spread aloft our sails; they are too torn and tattered by the tempest. Neither is it a time to resort to desperate measures and call all hands to the pumps to save the ship. Rather it is a time to cast anchor and to wish for day.

In the political context of the post-war period, Coats's counsel of caution in his allegory of the safe haven, undoubtedly what he hears Eliot advising his readers, carries important tactical instructions on how a frightened intelligentsia might comport itself in dangerously uncertain times. He continues:

That is what Mr. Eliot does for us. In our troubled and tempestuous age, he pro-vides us with an anchor, an anchor of the soul, which is all the more sure and steadfast because it enters in that which is within the veil. Far more than in Matthew Arnold's day, we seem to be hovering 'between two worlds, one dead, the other waiting to be born'. Mr. Eliot does not profess to foresee the future. But what he does offer us, perhaps because he is more sure of it, is eternity. That is enough to go on, for the present. (118)

Like Thielicke's wary students in Germany, many of Eliot's readers, having been seduced by the intellectual and rhetorical debauch of the 1930s, were acutely suspicious of all ulterior motives and the easy fluen-cies which conveyed them. One of the poem's greatest achievements, from this perspective, is how it sets such a reader's mind to rest, disarms it, in effect, in order to get on with the tasks of solace, persuasion, and, finally, the construction of a guiltless re-entry into established society.

In this respect, then, I would like to explore a second aspect of the essay on the 'classic' that strikes one immediately: the way Eliot implies, that is, constructs silently, an ideal reader of the classic work of literature. Eliot was highly conscious of the fact that the contemporary mandarin reader of his essay was one whose primary reading experiences and training were largely contaminated by the reading habits and expecta-tions of a century and half of romanticism. Such a reader must be taught *how* to read, not simply *what* to read. He must be informed what is expected of him as a reader of Virgil and of the essay in question.

This is, of course, an old modernist task. Ezra Pound, the advocate of the armed struggle in matters of criticism, spent his entire career as a literary critic re-writing again and again, and with increasing pugnacity, *The ABC of Reading*. Eliot was the better strategist in the immediate context. Eliot was more patient, and more shrewd. He had come to understand, over the years, that Pound's outspoken aggression very rarely met with success, indeed it often met with open hostility and resistance. Eliot's indirect appeal in the essay is not to a *competing* 'classic' standard to set against the 'romantic' legacy; Eliot cannily dismisses that whole burnt out quarrel in the first two pages of the essay. He simply assumes that the 'classic' temper *is* the cultural inheritance with the deepest draw in 'the mind of Europe' and that other legacies are merely parasitic encrustations which over time have grown so dense they obscure the classic core. It is to that core that Eliot quietly appeals, arguing that it encompasses all experience. His judicious reference to Dido and Aeneas, as discussed above, underlines the inclusiveness of the classic in a matter of feeling which the 'romantic' has always taken to be within its own special competence. The calm confidence with which Eliot deploys his assumptions and the arguments based on them is difficult to resist. This suavity is a far cry from his more boorish deployment of the same argumentative tactics in *For Lancelot Andrewes* and *After Strange Gods* a decade earlier.

Eliot also positions the reader in a framework of assumptions that the reader finds difficult to oppose in another way. Knowing that a reader might find the principal term of his definition of the classic – 'maturity' – too slippery or innocuous to be useful, he admits candidly – and the show of candour is intended deliberately to disarm us – that he cannot really define it.

To define *maturity* without assuming that the hearer already knows what it means, is almost impossible: let us say then, that if we are properly mature, as well as educated persons, we can recognize maturity in a civilization and in a literature, as we do in the other human beings whom we encounter. (55)

The analogy between recognizing maturity 'in other human beings' and, therefore, being able to recognize it, without any further evidence, 'in a civilization and in a literature' is a brilliant touch, especially if you believe that your readers are already subconsciously disposed to believe such assertions. Indeed they probably *want* to believe them, although their conscious culture, that is the romantic distractions that obscure the classic temper, might incline them to other professions. Eliot's rhetoric here is characteristic of his polemical style. We are not being asked to weigh an argument, but to become aware of what is already inside us. If we pay it heed, this thing which we already know will make us see that what he is saying is not controversial in any respect. He is simply recording cultural givens.

We are in position to understand the rhetoric of *Four Quartets* when we have grasped this point. Eliot wants us to accept that *Four Quartets* is not just a 'position' or 'perspective' on matters of art, history, and religion, least of all a self-indulgent excursion in lyrical autobiography, but has set itself, like Heidegger's *Being and Time*, a sterner task, the task of describing what is, of describing the real.[10] For a generation of well-educated and weary mandarins, whose beliefs in the various isms had been knocked about by historical realities indifferent to their sentiments and ideas, a strategy which assumed that they too had arrived at this kind of 'maturity', out past the gravitational pull of mere 'argument', was bound to appeal. This is certainly what F.R. Leavis, quickly responsive to the poem's ontological thrust and its anti-rhetorical rhetoric in 1943, grasped when reading 'Burnt Norton' in 'T. S. Eliot's Later Poetry' (*Education* 96). This is why 'Burnt Norton' begins with two epigraphs from Heraclitus and in the voice of the practised professional philosopher. And, futhermore, 'Burnt Norton' provides the rhetorical blueprint for the three poems to come. In 1935, Eliot may not have yet conceived of sequels to it, but when in 1939–40 he turned back to 'Burnt Norton', the map for the journey's continuation was already in place.

The opening propositions about 'Time present and time past' achieve their authority in two ways. The professional philosopher, settled in his fellowship, is no mere peddler of rhetoric or sententious whimsy. This is a voice which assumes, as primary principle, that it bows before the government of reason alone. It is a voice which is not 'merely chattering' (BN V 194)[11] and which reminds us, not only of the ancient lineage to which it belongs, a lineage that extends back in time 2,500 years to Heraclitus, but also of the listener's own past, the innocent and calming memory of our own first schoolroom or lecture hall.

In the concrete historical circumstances in which the poem was initially read, this measured, familiar tone of voice is very important. It immediately acts to disarm readers wary of both the extraordinary power of words to seduce and of the impact of new radio and film media in the propagation of ideology and power. It does not really sound as if it is trying to convince us of anything. The opening propositions seem to be turned inward toward the speaker; the philosopher with his careful probing speech, his 'perhaps', his 'if' and his 'but', his painstakingly accurate delineation of tense and aspect calms us, because we recognize in this presentational mode, the style of truth in 'our' tradition. This is a voice we remember from an older academic world not yet retooled for the Cold War in the 1950s. The fact that the passage reminds us that we must learn to leave off feeling disconsolate about 'What might

have been' and endure, for better or worse, 'what has been' and, therefore, learn to accommodate ourselves to 'what is', also speaks firmly and
concretely to the situation of the 'burnt children' of the 1940s.

The second way in which these opening lines convey authority develops from the notion that they are not addressed to an audience at all, but
are private musings. They do not constitute an argument to which the
philosopher is strenuously appealing for our assent. And, of course, they
are doubly effective for that. The voice's calm, which is meant to convey
inner composure, has also about it an element of weariness and resignation. There is no heuristic excitement here, the mounting intensity of a
mind at full stretch, having worked its way towards philosophical revelation. Any inkling of energetic entreaty is the false note that wrecks the
effect. The plangency suggests weariness and resignation, truths realized
after great struggle. This finely crafted reserve accurately echoes the
weariness not only of those who have passed through the 'hurricane' of
war, but also those for whom the war crisis was only a prelude to the
deeper crisis of nihilism which followed it. In the communicative ambience created by these donnish accents, the Heraclitean fragments play a
vital role.

The commentary on Eliot's use of the two epigraphs from Heraclitus
with which 'Burnt Norton' opens is voluminous and diverse. Raymond
Preston has reported that Eliot's own sense of their significance lay in
their 'poetic suggestiveness' (viii) which, typically of Eliot on his own
work, deploys resonant banality as a way of avoiding having to say
more. Others, of course, have stepped forward to fill the interpretative vacuum. I do not want simply to repeat their work – Clubb,
'Heraclitean' 19–33, Grover Smith, *Poetry and Plays* 255–56 and
Reibetanz, *Four Quartets* 19–22 for example – but it is important to note
that most of this commentary on the epigraphs is thematic in nature. My
question does not ask again how these philosophical fragments engage
the themes of 'Burnt Norton' and, subsequently, the sequence as a
whole, but inquires into the rhetoric of the epigraphs, and, more specifically, asks how this initial poetic decision positions the reader politically?

To begin with, the first epigraph attempts to obliterate the validity of
individual perspective. The translation of the whole fragment from Diels
is as follows. Eliot cites only the second part.

Therefore one must follow (the universal Law, namely) that which is common
(to all). But although the Law is universal, the majority live as if they had understanding peculiar to themselves. (Freeman, *Fragments* 24–25)

We learn from this that an individual subject cannot gain knowledge of the *logos* on the basis of being a unique and separate being. The epigraph declares that most men act as if they have insight of their own, rather than resigning themselves to their inherent partialness, and, thus, recognizing and accepting the universality (and one might add comprehensiveness) of the *logos*, that which is common to all things, both valid for things as such and accessible to all men.

Now this word *logos* presents many problems of translation from the ancient Greek, not the least of which are the Christian accretions of meaning; Heraclitus may have meant something like 'the universal law of things' by the word. The Christian resonance would not have been lost to any educated contemporary of Eliot's, and it is very important to his purpose. Why? Partially for the same reason that when discussing Virgil's 'destiny' Eliot is able to repeat blandly the old *trecento* commonplace about the author of the *Aeneid*, namely, that he unconsciously complied with the dictates of Divine Will, so that 'the machinations of gods . . . are themselves, we feel, only instruments of a greater inscrutable power' ('What is a Classic?' *OPP* 62). Heraclitus, too, has hit the Christian nail on the head without realizing it, and this at the dawn of thought, not only pre-Christian, but pre-Socratic as well. In a moment of crisis in Europe, this return to the origin of European thought, the birth of authentic reason, when we are asked to believe that it was most in contact with the *logos* and with itself, suggests two things: firstly, a notable appeal for philosophical legitimation through the startling return to an original or radical philosophical moment (Heidegger's own return to the pre-Socratics in the cultural politics of the 1920s, and later more vividly in the 1940s, is a crucial point of reference here) and secondly, a subtle, and unexpected, foreshadowing of the poem's doctrinal agenda.

The epigraph also stresses the notion of what is 'common' to all. The Greek word for 'common' in the fragment sounded very similar to a Greek phrase meaning 'with rational awareness'. The pun stresses the natural connection between *thinking* 'with rational awareness' and allowing one's thoughts to be guided by 'what is common' (Kirk and Raven 188). Through Heraclitus, Eliot affirms, as he does in the essay on the 'Classic' in different terms, the essential correspondence of thinking and that which is the proper object of thought. We already know what is necessary and how to attain it, but we have forgotten the path and the goal. The epigraph silently insists, then, that the wisest among us must adopt a posture of radical receptivity to the divine utterances of the *logos*, something akin to Heidegger's continuous insistence that philosophy must learn again how to listen, 'be attuned to', the authentic voice of Being.

These two points are further reinforced by the second epigraph from Heraclitus: 'The way up and down is one and the same' (Freeman, *Fragments* 29). The new element in this second Heraclitean fragment is that it presents itself as recovering from the dawn of thought itself, the language of paradox, which the poem will deftly deploy as the language of transcendental experience, as the primary attribute of a higher episte-mology as yet uncontaminated by the corrosive vocabularies of contin-gency, the lesser reason of European skepticism and its final conquest of 'the mind of Europe' in the seventeenth and eighteenth centuries in the form of the Enlightenment.

The epigraphs and the donnish accents with which the poem opens give way at line eleven – 'Footfalls echo in the memory' – to an authority of a very different kind, but finely and cleverly achieved after the opening *bona fides* and confidences have been adroitly displayed and the reader positioned for further edification. From line eleven to the end of BN I, a new modality of feeling and a new discursive procedure emerges from the theme of origins which the invocation of Heraclitus and the schoolroom proclaims. The drama of primordiality is now pushed further back in a new way, no longer as knowledge, but as personal expe-rience suddenly and richly recollected. The events in 'our first world' bring into the poem's rhetoric the lyric intensity of the imagist intelli-gence, no longer as the radical departure of early modernist aesthetics, but as part of the rehabilitative programme for the retrieval of the real.

As the passage ascends steeply towards its visionary climax, the poem reaches and swings past, as far as the reader is concerned, its first crucial juncture. If the donnish opening has done its proper work of preparing the irresolute and distressed mandarin reader, then the vision glittering 'out of heart of light' (190) consolidates the poem's rule. It does this not as some easy half-mystical escape from reality, but in the name of reality itself: the speaker abruptly challenges the reader after the ravishing and seductive visions have disappeared: 'human kind / Cannot bear very much reality' (190) arrives like a cold bath in November. Having calmed and beguiled us, the speaker turns to us abruptly with the brutal truth about our condition, not to punish our waywardness, but to bring us to a knowledge of the obvious, or to put it another way, a knowledge of what is 'common to all'. We are left to draw the conclusion on our own that this voice is the one that speaks out of the abyss, that has 'experienced and endured' the world's night and is therefore the voice qualified in such a time to offer direction, firmness and worthy solace. The restoration of the philosopher in the last three lines returns us to the imperturbable repose of the seminar room. How could a mind in distress and in search of authority and consolation not succumb to such an approach? Perhaps not yet in 1936, but certainly in the 1940s (cf. Jenkins, 'Errant Elitist' 9).

Eliot's evocation of 'our first world' and the semi-mystical experiences in the 'garden' made a lasting impact in the 1940s. As late as 1949 the imagery and structure of the passage had achieved a kind of hieratic status among the minor poets. And, typically of most earnest imitations, we can note, in the following example, the usual exaggerated effect as a way of signifying intensity of vision when it is conspicuously not there:

> They are moving inwards; the circle is closing.
> Tonight I have heard them again among
> the houses, a million voices rising as one
> in the darkness, hounding our lives with their
> pitiless tongues, the voices of leaves and children
> crying, as children cry, for light – where is
> no light; for love, where there is only silence:
>
> and under my feet stars like dead leaves falling
> under my feet the bloodless faces staring . . .
>
> . . .
>
> Look into their eyes and faces if you dare
> and, if you dare, describe a victory. (Sergeant 83)

The final lines are meant to evoke the 'reality' – 'if you dare' – of which humankind cannot bear very much. The poem's title, 'Man Meeting Himself' at least comprehends the basis of Eliot's original as in some ways involving self-recognition and self-discovery. In the hands of Howard Sargeant, the Eliot routine reaches its nadir.

Stephen Spender's situation is typical in another more clever way. It reveals the kind of consciousness to which Eliot's words were particularly aimed. With the defeat of the Left in Spain and elsewhere and with his own frustratingly tangled relations of mutual suspicion with the British Communists and the working class movement in general, Spender began to abandon explicit political commitment during the decade's closing years. This process culminated in May 1939 with the publication of his pamphlet *The New Realism* in which he fell back disgustedly from radical politics to a position in which the artist's 'duty' was re-defined.

The artist, Spender argues, should not concern himself with changing the world, but simply analysing and understanding it from a distance. And he can only do this by writing with honesty and truth about the kind of intimate life he knows best (23–24). It is a matter of staying away from the 'outer rim' of life where political engagement is located. The centre of a writer's 'real interest' lies closer to home. 'The duty of the artist is to remain true to standards which he can discover only within himself' (12). This inward turning with its attendant political quietism and conformism is a solution typical of the mandarin sensibility in the time I am discussing and it comes up again and again. It is the style of the mandarinate which Harold Rosenberg referred to in the 1950s as 'the new 'quiet', domesticated generation one reads about in the weeklies' (*Tradition* 241). Auden's situation is also well known. Day Lewis's 'The Poet' (1943) makes the inward turn explicit and the collection from which the poem comes, *Word Over All*, returns to the stratagem of retreat again and again. Cyril Connolly's highly successful scrapbook, *The Unquiet Grave* (1945) published rather melodramatically under the Virgilian pseudonym 'Palinurus', also declares the inner life the last possible refuge of consciousness. Art as interiority makes a safe harbour from the risky political business of mass society.

The opening movement of 'Burnt Norton' possesses the careful rhetorical craft to captivate a reader like Spender. It does this by positioning itself as the inescapable knowledge towards which the perplexed have always been tending anyway. Its craft acts to allay the prickly defensiveness and private despondency of personalities not only convinced of their own idealism and good will, now thwarted by the intransigence of history, but spooked by the possible consequences of their acts.

The poem also suggests new modalities of Being to fill the void left by the unravelling of political commitment and of the bits and pieces of identity which, entangled with the posturing of the past, have gone down with it. The return to the primal scenes of consciousness, the scenes enacted in 'our first world', provide both a first destination for the 'strategic withdrawal' into inwardness and the starting point in the reconstitution of identity on a new footing. In this process, art plays a decisive role.

The continuity of identity for this generation lies, then, in the programmatic identification of inwardness and art. History is replaced by art as the epistemological groundwork, as the master science of knowing, not because of some general modern shift in consciousness, but in order to throw the state's bloodhounds and witchhunters off the track. Individual identities no longer have pasts that continuously define them, they now have 'roles'[12] defined by their present relationship to dominant ideology. Narrative continuity of the single life and of society gives way to lyric in the one, and spectacle in the other. Later biographies of the central actors become controversial because they seek to find the narrative thread in lives which no longer develop along a single path, but zigzag through the political minefields of contested creeds. The controversy about David Leavitt's and Hugh David's 'lives' of Stephen Spender, Auden's care in destroying the trail of his past, the fracas over Lillian Hellman's *Pentimento* some years ago, and even the secrecy surrounding the documentary traces of Eliot's life are all symptomatic of a time in which personal histories are no longer temporal sequences, but a species of absurdist drama, a series of stages with sets, costumes and scripts, with this enabling postulate, that the actors must try to forget in Act II what they did and said in Act I.

Having turned its readers firmly but consolingly towards the safe haven of inwardness, 'Burnt Norton' attends in the second section to a more positive programme, the formulation of a metaphysical foundation for aesthetic consciousness, the famous 'still point in a turning world' (191). But it must do this first by establishing its own artistic authority in a new mode, in an apocalyptic lyric of visionary power. The goal here is to consolidate not only the autonomy of inwardness, but its sovereignty, that is to say, to assert the separation of 'inner freedom from the practical desire, / The release from action and suffering', the release from compulsion (191).

The latent political content of French symbolist aesthetics begins to show itself only under the appropriate historical conditions. It becomes visible in Eliot's apocalyptic 'Garlic and sapphires' lyric that opens the section (190–91), but only when we read the passage as readers in history, when we read it, in the 1940s, in the context of an age of increasing political regulation and continuous state surveillance. The arrival of the 'New Apocalypse' group in London in the early 1940s – Henry Treece, Nicholas Moore, J.F. Hendry and others – with the resulting retreat from the social realism of the 1930s, is not then much of a surprise under the circumstances. The allusions in the lyric to Mallarmé's 'Le Tombeau de Charles Baudelaire' and 'M'introduire dans ton histoire' are the key reference points. The following abstractions, which develop the dialectic of 'still point' and 'turning world', now exploit Heraclitean paradox as the foundational language of an old epistemology charged with a new significance by historical circumstances. It is important to point out that Eliot's programme here is to lead secularized consciousness *through* the aesthetic towards the religious awareness which lies beyond it, towards the doctrinal treasure of the whole sequence. For Christian readers this is the hoped-for prize, for most others, less interested in religion, like Maurice Bowra as quoted above, or Spender, it is the consolidation of the autonomy of inwardness and of its relationship to aesthetic consciousness that is the desired goal. Eliot's evocation of French symbolism reminds the reader of the distinguished ancestry of such ideas.

At this juncture, Eliot's poem undergoes a systematic misreading, or, at least, a partial reading limited by the requirements of what might well be called the instinctual politics of a wary readership. The line with which the second part of 'Burnt Norton' closes – 'Only through time time is conquered' (192) – may have a clearly transcendental significance for Eliot, but for a secular mandarinate its significance lies closer to home. For a generation who feels itself wounded by history, someone who holds up the possibility of the conquest of history through a form of inward renunication without the necessity of actually having to perform any particular concrete actions, that is, not to have to renounce one's privileges, cushy jobs, creature comforts, social position, etc. or the desire for such things, is perhaps someone well worth listening to. Under these conditions, the sundering of inner and outer is noiseless and complete. In this respect, Eliot's form of renunciation as a completely inward event unintentionally summons the bad faith of his readers. Nothing need be materially renounced. Harry in *The Family Reunion* can still leave on the redemptive journey to the desert, but he can do so with car, chauffeur, and a forwarding address at his bank. The externals carry on as before; we are asked to believe that only the inner man is transformed. This state of affairs may be genuine as far as Eliot is concerned, although there is something unsettling about such a radical commitment of the private self that makes such little visible impact on the public persona.

Gordon spends a good deal of her *Eliot's New Life* trying to explain this phenomenon. It seems we can continue with all the privileges of a successful or privileged life intact, but, our atonement for both our nature and our specific past sins must lie in the private knowledge at the end of the day that such lives 'all go into the dark':

> The captains, merchant bankers, eminent men of letters.
> The generous patrons of art, the statesmen and the rulers,
> Distinguished civil servants, chairman of many committees,
> Industrial lords and petty contractors, all go into the dark . . .
> (EC III 199–200)

And all we are asked to renounce is hope and love ('for the wrong thing' [200]), but not our membership in the club, or country house weekends, the offices we hold, or our little fragment of power. It turns out that nothing outward needs change at all, that the *knowledge* of the 'the dark' into which we all go and the self-dealt and self-managed contrition comprises sufficient propitiation for carrying on with business as usual. Which of the perplexed 'sea-waifs' of the 1930s could easily disregard such safe harbour and an intellectual flag of such conspicuous convenience?

The third section of 'Burnt Norton' might speak to a secular mandarin like Spender for these and other reasons. Spender's admiration of Eliot never wavered even in the years of the younger man's public involvements with the Left (see *The Destructive Element* 1936). He was also a Faber author and the influence of Eliot was no doubt more direct for that. In fact, the master's touch can be seen rather well in the title and the final poems of Spender's 1939 verse collection called *The Still Centre*. In the closing section of the book, Spender's poems of the late 1930s, Eliot's influence is pervasive, as it was during the whole of the 1940s, the years of changing allegiances. But it is an influence that Spender has either entirely misunderstood, or deliberately misread.

It is useful to Spender to mimic some of Eliot's intellectual and verbal mannerisms. The first poem in the final section 'Darkness and Light' engages explicitly with the renunciatory rhetoric of BN III, but stops short of Eliot's more radical professions. For one thing, Spender's poem adopts Eliot's use of paradox, which Eliot absorbed from the tradition of European mysticism. Spender, of course, is no mystic, but in the retreat from his former position on the Left, he finds a certain tortured vagueness of phrasing, which seems to acknowledge visionary possibilities and deeper commitments, useful.

> To break out of the chaos of my darkness
> Into a lucid day is all my will;
> . . .
> Yet, equally, to avoid that lucid day
> And to preserve my darkness, is all my will.
> . . .
> The world, my body, binds the dark and light
> Together, reconciles and separates
> In lucid day the chaos of my darkness. (77–78)

When set beside the lucidity and passion of Eliot's BN III Spender's 'Darkness and Light' pales, as it goes about the awkward business of avoiding being pinned down. These lines are far more concerned with pushing the author away unscathed from his youthful affirmations, by adapting, as protective colouring, Eliot's paradoxical discourse of inwardness. Spender's new gibberish helps in the defeat of what can only be called his old gibberish.

But it is not Eliot. It is mimic-Eliot. Spender has read and taken in the first half of BN III, but not the second half, the Eliot half. The first half repeats the conventional contempt of the world of the inner-directed religious consciousness, made over by 'the new realism' as a character-izing attainment of aesthetic consciousness. The second half is Eliot's more radical confrontation with nihilism. It is the part which makes him Heidegger's contemporary rather than Spender's. But we ought to keep Spender's use of Eliot in mind because such responses go a long way to explaining Eliot's extraordinary authority in the 1940s and 1950s, and, equally, his ultimate irrelevance. They explain the weird situation of a great cultural spokesman to whom everyone lent an ear in the late 1940s and 1950s, but to whom, finally, no one listened.

Spender is not interested in Eliot's radicalism at all. In *The Still Centre*, he is not moving from a political to an apolitical stance; he is steeling himself to engage in the new cultural politics of the post-war, the ideo-logical politics of Daniel Bell's slogan, 'the end of ideology', an unpoli-tics more thoroughly political than his earlier involvements, involvements which increasingly take on the character of costume drama. This new 'politics of the unpolitical' (to repeat Herbert Read's phrase) will eventually lead Spender into active and self-righteous participation in the Cold War, the cultural politics of the Congress of Cultural Freedom, and the *Encounter* circle with its hidden agendas and its shady budgets drawn from the American intelligence services (Hamilton, 'Spender's Lives' 79–80).

But BN III does not only renounce the 'daylight' which conjures 'beauty', it also abjures the lesser 'darkness, in this twittering world' (193). Engagement with ultimate questions for the religious consciousness comes with the more radical 'darkness' by which the individual penitent, in the spiritual exercises described by St. John of the Cross for the first episodes of purification in the dark night of the soul, empties and cleanses 'the sensual' and 'the temporal' (192) as the precondition for the descent 'Into the world of perpetual solitude' (193). If 'beauty' and the rudimentary exercises of personal purification cannot bring us back from the abyss, the mere social world then, 'filled with fancies and empty of meaning' and symbolized by London's 'gloomy hills,' pointedly listed at the end of the first half, can hold absolutely no hope.

BN III does not simply reject the weary routines of 'everydayness', 'this twittering world', and the traditional forms of salvation from the 'tumid apathy', but rejects experience itself (cf. EC II 199, lines 81–83). Eliot requires us to understand that we must 'Descend lower' towards something the poem calls the 'Internal darkness' (BN III 193, lines 117–129), which corresponds to a more radical stillness than can be imagined in a world bound to longing and desire ('appetency'), moving 'on its metalled ways'. The ominousness of tone which enters the voice as we traverse the silence between the two halves of the third section takes us past the familiar critique of the ephemerality of the world, into the metaphysical darkness of 'that which is not world'.

On the evidence of Spender's poetry in response to *Four Quartets*, Eliot's complexity of vision does not seem to have been translated to the younger man. This was typical of the mandarin reading of or reaction to Eliot's work. Spender seems more interested in the style and mood of Eliot's metaphysical reflections, rather than in the thing itself. Eliot's gravity becomes a kind of badge of affiliation. By mimicking these tonalities and devices, Spender borrows a serious man's seriousness in order to announce his new public role, after the retirement of the old one. He does not arrive at this state as a religious convert or as a radical metaphysician, but in the role of the former activist newly spiritualized, happy now to have escaped the compulsions of time. Having been 'hounded by external events' in the 1930s (*World Within World* 137), Spender, as the Cold War began, settled into the kind of occupations, interests and beliefs for which someone of his class, education and other attainments was destined in the first place. In this new mood, he can now take them up guiltlessly. This transition was accompanied by a flurry of gestures of despair and soul-searching of which his poetry in the 1940s (see especially his *Returning to Vienna*) and his autobiographical re-narrativizing of his own past, *World Within World* (1951) are replete.[13]

The third section 'Burnt Norton' has been very well and vividly expounded by many of Eliot's critics. The references to Dante's voyage to the underworld, the tradition of the *via negativa* in European mysticism, especially in the work of St John of the Cross, are no doubt important points of reference and of construction, but they cannot explain the significance of these lines to Eliot's contemporary readers (but see Hay, *Negative Way passim* and Murray, *Mysticism* 257–62). It was only to be expected that a learned poet, who had never made any effort to wear his learning lightly, and had made allusiveness a principal axiom of his poetics, would not now abandon his technique of intertextual assemblage. No, it was not this that reverberated with his mandarin readers, although it was not entirely irrelevant to the work of fabricating the poem's authority. Eliot's succinct programme of renunciation of the world as a vale of distraction appealed on a number of levels, no matter how completely moments of 'lucid stillness' or the seeming 'permanence' of 'beauty' might hide from us the world's undeniable transience (192).

This is the point of section IV of 'Burnt Norton'. The enchanting moments of vision, of 'sunflower' and 'kingfisher's wing', cannot hide from us that 'Time and the bell' will bury the day. These moments of lyric intensity may *seem* permanent and real, but are not. They may even carry us to the threshold of the eternal, but they cannot take us there. As one might expect, the whole poem insists repeatedly that the 'time of chronometers' is an illusion. The three parallel movements, EC III, DS III, and LG III, will elaborate this idea three more times with more concrete detail and, therefore, clearer social meanings.

But in these passages Eliot can be heard to be saying something else as well, something less metaphysical, and of more practical moment to mandarin readers. For Day Lewis's 'sea-waifs', it is not the world as such that is to be renounced, after all, actual material life, according to the poem and to Eliot's own example, goes on more or less unchanged. Renunciation occurs in the silence of interiority; this means abandoning ideas of significant action in the world, letting go the illusion that any involvement in the world matters in the scale of ultimate things. The very subtle metaphysical speculations of the closing lines of BN V in which Eliot lucidly expands on the theme of divine 'Love' as 'itself unmoving . . . Caught in the form of limitation / Between un-being and being' (195) is all very well, but what of the 'sea-waif' who cannnot follow him towards the bliss of Christian piety?

For the lost soul in a destitute time, there is the fact of interiority itself as the safe refuge, and art as its ground and architecture. This does not necessarily mean accepting the poem's treatment of art. There, art is a ravishing prologue to the divine which an inwardly-active humility must empower the artist to relinquish on the road to God. The perplexed exile, however, can only hear that art is our sole possession, the pervasive sum total of a saving inwardness. The line begins

> Words move, music moves
> Only in time; . . .

but there its vital meaning ended for most readers in the 1940s. The mandarin elites were condemned to make their way in time, to find a

way to live in history. To be told, banally, that 'that which is only living /
Can only die' (194) merely required the show of pious assent before the
resounding cliché, while carrying on with the business of sorting out
one's safe haven in the world.

A certain detached priggishness of tone, the occasional controlled
outburst of restless torment to convey *angst*, some weary gestures of
resignation, and the subdued wariness of the middle class mandarin
keenly aware of the impression he's making, delineate the favoured style
of this new climate of feeling adapted from Eliot's work. The ease with
which Spender acquired these new artifices (to replace the old ones) was
only superseded by the dexterity with which they were secured by less
notable personalities. For a poetry-writing BBC mandarin like Rayner
Heppenstall, who had a lot of catching up to do during the war years,
taking stylistic possession of *Four Quartets* was not enough; his pastiche of
Eliot had to back up and take account of *Ash-Wednesday* as well.

> I have renounced already that hope. I renounce the sudden Whole
> And I will not hope any longer to live my days in the clothedness of
>   vision
> Accidents of the numerous daytime so hate. Yet no days live if still,
>   as I say,
> Timlessly long, still in the same thought, no more untied from
>   Time,
> Abroad on the red-bellied bowl of oil, I figure the string of the
>   small flame
> Of any dark chapel, staring aloft at an image painted last year.
>   ('Spring Song', *New British Poets* [1948] 94)

Heppenstall plunks plaintively on the Eliot keyboard – renunciation,
hope, the Whole, vision, stillness, Time, fire, chapel, etc. etc. – with little
evident passion and even less skill. The obscurity of these lines is quite
obviously their greatest achievement. Seemingly profound, deeply felt,
difficult and in their master's voice, or at least a passable imitation of it,
'Spring Song' provides just the right protective colouring for the worried
civil servant/artist. And in the same guarded way, publishing a distasteful little comic essay explaining why 'I am not in favour of the Working
Class' does not hurt either, in a time when every intellectual's political
loyalties are under scrutiny. In case this seems to accuse Heppenstall of
artistic hypocrisy unfairly, let's not forget that, like so many of his watchful contemporaries, he was rather brisk at spotting the bad faith of
others: existentialism, he wrote for example, 'is a handy rationalization
for those who wish to adopt pessimistic conclusions for temperamental

motives which they do not declare' (quoted in Blythe, *Components* 383).

The use of Eliot was evident also in the poetry of many other minor writers of the time. Most conspicuously Eliot's influence can be seen in a large-scale work like Frank Kendon's *Four Quartets*-like verse cycle called *The Time Piece* handsomely produced and promoted by the Cambridge University Press in 1945. This long poem is a tedious exercise in mimicry, from the epigraph – 'How great is that darkness' – to the by now ritual mention of Time, especially midnight and midwinter (LG I), stillness, rural England, children, and emptiness, as in the following lines that feebly echo the second strophe of the opening section of 'East Coker' illustrate.

> The school is empty, and the street is empty,
> And the stable's empty, and the only cool place
> Is the church, empty, with its door ajar.
> Houses are shut and all their kennels empty,
> Shops in full sun and shops in shadow deep.
> 'My shoes are dusty', thinks young Tom, . . . (48)

As farcical as this sounds, it is not meant to be biting parody. When one turns to the lines in EC I to which this doggerel alludes,

> . . . In a warm haze the sultry light
> Is absorbed, not refracted, by grey stone.
> The dahlias sleep in the empty silence. (196)

one begins to appreciate how the uncertain atmosphere of the time, the pressure of conformity, the example of *Four Quartets*, and the weight of Eliot's authority comically discomposed otherwise serious people like Kendon.

The secret was to live and write and think safely in history, and to live richly, variously and without niggling regrets, or a sense of personal disgrace. 'Burnt Norton' defines a way one can do this in a destitute time, the kind of dead end in history MacNeice defines in his 'Epitaph for Liberal Poets' in 1944 ('. . . There is no way out, the birds / Will tell us nothing more' [*CP 1925–1948* 232]). Aesthetic consciousness, the artifice of eternity, is the primary groundwork:

> . . . Only by the form, the pattern,
> Can words or music reach
> The stillness, as a Chinese jar still
> Moves perpetually in its stillness.
> Not the stillness of the violin, while the note lasts,
> Not that only, . . . (194)

For a secularized and aestheticized mandarinate 'the stillness of the violin' was enough. It was Eliot who needed more. For Auden, however, music itself, in all its earthbound forms, provided a political solution to what he had come to experience, uncomfortably, as the compulsions of historical Necessity. In the new conditions of watchfulness, conformity and the political witch-hunt after the war, freedom to oppose carried with it enormous risks. Music, 'in / Its formal way', ('Music is International' [1947], *CSP* 228) and this is the key phrase, might conserve something resembling freedom, not freedom as the necessary pattern of an active agency, but, at least, in its formal way, as 'the free play of intel-lect' among friends and intimates, the place where 'the Just / Exchange their messages . . . Beleaguered by the same / Negation and despair . . .' ('September 1, 1939,' *EA* 247; and see Edwards 207). Or put more ardently in 'Anthem for St Cecilia's Day' (1947)

> O flute that throbs with the thanksgiving breath
> Of convalescents on the shores of death.
> O bless the freedom that you never chose. (*CSP* 175)

The use of music as an emblem of freedom in Auden correlates with Eliot's use of music as the rarest form of aesthetic cognition and of a saving aesthetic detachment in *Four Quartets*. Music is Eliot's central symbol of the aesthetic state as such, the closest an earthbound intelli-gence, bent on practising gestures of renunciation, can get to the divine. It is in this context that Eliot's use of quartet as the appropriate musical analogy for the poem, takes on its most interesting social and political colouring.

From the moment that Helen Gardner in her first book on Eliot decided to make 'The Music of *Four Quartets*' (chapter 2) the formal axis of the poem, with Eliot's implicit support, much has been written about music and Eliot's final masterpiece. The general tenor of this writing attempts to identify the musical form or forms which the poem most resembles. Most identifications refer to the string quartet in its heyday in Vienna at the turn of the nineteeenth century (Howarth, Gross, and Alldritt, *Chamber Music* 27–33), and, occasionally, the practice of Bela Bartók and his extraordinary quartets (Kenner, *Invisible* 261) which were widely performed and recorded in the 1930s.

The weight of opinion has fallen on sonata as the musical form which most approximates 'the underlying pattern of Eliot's four poems' (Alldritt, *Chamber Music* 28). It is the 'sensuous embodiment of the dialec-tical relationship of opposed terms' in classical sonata form (Barford,

Keyboard 81) which is the engine of development both in the musical form itself and Eliot's poems. Keith Alldritt has put the matter most trenchantly, in comparing *Four Quartets*'s 'four voices' to the sound world of the classical quartet.

There are four voices in the poem and, since they are very much voices for social performance, the principle of instrumentality asserts itself as strongly in this writing as in the musical form itself. And the fact that there are four parts, four voices, means that each individual one is only a version. The full account, the complete version is the sum and interpretation of all four performances. (39)

The four 'voices', which correspond to the four instruments in the quartet, are described as four 'verbal roles', that of the don or lecturer, the visionary, the urbane conversationalist and the conjuror. The 'rapid and complex interaction of these four voices' (39) for the purposes of contrast, tension, debate and discussion accords well with the social character of the quartet in the Vienna of the mid and late eighteenth century (Adorno, *Sociology of Music* 86). It was a time when Mozart, Haydn, Dittersdorf and Wanhal collaborated for a short period in the making of a chamber music 'of intimacy and unity' (Alldritt 32), a music for friends and colleagues, rather than the public grandiosities of court or concert hall.

The quartet, then, seems essentially a semi-private matter, 'four expert players assembled in a fairly large room, and performed for the benefit of a few connoisseurs' (Barrett-Ayres *Haydn* 71, quoted by Alldritt). As lively and significant as its Viennese origins are, the quartet, in its contemporary decline, is referred to disconsolately by Adorno as having become 'an art of experts' (102) and mandarins, an art to be savoured in 'the precarious haven' where 'the reality principle' is held at bay, an art which has been rendered, at the end of the day, 'good for nothing' (103), occurring in the same place, one assumes, where Auden, in his tribute to Yeats, discovered, rather less sardonically than Adorno, that 'poetry makes nothing happen' (Auden, *EA* 242).

Perhaps it is worth observing that the late eighteenth-century Viennese ethos suggests also the arrival of a new relationship between artist-intellectuals and modern society. The quartet begins as an artform which can be relished primarily by the initiates of the comradely circle. In societies already fracturing under unavoidable political and economic pressures, 'connoisseurs' who find a happy niche, or sequestered haven, protected from forces which threaten and break an active civic freedom and the old status order of inherited privilege, may feel themselves to be lucky indeed, at least 'while the music lasts'.

If *Four Quartets* reminds us wistfully of the original culture of the Viennese quartet, as Alldritt and others think it does, it does so because of the desire for intimacy and trust which it hopes to establish with its own primary audience.[14] This is a capital point. Alldritt describes this felicitously as the quartet's continual questioning of 'the extent of its audience' and its inevitable allusions 'to an uncertain negotiation, a suspension between the utterly private world of the composer and the public world of the concert hall' (32). But this interrogation of the audience's extent does not occur in a historical void. How can it? How does a poem whose very form assumes a particular kind of audience in time and place square with the view that we must let 'the concerns, the moods and ideas' of the 1940s, in short, the concerns of that specific audience, 'recede from us', in order, as Alldritt argues, to appreciate 'the acts of language' which make it up (128)? Could such a thing possibly be said about Shostakovitch's contemporaneous string quartets, the greatest quartet literature of the twentieth century? Were Shostakovitch's 'acts' of musical language, neatly separated from the 'concerns' of his audience, all that spoke to the Soviet intelligentsia in the Stalinist darkness which had come to engulf their public sphere? Shostakovitch knew the extent of his audience well – intellectuals, the liberal-minded *nomenklatura*, the artists – and he understood the private confidences and the intimacies of the suburban *dacha*. These mutual recognitions between composer and audience gave him leave to write candidly of the encompassing tragedy. His audience knew only too well what the music was saying.

The disposition of Eliot's poem to address a certain audience within an ethos of intimacy and trust is the product of deliberation, a part of Eliot's concrete rhetoric. This approach to an audience carries with it the aura, the justificatory body language, of an affirmative philosophy that turns its back decisively on what Heidegger dismisses in *Being and Time* as 'the ontic sphere', mere routine existence in the prison of average everydayness (69), the sphere of abandonned hope, of 'fruit, periodicals and business letters' (DS III 210). But this disposition to 'concernful' intimacy in the inner circle carries with it important political messages as well, that are obscured by the theo-ontological style in which the culture of the inner circle is tendered. For one thing, it encourages, in a spirit of resignation, the intelligentsia to detach itself from the public sphere, now in the 1940s and 1950s dangerously the arena of surveillance by watchful ideologues and 'witch-hunters', characters much like Winston Smith's tormentor, O'Brien, in Orwell's *Nineteen Eighty-Four*. Indeed Orwell's novel thoroughly anatomizes the culture of the frightened mandarin in the society of total surveillance. Certainly Orwell exaggerates in the case of the Atlantic democracies, but who can doubt that Orwell's vision doesn't already convey the distress of 'open' societies suffocating in the claustrophobia of the Cold War.

Eliot's rhetoric administers consolatory Christian ideas and practical quietism in the only privileged language left for secular humanist intellectuals after the verbal debauch of the 1930s, namely the language of *symboliste* art, for which music stands as the rarest cognitive form. And *Four Quartets* disposes itself towards its audience by accepting silently, yet knowingly, one view of culture which suggests that, in times such as these, increasingly razed by the market form, by the mass culture of mass societies, and by the traumas of total war, the mandarins need a protected enclave where their own cultural exchanges can be intimately and freely transacted beyond the gravitational pull of power and its blunt demands.

Such an enclave is the concrete place where one can achieve, in history, the inner freedom from practical demands, from the demands of practice. It is the enclave for which the quartet form seems to be precisely fitted. Adorno's description of the quartet's internal dynamics underlines the point. Its 'vital element' accomplishes a subtle

. . . work with the themes and motifs or its echo, that which Schoenberg called 'developing variation': the dialectical spirit of a self-engendering, self-negating, but then, most of the time, newly self-confirming whole. In such a spirit even the utmost chamber-musical intimacy clings to its relation to social reality, from which it withdraws as though in horror. (*Sociology of Music* 89)

And, in this enclave, music itself and music as the emblem of art as private and inward plays a special role. As the so-called 'music of inwardness', chamber music cannot by this definition 'intervene in reality' (89–90) and so suits the politically and psychologically supine. The mandarins are not so much 'connoisseurs' in Barrett-Ayres sense as like-minded colleagues needing succour and consolation in a threatening time, although the capacity for connoisseurship is vital to their general aesthetic training and to their own needs for self-congratulation (cf. Adorno, *Sociology of Music* 95).

In addition to the semantics of opposed terms in sonata and *Four Quartets*, a second musical condition, akin to Adorno's 'vital element', prevails in the poem. The patterns of recurring images and other motifs which Gardner first noted in the 1940s can only be understood in musical terms:

One is constantly reminded of music by the treatment of images, which recur with constant modifications, from their context, or from their combination with other recurring images, as a phrase recurs with modifications in music. These recurring images, like the basic symbols, are common, obvious and familiar, when we first meet them. As they recur they alter, as a phrase does when we hear it on a different instrument, or in another key, or when it is blended and combined with another phrase, or in some way turned round, or inverted.

(*T. S. Eliot* 48)

The example which Gardner cites in illustration is the image of sunlight which recurs again and again through the whole sequence, each time taking on changing significations in the accumulating structure of references. As noted in the previous chapter, there are many more of these motifs all through the poem. Indeed this is the principal property of the artfulness of the poem, of the poem as artefact. What this particular feature does in the array of the whole poem is draw disparate parts into discernible unity. There is no wastelandism here; cohesiveness and coherence co-incide fully, deliberately. The end is implicit in the beginning. The wheel of the turning world is not only a metaphysical symbol in 'Burnt Norton', but a trope for the poem's completedness, for the sense of a finished and closed artefact.

Gardner concedes that *Four Quartets* is undoubtedly an important poem in a philosophical sense, but its whole effect surpasses ratiocination, not as Leavis would have it by transacting the business of thought more radically than the ontologist, but by conceiving of its task in higher terms, namely, the transforming of 'life into art', giving us 'a sense of beginning and ending, of the theme having been fully worked out' (Gardner, *T. S. Eliot* 47). Alldritt too sets aside the poem's intermittent references 'to matters of thought, philosophy and belief', in favour of the admirably 'strenuous, subtle, patiently careful workings with language' (12).

The poem's surefooted purposiveness in the matter of craft, never allowing the variations to lose contact with the secure structure of thought and figure, which makes us recognize them as variations, affords the high satisfaction that complexities, conducted to inevitable closure, accord. Gardner's applause for Eliot's consummate artfulness elevates her account to the kind of disciplined tautologies of which Eliot himself was the ironic master:

The strict limitations of the form make possible the freedom of the treatment. The poet can say what he wishes because he must say it in this way. (47)

Buoyed by such warm exultation, I hesitate lugging the discussion back to earth, to the political dilemmas of the 1940s when these words were written. I suppose I must say that I know of no better example from this period which so capably, but unconsciously, delineates the epistemological slant and hothouse ambience of the mandarin enclave. It is a criticism which has been so thoroughly colonized by the work of art under examination that it can no longer operate on its own, but needs the poem as primary life support system. It circles back on itself tracing the lineaments of the poem's self-referring, inward-gazing elements, strenuously recommending Eliot's mastery, and his impenetrable polish, in the highest possible terms.

The problem, if there is a problem, seems actually a simple one. Gardner accepts as given that the artefact she examines correlates strictly with Eliot's purposes, that the proffered work carries no significance other than that which the poem assigns to itself. The possibility that it fulfils a concrete ideological function in society, for a determinable set of readers, a function that even Eliot might not completely control, is alien to her way of seeing, as it is to mandarins who have come to accept their sequestration as a natural or inevitable condition. What she does is to follow the poem's own lead in marking out what someone might call a 'happiness in hiding' for demoralized mandarins living through uncertain times. Music, in this configuration of society, is the name and sign of that happiness, the name and sign of a sublime, but sheltered, transcendence. Kevin Barry has written the history of the origin of such attitudes towards music and the philosophical ideas which support them in the eighteenth and early nineteenth centuries.

The quartet form, with its free play of familiar and intelligent voices, within a strictly limited formal space, and with its predisposition to developmental self-absorption in the 'conversation' among the instruments is precisely what the doctor ordered for those in need of escape and consolation. In fact, Barry's repositioning in the late eighteenth century of the advent of that view of poetry we commonly associate with nineteenth-century philosophers and poets like Mallarmé, the view that sees poetry in musical analogies rather than in terms of the classical doctrine *ut pictura poesis*, suggests affinities to the coincident rise of the quartet at the same time.

The notion of music as a language of empty signs, ideally separated from the world of mundane reference, is crucial here. Music embodies a pure language of form which subsists without positive terms, and which shifts aesthetic experience from the contemplation of the beautiful to the experience of the sublime, as a mode of experience surpassing all forms of sensuous cognition. This development occurs in precisely the moment in the history of music when purely instrumental works, a music free of definite scriptural or literary programs, starts to come into being. The aesthetic which rationalizes this change in musical practice and taste began to be discussed in the mid eighteenth century, so that the *symbolistes* were working from a tradition of musical thought in the mid-nineteenth century that had been in existence for a hundred years.

At the moment when eighteenth-century epistemology noticed that the signs of music evade the categories of distinctness and clarity of ideas, it became possible (1) to locate the significance of music in its composition, in its structure or source; and (2) to locate the significance of music in emptiness, in its absence of meaning, and therefore in the act of listening, in the energy of mind which its emptiness provokes. (Barry, *Language* 65)

Four Quartets, as a culminating artefact in this development of music as pure signifier, corresponds impeccably with the political requirements for artistic expression in the 1940s and 1950s, namely, for an art of maximum internal complexity and expressiveness, but which recoils from 'social reality . . . as though in horror'. It is for these reasons that Tolstoy 'rebuked chamber music in the work named after one of its great items', that is to say, 'The Kreuzer Sonata' (Adorno, *Sociology of Music* 88).

It is Beethoven's late quartets which are mentioned as Eliot's primary musical models, especially Beethoven's Quartet in A minor, Op. 132 (Howarth 324).[15] I have no doubt that these speculations are more or less correct as far as they go. Yes, Eliot did love Beethoven's late quartets and was listening to them during the crucial years of composition of the poem and, yes, he knew Bartók's quartets as well, and, of course, he did end up calling his late masterpiece by a name which invites the analogy in the first place. But we know also that drawing strict parallels between a verbal artefact and a musical one, or to works in the other arts for that matter, is always an approximate business. Most critical approaches to Eliot's *Four Quartets* that suggest the analogy, don't really do very much with it. They go about the business of interpretation in traditional ways that could have very easily proceeded without the drawing out of the musical parallel in the first place. Gardner's concluding chapter on *Four Quartets*, 'The Approach to the Meaning', could have very easily been written without the benefit of chapter 2. Indeed Stephen Spender, in his book on Eliot, advises prospective readers of Gardner's book to get down to the nub right away and 'begin with the last chapter' (*Eliot* 154).

And, although Alldritt airs many interesting and serviceable matters of musical and literary history, his reading of the poem, at the end of the day, seems more usefully informed by the *symbolistes*, by Heidegger's *Being and Time*, and, principally, by the critical tradition of close verbal analysis we associate with F. R. Leavis. Music, in these accounts, stands for a certain cognitively satisfying complexity and the clean sequestration of the artefact from external contexts, which are seen at every turn as threatening to plunge the work into the confusing domains of history and ideology.

III. FREEDOM IN HISTORY

When we turn our attention to the three quartets written and published during the war, the whole sequence's rhetorical design comes more fully to view. With the metaphysical foundations in place in 'Burnt Norton', 'East Coker' now broaches more concretely the question of Time in its manifestation as history. And our attention as readers in the 1940s is more tellingly focused. Eliot's meditation on history threads in and out of the whole cloth of *Four Quartets*, concluding in the explicit propositions of 'Little Gidding III'. The ideological terrain which the poem occupies acts to dislodge materialist and positivist conceptions of history that one might find in a liberal, humanist intelligentsia schooled on the ideas of the Enlightenment. Eliot, as is well known, is not only sceptical of, but aggressively opposed, to all those Whiggish views of the past which emphasize its chronological, empirical, progressive and ameliorative character (Thomas, 'Culture' 157; Miller, 'Submission' 448–64; Jones, 'History' 31–48; Moody, *Poet* 72, 256). From 'Tradition and the Individual Talent' in 1919 to the publication of *Notes towards the Definition of Culture* in 1948 his views are not entirely unchanged, but there is a notable consistency about the necessity of holding transcendental notions of history. Eliot's views essentially contest the received positivist and materialist traditions of the Enlightenment and the consolidations of the efficacy of historical knowledge in the works of the great nineteenth-century historians. But that is not all.

What needs to be displaced as well is the associated notion that narrative is the human discourse best organized to convey historical reality. When significance in history is located only in those moments where it intersects with eternity, then narrative history gives way to what can only be called, in the world of discursive representation, history as lyric repetition, history as a usually dreary sequence sometimes ecstatically disjointed by the sudden 'shaft of sunlight' which for an instant – 'Quick now, here, now, always' – registers the presence of the divine in and out of Time (BN V 195).

This is the familiar distinction between history as *chronos* and history as *kairos*, between time as a mere succession that just goes on and those intense moments of revelation in which time stops, when things or events are charged with a 'seasonal' meaning, 'a meaning derived from its relation to the end' (Kermode, *Ending* 49).[16] For Eliot, 'history is a pattern / Of timeless moments' (LG V 222), those moments are moments of personal vision and private meaning *and* moments of Christian revelation. It is to this latter stage that the poem hopes to bring consciousness, that is to say, the stage of lifting consciousness free of entanglement in 'chronos'.

For readers in the 1940s, history as aestheticized 'kairos' no doubt held ample appeal for quite different reasons than the task of preparing oneself for Christian revelation. By lowering history to a level of diminished significance, one might more easily come to dismiss it. History is no longer seen as Necessity, the all-encompassing 'dangerous flood / . . . that never sleeps or dies' (Auden [1935], *EA* 157), but might be observed from a distance as 'time's flow' which we can 'escape' and upon which we can settle 'like a bird' or 'feathers', making, if nothing else, 'one devoted / Gesture of permanence' as 'our wish' against its senseless successiveness (Day Lewis, 'O Dreams, O Destinations' [1943] *CP 1954* 216). Such a view authorizes the serviceable obliteration of personal history by a kind of divine act of reification, in the sense that the 'experience revived in the meaning' of an event or an action 'Is not the experience of one life only / But of many generations', which, at the end of the day, 'is probably quite ineffable' anyway (DS II 208). And just like that, the notion of history born in the Renaissance, philosophically grounded by the Enlightenment, and consolidated empirically by the 'higher criticism' of the nineteenth century historians, is 'disappeared' at a stroke.

'East Coker' accordingly rescues contemporary readers from these epistemological traditions, and relieves them, in the process, of social and political responsibility in the present. Dynastic time – 'In succession / Houses rise and fall' (EC I 196) – the rhythm of the generations, the persistent return of the old as the new and back again, this sense of time as ceaseless reiteration implies the illusory character of liberal notions of progress and the ideals of human perfectibility. Eliot's cultural criticism in the period, principally his *The Idea of a Christian Society* published just months before the first appearance of 'East Coker' and his later *Notes towards the Definition of Culture* (1948) re-inforce the poem's implications.

For Eliot, history is not epistemologically negligible, but its status is emblematic rather than empirical, bewitchingly free of particular narratives, concrete events and necessary obligations. The evocation of the country dance with which EC I concludes offers essentially the same static vision of a harmonious Elizabethan England with which *For Lancelot Andrewes* opens. It is the old Tory vision of a staunchly comfortable, unchanging, hierarchical rural culture which, in the discourse of Tory nationalism, persists continuously in the nation's collective psyche even if it can no longer be found in the real world. As I suggested in my first chapter, such historical simple-mindedness could not go unchallenged in the 1920s and 1930s. In the changed conditions of the 1940s, the dancing countrymen 'In that open field . . . Holding eche other by the hand or the arm / Which betokeneth concorde' comprised an irresistible vision of communal harmony and solidarity. This was no longer an 'interpretation' of English history which might set professional historians at odds, but a vision of England which exactly coincided with a particular variety of cultural propaganda in wartime.

I am thinking of the sort of wartime and post-war attempts to raise morale that we find in countless books, radio broadcasts, popular verse, newspaper columns and features, pageants (like the one in Virginia Woolf's *Between the Acts* (1941)), and films, a film, for example, like Michael Powell's *A Canterbury Tale* (1944), with its linking of contemporary people caught in the maelstrom of war and the ghostly company of Chaucer's pilgrims representing the persistent heart and soul of England. This use of the English literary past as an ideological bulwark during war was particularly visible in Shakespeare productions and some Shakespeare scholarship. Under this latter head I have in mind, for example, a good deal of the work on Shakespeare by G. Wilson Knight in the 1940s.

A series like the 'Macmillan War Pamphlets' also functioned within and helped cement the same nationalist mythology. The ten pamphlets published up to the end of 1941 constitute an accurate roll call of British middlebrow culture. The series included authors like A.P. Herbert, Ronald Knox, C.E.M. Joad, Hugh Walpole, Harold Laski, J.R. Clynes, the Dean of Chichester, A.A. Milne, E.M. Forster and Dorothy Sayers. Liberals and conservatives, mild socialists, Broad Church clergy and popular authors participated in the common task. The only major popular figure missing from this representative list is J.B. Priestley. The Macmillan pamphlet by Sayers, *The Mysterious English* (1941), parallels Eliot's evocation of the essential Englishness of the English community in 'East Coker'.

During the 1930s, Left intellectuals and political activists would have dismissed such rhapsodic nationalism as Tory obscurantism, more or less steeply inclined towards some native form of fascism. In the mid 1930s, Auden and Isherwood satirized, in Pressan Ambo, the traditional English village in *The Dog Beneath the Skin* (1935) in just these terms. Quite obviously in 1941 such a reaction was no longer possible. 'East Coker' allowed hesitant intellectuals and mandarins, who wanted to forget that they had ever found the satire of English life in *The Dog Beneath the Skin* not only funny, but more or less accurate, to endorse the mystical nationalism to which a good deal of the middlebrow audience seemed steadfastly devoted in wartime.

In 'East Coker', Eliot made such sentiments available at the level of the highest cultural achievement to an arrested elite who no longer had a stomach for clever contentiousness, whose characteristic mood in the 1930s had consisted, according to Day Lewis, of the 'volatile / Mixture of hero-worship and disrespect' ('A Letter from Rome' [1953], *CP 1954* 325), hero-worship of the brooding outsider (like T.E. Lawrence) and disrespect for the conventional pillars of established society. With the passing of that mood, the old tribal atavisim – 'Round and round the fire' (33) – takes on an inconstestable priority, and what might have seemed the stuff of oafish hilarity to clever young men in 1935 – 'Lifting heavy feet in clumsy shoes' (36) – now soars as the historical sublime in affirmation of 'ancient' tribal values. Eliot's appropriation of some phrases in Tudor English from Sir Thomas Elyot's *The Boke Named the Governour* clinches the effect, connecting the present with the essentialized past through the 'common genius' (LG III 220) of the English tongue in one of its greatest and most definitive periods. Here the political potential of the first epigraph from Heraclitus is exploited concretely within the context of a particular historical reality. 'England', like Heraclitus's mysterious 'logos', speaks through us whether we like it or not and tethers us to what is common to all.

The cult of Shakespeare during the war and after – Duff Cooper's *Sergeant Shakespeare* for example, or G. Wilson Knight's gruffly patriotic pamphlet *This Scepter'd Isle*, or E.M. Forster's pamphlet *Nordic Twilight* that contests the Nazi recruitment of Shakespeare to nordic culture, or the vogue for *Henry V* – and other references to Elizabethan England – the defeat of the Spanish Armada for example (Sayers, *Mysterious* 13) – were attempts to bind England as an ideological community during the war crisis. Whatever other effects and meanings it carries, Eliot's high-

brow evocation of that dimension of the common culture of England in
'East Coker I' helped to gather his displaced 'sea-waifs' into the national
community as defined for the popular culture by its bestselling authors.
Eliot's reference to *The Boke Named the Governour*, a more learned and
refined reference than, say, Wilson Knight's more middlebrow appeal, a
reference not notably available to a general readership, is more or less
available, however, to a mandarin elite, and functions to help consolidate
the top end of the same national cultural community. It functions ideologically to bring back into the fold an intelligentsia alienated from the
national community in the 1930s.

Having been incorporated by such a vision of the English past, how
could a reader then resist Eliot's more telling negations of history in the
third sections of 'Dry Salvages' and 'Little Gidding'? In the former, the
employment of the *Bhagavad Gita* and the *Upanishads* as the intertextual
lever by which the universe of a secular, humanist intellectual might be
moved is brilliant. The point about detachment which Eliot makes in DS
III could be very easily made by the use of references entirely within the
European tradition. But the use of an Indian text helps to universalize
the point and taps also into an issue very dear to left-liberal political sentiment in the 1930s and 1940s, namely the moderate anti-colonialist sym-
pathies for Indian independence. I refer here to the sort of support
George Orwell gave to Indian voices during his BBC years.[17] Eliot's
Indophilia seems to share, with more progressive opinion, an essential
respect for Indian culture and thought, while at the same time, and this is
the primary ideological effect, assuring the secular progressive that
renunication of and detachment from history and worldly action is the
only saving stratagem in difficult times, not only according to European
traditions, but to Indic ones as well.

Of course, Eliot's argument in DS III is a good deal more subtle than
simply a counsel of detachment from the world. Eliot's views are conditioned by his Christian consciousness of death as the destination of the
purely human variety of Being and of the metaphysics of 'the moment
which is not action or inaction' (DS III 211). But the preparation, in a
redemptive spirit, for 'the time of death' also makes for politically useful
advice, on a lower plane, to those perplexed by the unpredictable twists
and turns of history.

> Fare forward travellers! not escaping from the past
> Into different lives, or into any future;
> You are not the same people who left the station
> Or who will arrive at any terminus . . . (DS III 210)

Those actions, beliefs, and events which constitute the past should not be seen as constituting a matrix of determinations which the subject can never escape. Neither should 'the future' be seen nihilistically as the kingdom of ceaseless self-fashioning. For those who needed a way of distancing themselves from past commitments, watching them disappear, 'While the narrowing rails slide together behind you', made a great deal of tactical sense. The fact that Eliot seemed to be saying that future commitments in the world were not matters of concern either, helped to diffuse the embarrassment or shame of watching yourself turn your back on the idealisms and affirmations of youth. And this is accomplished in the name of both 'reality' and a rich interiority sustained by aesthetic consciousness.

For Eliot, 'time is no healer' (210) and there is no redemption either through 'action or inaction' (211) in history. While we are in time we can only 'Fare forward' detachedly, having 'heard' finally the voice of our true calling (of our being called to death).

> At nightfall, in the rigging and the aerial,
> Is a voice descanting (though not to the ear,
> The murmuring shell of time, and not in any language) (210)

This is Eliot's exalted formulation of Christian heroism in a destitute time; the subject, like Dante's famous boat (*Paradisio*.II.3), must make its way forward, but it must make its way singing. When seen, however, from the perspective of aesthetic consciousness as the safe refuge from history, the Christian metaphysics in these passages provide a convenient blind for those whose goal is not heaven, but a secure place in established society. The musical 'voice descanting' dismisses the notion of history as necessary narrative both in the individual life and in the collective life of a society. The Christian metaphysics which Eliot intends us to affirm can be quietly 'affirmed' (as this seems to cost very little) and, then, just as quietly set aside for the inner detachment of the enchanted singing.

In 'Little Gidding III' the issue of detachment is broached again explicitly. Memory's use, he writes, is

> For liberation – not less of love but expanding
> Of love beyond desire, and so liberation
> From the future as well as the past ...   (219)

In the end, history may be 'servitude' and/or 'freedom', but it doesn't seem to matter which, because in the transfiguration of experience 'in another pattern', history, we are told, vanishes. Thus, the strife which appears to divide parties and factions on one level, in fact unites them on another. The poem reproves the epistemologically naive in an indulgent voice, like a wise parent patiently explaining to a well-intentioned, but erring child the difficult facts of historical life:

> These men, and those who opposed them
> And those whom they opposed
> Accept the constitution of silence
> And are folded in a single party.   (220)

The ideological effect here is to appeal silently to mandarins who believe themselves to be above faction, that they are capable of that refinement which attends to higher ends. Eliot, by urging the transcendence of history, ministers to readers who feel themselves to be wounded by history, readers who feel they have seen the destruction of Europe by political division, by class struggle, by the various contending 'isms' of the 1930s and who now seek release from the weight of the past and from the discourses which fix past words and actions in the amber of narrative causality. The poem ends this long meditation on history, that begins in 'East Coker' and culminates here in 'Little Gidding', with the consoling words of the sage: 'And all shall be well. . .' and so forth (219).

One might add as well that Eliot's evocation of the English Civil War in the seventeenth century connects with the reference to Tudor times in 'East Coker'. The references to the journey of Charles I to Little Gidding in sections one and three, and, in three, the allusions to Milton ('one who died blind' [220]), Crashaw and other victims of the wars are part of the integrative design. They depoliticize the seventeenth century struggles which still have the disruptive power to set people at odds in succeeding centuries, including our own.

The fact is simply that the Civil War of the seventeenth century, in which Milton is a symbolic figure, has never been concluded. The Civil War is not ended: I question whether any serious civil war ever does end. Throughout that period English society was so convulsed and divided that the effects are still felt.

(Eliot, 'Milton II', *OPP* 148)

This, written in 1947, I take to be Eliot's final opinion about the matters which he raises in 'Little Gidding III'. They are not substantially different than his opinions about these matters, and Milton's place in them, in an earlier, and more famous, condemnation of Milton in 1936. In 1943, in conditions that require the ideological integration of all cultural figures to the gathering in of the national community, a way is found of including even the hated revolutionaries of old. Milton, too, is 'folded' into the single party, just like the 'revolutionaries' of the 1930s, who also have their place in English society, whether they like it or not, and help to constitute something Eliot calls 'the silence', the harmonies of assent.

The conciliatory and self-revealing tone of voice is very important, for the same reason that the broadcasts to the Germans in 1946 required the utmost tact in approaching a devastated audience. These passages in LG III are Eliot's invitation for inclusion. But they are not cast as alternatives from among which the reader must decide, they are cast as our inescapable fate. We are already part of this movement of reconciliation and all we have to do is to let ourselves go. Coming at the end of *Four Quartets*, this is a compelling 'argument' and the compassionate reference to Milton is absolutely brilliant. Eliot's use of the Miltonic fragment – 'O dark dark dark' – in EC III contributes to the establishment of the speaker's generosity and openness of spirit in sympathetically recalling a poet whom Eliot had denounced in the past.[18]

It is an important part of the poem's rhetoric of inclusion to engage in moments of self-revelation and confession. Of course, all works of art are 'confessional' in one way or another, all acts of language are species of self-display and self-revelation in some form or other. Eliot makes self-revelation and confession a *thematic* concern of *Four Quartets*. This is one of the roads he takes to arrive at one of the poem's crucial Christian destinations, humility. Eliot's strategy here is to use the confessional mode as a way of opening new areas of feeling that originate in an exacting self-scrutiny. This voice takes us wherever self-examination may lead, no matter how arduous. Here the poem's voice establishes the *bona fides* of its own genuineness. This is the baseline from which the poem hopes to earn the treasure of an authentic humility. A good deal of the critical commentary on the poem for the last forty years tries to weigh Eliot's success in this enterprise. I am not concerned with that. My interest in this aspect of the poem is the kind of effect which such a rhetorical slant has in the project of persuasion and the administration of solace.

It is a very disarming thing to have a poet turn around after a stunningly magnificent performance in the apocalyptic visionary mode – the first part of EC II for example, 'what is the late November doing . . .' (198) – and write it off as 'not very satisfactory' and 'worn-out'. It certainly undermines the satisfactions which mastery of an art or a knowledge are supposed to give us. In a sense what it teaches is not necessarily humility, unless we are set on the course Eliot insists he is pursuing, but teaches that mastery can take many forms, including, paradoxically, its surrender. The poetry does not matter because individuals ought to be directed to other ends which poetry cannot finally comprehend. We are

meant to read these lines about poetry and its limits in close conjunction
with the lines about music in 'Burnt Norton V'. Art in these formulations
is simply the limiting case in the pursuit of higher aims.

These points are reprised and developed in EC V in which the confessional note is expanded and even touches, coyly, on the autobiographical. Confessional inflections provide, in the context of self-examination,
an authoritative style for exploring interiority in a new way. While
emphasizing failure and the fragility of the psyche's resources, the poem
in this mode nonetheless deploys powerful motivic and rhythmic capital
in the making of an appealing subjectivity; but the effect is essentially
anti-lyrical, even prosaic. The sections that begin in the confessional
mode constitute a kind of intellectual shoptalk, after the poet has
shrugged off the costume of lyric and visionary intensity, walked backstage, settled in a chair and gently scoffed at his own performance. The
celebrated author, it seems, has taken us into his confidence. The professional philosopher's voice in 'Burnt Norton' specifies similar intimacies,
but in a more socially recognizable inflection. It is not a voice that can
sustain the rehabilitative task of the whole sequence. The disarming
candour and intimacy of 'That was a way of putting it . . .' (EC II 198) or
'So here I am, in the middle way . . .' (EC V 202) not only pays the reader
the flattering respect of taking him into the speaker's confidences but
also puts the reader, superbly, in his place. After 'East Coker', this rhetorical situation is repeated again in DS II – 'It seems, as one becomes older,
. . . (208) – and again, more compellingly still, in the parallel movement
of 'Little Gidding II' – 'In the uncertain hour before the morning . . .'
(216). This is also very much the mentoring style, it seems, of Eliot's personal relations with younger writers during his years as a publisher,
according to their memoirs and recollections.[19]

In this complex rhetorical structure the point I made earlier about
Eliot's essay on the 'classic' completes Eliot's rhetorical design. He does
not present his 'argument' or persuasive intent *as* persuasion but as
something that we already know, the undeniable givens, he would say, of
our human nature and, with more urgency for his contemporary
readers, the inescapable truths of our current condition. In other words,
what we have backstage is the great man in intellectual and artistic mufti
(in both senses of the word), plainly speaking the simple truths which are
common to all. The verbal traces of the shared assumptions of an educated mandarinate and a common stylistic ethos are everywhere visible
in the passage in DS II (lines 87–125) mentioned above, for example, not
only in phrases like 'as one becomes older', 'I have said before', 'Now, we

come to discover', but also in the conspicuous presentation of banalities and commonplaces, the superficiality of 'the popular mind' for example, or the impermanence of time, or the inevitability of change, and so on (cf. Perl 157–58). The same kind of detailing occurs to the same affect throughout the whole sequence. The implied context of situation with its shared assumptions, confidences and goals provides enough 'argumentative' force to beguile a relatively small mandarinate lost in mass society in a period of crisis. Eliot's authority and reputation, as artist, as man of affairs and as thinker, does the rest. Hugh Sykes Davies later recalled 'the Eliot effect' in just these terms.

He had spoken to the condition of a very small minority, but to them with enormous force, giving a new perspective to the world of eye and ear, and inner contemplation. His poetry was, indeed, a weighty and discernible part of that internal duologue which is the ultimate reality of mental and spiritual life; many of my generation, when we thought, or felt, or thought that we felt, would find its phrases there already, in our own heads, before we could find words of our own. (in Tate, *T. S. Eliot* 361)

This is precisely the power of *Four Quartets* in its time. But it was a power that could best work on a certain kind of reader with an education and an elevated view of himself, who was in need of a certain kind of necessary succour. This reader needed to feel that in the darkness of the 'world's night' there was a quiet, safe place in which to withdraw, which did not cost much in terms of self-esteem when the established order demanded visible displays of loyalty, and a place which carried with it a spiritual aesthetic charge of some magnitude in order to ground otherwise groundless existence in a defensible absolute. To the majority of the general public in the 1940s, on the other hand, this was all too bookish and oppressive. The masses were in need of a different kind of intellectual and spiritual uplift. This was well supplied by C.E.M. Joad, J.B. Priestley and the Dean of Chichester.

It is in the second section of 'Little Gidding' that we see the extraordinary final effect of the confessional mode in *Four Quartets*. Having been accustomed in each of the preceding quartets to expect a kind of conversational lowering of the temperature after the lyrical opening, Eliot's adaptation of Dante's *terza rima* is both surpising and inevitable. Lying, tonally, somewhere between the freer fluencies of 'That was a way of putting it . . .' and the prosodically compressed and rhymed lyric mode, this is impassioned, metrical speech, yet with all the rhythmical virtues of supple, heightened prose left intact. This stylistic vehicle is chosen as the best way to convey, finally, naked confession, confession of the ghostly, composite 'master' which we are now asked to overhear. The style conspires again to encompass us in a series of incontestable givens. These are not presented as contentious matters, about which we can have opinions and views; these are truths through and through. The poem implies that they can only be acquired by the greatest self-discipline and detachment from self and the world. They constitute the clearest possible statement of what exactly this 'reality' is which humankind cannot bear very much of: 'Let me disclose the gifts reserved for age / To set a crown upon a lifetime's effort' (lines 130–31 and *passim*). It lies, no doubt, not in some exaggerated sense of great evil, but closer to home, in consciousness of our simple deceits, lusts, impotence, in short, all our own ordinary wickednesses. It ends with rending pain (line 139) and spiritual exasperation (line 145).

This sense of an heroic stripping bare of all personal artifice, which spoke with so much authority to the 'burnt children' of the 1940s that it led to ceaseless imitation for a decade, has been prepared for in the preceding quartets. It is already present in embryo in the experience of 'enchainment' to desire and 'the weakness of the changing body' in 'Burnt Norton II' (192). It is given a bloated life as epic simile *en double* in 'East Coker III': 'As, in a theatre . . . the bold imposing façade are all being rolled away' and 'as, when an underground train, in the tube, stops too long between stations . . . And you see behind every face the mental emptiness deepen' (200). And again the faces, in 'Dry Salvages III,' relaxing 'from grief into relief' (210) on yet another train journey. But it is in the final quartet that this line of development reaches its most consummate and classic formulation. The approval of fools and the public honours heaped on a smiling public persona that is no longer gravitationally constellated with the authentic self thoroughly exasperates the spirit (LG II 218–19). Only the most drastic measures of self-scrutiny, renunciation and atonement can bring about the 'at-one-ment' which restores us. The closing reference to 'that refining fire' in 'Little Gidding III' (219) which brings about the long sought-for restoration, prepares the reader for the sublimity of rose and fire to come.

In each of these cases, where a kind of confessional mode of personal exposure, or at least something that reads and feels like personal exposure, marks the emotional centre of each quartet, the attack on history and the disdain with which all existential possibilities are dismissed, follow closely on its heels. The secular humanist may not follow Eliot into the next stage of the Eliot programme, that is the step towards the divine, but such a further step is not actually necessary for mandarins who are interested in finding a viable security in the world. In the ascent towards the divine, *Ash-Wednesday* has already affirmed that aesthetic consciousness must be reluctantly disposed of, but this comes well after all the materialist and historicist labyrinths have been abandoned along the way. Here, finally, is what an increasingly uncertain and watchful mandarinate found in the Eliot of their construction. For one thing he was the apologist for an exact, self-referential and autonomous art – 'where every word is at home, / Taking its place to support the others . . . The complete consort dancing together' (LG V 221). He also seemed to be saying that one carried on nonetheless with the life for which an indifferent fate had chosen us, recognizing that one could not put any faith in history, in politics, in action, because to believe in the efficacy of action, personally or collectively, is to blindly 'step to the block, to the fire, down the sea's throat / Or to an illegible stone' (222).

That a 'quiet generation' of conformist intellectuals, 'organization men', shrewd careerists, wary, watchful mandarins, came to characterize many in the professions, the academy, the arts, and the trans-national bureaucracies of the North Atlantic world after 1945 should not be all that surprising (cf. Rosenberg 241–58). What was remarkable about these intellectuals on tiptoe was how thoroughly aestheticized they had become, not only in the personal cultivation of the arts, especially music, but also in the way these counsels of detachment and accommodation affected all areas of knowledge in the North Atlantic world. Part of this 'management' of the 'mind of the West' occurred as a result of the routing of public monies to support the arts, scholarship, intellectual life in general, through the new Cold War systems of patronage, the national arts and research councils, the foundations, endowments for the arts, and so on for the incorporation of intelligence and bohemia as new conscripts to the conventional ideological state apparatuses of the North Atlantic alliance.

How the political energies of the intelligentsia in the 1930s were channelled into two seemingly contradictory, but comfortably accommodated, ways of living in mass society is the untold story of the inner life of the North Atlantic mandarinate during the Cold War. This bisected existence was fashioned, on the one hand, by conformity to the practical demands of power and, in many cases, recruitment to its service, and on the other, the construction of aesthetic consciousness, not as art for art's sake any more, but, more desperately, as the new ground of Being in postmodernity, which came to represent both the zenith of human freedom and the new aestheticized domain of personal ethics. 'Politics' was banished to the 'the public side of [the] mirrors', the frenzied arena of 'resentments and no peace' (Auden, 'Memorial for the City', *CSP* 293). Eliot's *Four Quartets* did not cause these changes alone, nor did Eliot, one assumes, intend them as a specific effect of the poem. But as the most authoritative work of literary art written by the most celebrated author-sage in the 1940s, *Four Quartets* helped to re-orient subjectivity and to establish, despite Eliot's explicit doctrinal purposes, the new ideological conditions for what was to come in North Atlantic culture for the next three decades.

CHAPTER SIX

White mythology: the comedy of manners in Natopolis

In the period after the war, when he had achieved the status of a world celebrity, Eliot was not in the least optimistic about the future of the human prospect. He had survived into the nightmare world of the 1940s within which he increasingly felt himself to be an alien. He had never been fully 'at home' anyway, but this was something new. In this respect he was like Pound. But unlike Pound, he had managed to land on top of the heap, rather than in a wire cage awash in floodlight. Yet his dejection was not simply composted from the normal reactions to the common difficulties of aging. His despondency was related to a number of other matters. He had become particularly aware of the frustrations of trying to be a good Christian *per se*, and a good Christian in increasingly unchristian times. Eliot's biographers have chronicled these spiritual predicaments in detail. They have also recorded the tensions in his personal life which the death of his first wife precipitated in 1947.

He was disturbed by external events as well. Concern for the new role of 'culture' in the social and political arrangements after the war led him to write *Notes towards the Definition of Culture* as a polemical defense of that conservatism that runs from Burke, through Coleridge and Carlyle, to Eliot himself (Williams, *Culture and Society* 229). His distress in the new world which began to emerge after the war is evident in certain small ways, as Ackroyd notes, in his correspondence with friends for example, or in his use of the pseudonym 'Metoikos' or 'resident alien' for his last piece in *The Christian News Letter* (272). Ackroyd enlarges on these feelings:

His depression had been caused at first by what he considered to be *the disturbing condition of the victors after the war*: he was uneasy about the foreign policy of both England and the United States, as well as about the intentions of Russia. But his gloomy prognostications were also of a more general kind, and in January 1946 he described a public world which was becoming more 'incredible' and a private world which was more 'intolerable'. The world was a less 'moral' place than it had been before the war: Germany and Japan had brought to a crisis the sickness which infected civilization, but their collapse had not cured it but left it raging everywhere. (Ackroyd 272, my emphasis)

The comments which Ackroyd quotes here about the increasing pressures on public and private life occur in a preface Eliot provided for a book published by Faber in June 1946 and in New York the following year. It is an anonymous work called *The Dark Side of the Moon* and surveys the political and human situation in Poland during the German occupation, as well as exploring the relations between Poland and the USSR both during the war and in its immediate aftermath. It is an attempt by the author (possibly Helena Sikorska, the wife of the Polish leader General Wladyslaw Sikorski) to communicate to English and American readers and, of course, to the political and military leadership in the West, the hard facts of life in a Poland unable to negotiate an independent path between the two powerful antagonists in the East. This book touches on the early stages of the historical and political record of that period which in Czeslaw Milosz's *The Captive Mind* (1953) we find the later intellectual and psychological account.

In his 'Preface' Eliot expands on the political and cultural dilemmas of the time. He is particularly troubled by the yawning split of individual existence into public and private spheres, not because the two are separate, which in his mind they always must be, but because neither of them are tolerable in post-war conditions (viii). He is also disturbed, as he was during this whole period, at the attempt to plan or 'engineer' the recovery and reconstructioon of Europe. For Eliot a revival of Christianity and a rebirth of the idea among Europeans of the integrity of European culture would go a very long way in bringing about, not the reconstruction of Europe, but its redemption.

He recalls the old network of historical and cultural relations among the nations of Europe that characterized their relations before 1914. Everyone belonged to the same club, so to speak, especially at the top end of the social scale, and therefore, everyone spoke the same language. 'There was always', he writes, 'a great deal that could be taken for granted: politics was one thing, commerce another, and intellectual relations a third'. There were also certain well-defined areas, principally in the political and military field, in which states agreed to disagree:

But we are now at a stage at which relations between nations, in peace as in war, become 'total'. The great powers and the nascent powers stretch all over the globe and comprehend a great variety of types of culture; issues between them extend deeper than ever before, and offer possibilities of much greater misunderstandings. (ix)

He is sceptical of the ability of the new agencies for the cultural management of a totalized globe, the 'Departments of Cultural Relations', UNESCO, the appointment to embassies of 'Cultural Attachés', the assembling of delegates for 'world congresses' and conferences, to establish concord and amity in a world gouged by lethal political divisons.

It needs saying that Eliot probably misunderstood the extent to which these noble sounding initiatives in the cultural field were often continuations by other means of the larger international political and military conflicts of the time. He seems to have thought that the arts bureaucrats were simply misguided in their premises, not that 'culture' had been reinvented politically as a new area of administration, and more ominously, a new arena of competition between states.

His pessimism in these matters echoes the pessimism in the 1940s of another intellectual of a rather different 'old school', also unable to feel at home anywhere in the 'administered world', Theodor Adorno (Jay, *Adorno* 45). Rather than Eliot's despondency about the vanishing of a dispersed, organic, traditionally rooted past, Adorno's dejection arose from a feeling of hopelessness in the opposite direction, the possible disappearance of an emancipated future. The new sense in the 1940s of society as a 'totalized' space, in which no aspect of social life, private or public, would escape scrutiny, management, or mobilization, required modifications in thinking, if emancipation were to remain the goal.

With the arrival of a society in which the sense of reality becomes a positivist projection of administrative categories, thought abandons itself to technique and to ever more subtle exercises in the classification of information, which becomes the base currency of intellectual exchange. Critical and speculative thought, Adorno called it negative thought, is always in danger of losing its autonomy and with it the power to comprehend the real. 'While thought relates to facts and moves by criticizing them', he writes, 'its movement depends no less on the maintenance of distance. It expresses exactly what is, precisely because what is is never quite as thought expresses it.' And essential to its always disjunctive role, critical thinking must contain, now more than ever, 'an element of exaggeration, of over-shooting the object, of self-detachment from the weight of the factual' (*Minima Moralia* 126). In this way, instead of mechanically reproducing the reality projected on consciousness by the sociopolitical machine, it can be displaced and comprehended. Orwell's *Nineteen Eighty-Four* dramatizes these predicaments in the 1940s. Those who celebrated in Orwell's novel a simple reflection of life in the totalitarian East did not comprehend the novel's wider critique of all closed systems of domination, including, in exaggerated form, the new totalizations of the West itself. 'The whole', in whatever form it comes, 'is the false' (*Minima Moralia* 50).

Yet, the administrative and technical means for the establishment and policing of the 'whole' have essentially defeated the traditional literary techniques of displacement of and resistance to the imposed symbolic order. I mean here the traditional techniques of displacement, namely satire, irony, hyperbole, litotes, etc. Adorno supplants Juvenal's remark – *difficile est satyras non scribere* (it is difficult not to write satire) – with its opposite, that in our time it is 'Difficult to write satire' (209).

The nostalgic blame this state of affairs on the relativism of values, the decay of conventions and norms, but they are wrong. The problem is far more radical; the satirist and ironist of the past were keenly aware of the difference between what ought to be and what is. With the arrival of the total political state, the difference has collapsed; what ought to be *is* simply accepted as what is.

Irony's medium, the difference between ideology and reality, has disappeared. The former resigns itself to confirmation of reality by its mere duplication. Irony used to say: such it claims to be, but such it is; today, however, the world, even in its most radical lie, falls back on the argument that things are like this, a simple finding which coincides, for it, with the good. (*Minima Moralia* 211)

Before the world's implacable settledness, irony falters.

There is not a crevice in the cliff of the established order into which the ironist might hook a fingernail. Crashing down, he is pursued by the mocking laughter of the insidious object that disempowered him. The gesture of the unthinking 'That's how it is' is the the exact means by which the world dispatches each of its victims, and the transcendental agreement inherent in irony becomes ridiculous in face of the real unanimity of those it ought to attack. (211–12)

Eliot's dismay in these matters was as profound as Adorno's. But his path was to initiate a new form for what Adorno calls, 'the transcendental agreement inherent in irony'. In this respect, *Four Quartets* spiritualizes irony by moving it out well past the gravitational pull of its origin in an earthbound tradition of satire, and, therefore, with its detailed commitment to the world. From the interior haven, somewhere in the outer space of pure subjectivity, the lifeworld seems like a dream, a nightmare fortress of delusions and phantoms. And yet submission to a hermetic distance from life was not necessary either. Here the paradox in Eliot's thinking is palpable. Eliot, the celebrated poet, the successful publisher, the distinguished platform speaker, did not advise an ascetic withdrawl from society. Instead, one must be *in* society, but not *of* it.

The worldly wise mandarin, more interested in making his way in the world than making his way out of it, took Eliot's paradox to heart. For the worldly, this paradox is not the achievement of a pious detachment from the coils of *maya*. It is more like a limited form of self-protection through the selective suspension of moral principles, a way of serving, in sporadic states of moral inattentiveness, the often morally dubious ends of power. To achieve this state of political dexterity, one must learn to get the ironic out of sight – thus Harold Rosenberg, ca. 1959, 'To keep a straight face has become an elementary health precaution' (242). In the seclusion of the comradely circle, among one's trusted intimates, if there are any, irony retires to flourish in the chamber music of the private joke. Your task, then, is to maintain the conditions in which it is possible simply to live a paradox, and then to try to forget that you are doing so.

Eliot's solution to the dilemmas with which the Cold War confronted the mandarinate was always to recall the social arrangements of the highly positional and rooted communities imagined by Tory ideologues as characterizing the English past. As a solution to the situation sketched by Adorno in *Minima Moralia* and, with Max Horkheimer, in *Dialectic of Enlightenment* (1944), Eliot's cultural criticism seems little more than wishful thinking. The way forward for Eliot remained, quixotically, that of keeping in their separate and proper orbits the elements which make up the total life of a civilization. Men of letters, as of old, should not concern themselves with politics or commerce. Those responsible for the production of material wealth or the political management of society should not set themselves up as arbiters of taste and culture. However, the calm serenity and obviousness of that older, unreflective world in which the clever younger son of a well-heeled, Brahmin family might be devoted to or amuse himself with philosophy or literature or sanctity, while others take care of business, was, after the years of confusion *entre deux guerres* ('Preface' x), gone for good.

Eliot, to put it bluntly, went on believing that somehow that world was still, like the idea of the classic, fundamentally intact, but buried by generations of persiflage and inadequacies of definition (see *Notes* 13, 21 *passim*). Only hamfisted cultural bureaucrats, attachés of cultural affairs, liberal sociologists and Labour politicians, with their programmatic misunderstandings and general imprecision of thinking stood in the way of the wider recognition of that old world's cogency and obviousness.

The tone of exasperation in *Notes towards the Definition of Culture*, as Raymond Williams has noted, is more appropriate to 'the correspondence column' of a daily newspaper, than to the court of rational judgement. Indeed, at times, Eliot 'is often dogmatic to the point of insolence' (*Culture and Society* 228). The dogmatism and the insolence are audible in the very title of the work in the famous use of the definite article. The lesson is not the more indefinite one of proposing a definition or plan of 'culture' for rational consideration and adoption in the task of its preservation. His culture is the one which, he feels, is always already there, and has been there for a very long time. It is *the* culture which those who should know better are ignoring deliberately in order, probably, to gain political advantage by flattering the masses (see especially his footnotes to pages 14–17).

The title is also provocatively unitary in a time when Britain was beginning its long, and very troubled, experiment with cultural pluralism as a result of Imperial and Commonwealth immigration. *Notes towards the Definition of Culture* offered not only many of the arguments in embryo one would hear in Britain during the Enoch Powell years for example, arguments that would reach their highest pitch among the cultural mandarins close to power in the Thatcher decade, but also the characteristic public posturing and tones of voice which have seemed to be as crucially important to the making of such arguments as the arguments themselves.

The style and tone in which Eliot's opinions are expressed in *Notes* come also as a result of the confidence with which he could now address the mandarin audience in 1948. Having intuited their buried conservatism as a class, even those who had made spectacles of themselves as leftists in the 1930s, he was able to depend on their inclination to believe or to pay lip service to his ideas, even though the world was developing in ways Eliot himself could not foresee. It was convenient at the time to agree with Eliot's prognosis as a kind of authoritative holding pattern, while, in the meantime, unobtrusively repositioning oneself in the new landscapes of power that increasingly bore little relation either to what Eliot was promoting or to what he consciously opposed. Eliot's occasional irritabilities in *Notes* might, then, be put down to his growing awareness that many of his sympathetic readers, though nodding in agreement, were not really listening. They had other problems to deal with. To master the tectonic shifts actually occurring beneath the surface of the North Atlantic world during the witchhunting years of the Cold War demanded the ethical nimbleness and accompanying survival skills one often finds among very clever, very frightened and very powerless people. *Nineteen Eighty-Four* made the more reliable weather report for these latitudes.

With a large majority of the English population having voted for fundamental change in the election of 1945, most members of the British establishment moved resolutely to the right (Howard, 'Masters' 32; Pryce-Jones, 'Cocktail' 220–25), positioning themselves on the sociocultural landscape for the inevitable pendulum swings of popularity. And, inevitably, with them came a large proportion of the mandarinate. This was certainly Raymond Williams's experience when he returned to Cambridge after the war: 'The movement to the right was specific to English intellectuals', he recalled in an interview with *New Left Review* many years later (*Politics and Letters* 61). And Eliot was very conscious of it, citing approvingly, and not a little bit smugly, the confirmation of his convictions in *Notes* 'from a point of view very different from that from which this essay is written, see *Our Threatened Values* by Victor Gollancz (1946)' (19n), a point of view which in the end did not seem to be so very different from his, no matter how radical Gollancz's politics had seemed in the 1930s.

In *Four Quartets* he had conducted a shaken mandarinate to the proper path, and provisioned it well with the appropriate inner resources for the journey back towards its 'natural' home in the upper reaches of a class-divided society. In that brilliant metaphor for the comfortable glamour of upper crust society, *The Cocktail Party*, this mentoring of the lost souls of the 1930s would be secured in the character of Sir Henry Harcourt-Reilly, the kindly psychiatrist/priest/guardian/benign 'big brother'/a benevolent O'Brien. Eliot had intuited that among the mandarin elites this was the political desire that dared not speak its name, the path they secretly desired to take anyway, but were constrained, like guilty children, by the barricades of their published words and their psychological investments in the political tantrums of the past.

The examples of this process of restoration and revision are many and varied. It was George Orwell in *Nineteen Eighty-Four* who put the matter of the rehabilitation and re-education of the lost mandarin soul in its most malign form. The drama enacted in the closing chapters of the novel between O'Brien and Winston Smith addresses in the most horrific and exaggerated terms the central dilemma of intellectual life in the post-war world, its Babylonian captivity to power during the Cold War. If we accept the generality of these conditions for the intelligentsia in the late 1940s and 1950s, Eliot's *Four Quartets* can be seen to function as a benign and voluntary programme of re-education for lost souls.

The poem's calming ministrations helped to dissolve the constraints of past commitments; it provided a transcendental vocabulary useful in rationalizing zig zags of belief and the nostalgia for the safety of privilege. It was a necessarily highminded 'strategic withdrawal' to the upper-middle class environment within which a mandarin elite knew it could flourish. Cyril Connolly understood the situation in his bones as he contemplated the post-war difficulties for an uncertain intelligentsia yearning for their main chance:

There is a decay in communication owing to the collapse of that highly cultivated well-to-do world bourgeoisie who provided the *avant-garde* artist – writer, painter, musician, architect – with the perfect audience.
(quoted in Pryce-Jones 'Cocktail' 217)

From there it was not a difficult path to take towards the historic compromise with power – towards a new kind of 'family reunion' – in the post-war era. Of course, not all intellectuals and writers were headed in this direction. Certainly Orwell was not, but by 1948 he was a spent force, not intellectually, but physically. And his greatest novel, *Nineteen Eighty-Four*, had already been recruited to do the business of the Cold War in ways which served to abridge and undermine his more serious purposes. In any event, these writers were in the minority, and seemed 'to be shipwrecked or marooned from the thirties' (Pryce-Jones, 'Cocktail' 239).

For the majority, these windings and compromises in the 1940s provided the basic training for re-inventing that relationship of intelligence with the 'well-to-do' which, it seems, had been lost in the 1930s (Hamilton, 'Spender's Lives' 80–81). It was also useful to have learned, in the Cold War context, to separate with surgical precision the private and public spheres. Auden's important post-war statement 'Memorial for the City', which culminates with just such an amputation, begins with the compulsory nod to *Four Quartets* as the period's master text by quoting Juliana of Norwich in its epigraph (see LG III 219, lines 168–70). The poem continues by revealing the prime lesson which *Four Quartets* seems to have offered the post-war intelligentsia, namely, learning how to 'know without knowing'. The lesson begins as metaphysics with Eliot's first epigraph from Heraclitus, continues as the epistemological ground of religious consciousness, and terminates in contemporary application as a political strategy. In Auden's line the phrase comes in the context of a saving optimism before unfathomable existence, 'As we bury our dead / We know without knowing there is reason for what we bear, . . .' (290). But the talent for 'knowing without knowing', born optimistically and ingenuously as the answer to nihilism, to the 'crow on the crematorium chimney' (289), becomes, when we are less misty-eyed about our condition, a very useful craft to have picked up for the 'cocktail parties' to come.

It was just around this point that Eliot's unhappiness with the time entered into a new and final phase, and it marks his concluding imaginative works, his last three plays. It was the phase in which all of Eliot's principles and views, except his aestheticism, were respectfully hailed and, then, simply ignored by all those well-educated, cultivated, re-integrated mandarins and intellectuals whom Eliot, in *Four Quartets* and other wartime writings, had helped get through the nightmare years of isolation and panic. Eliot's apotheosis in the popular media as the highest of brows on either side of the Atlantic certainly put him on a pedestal, but all his words, from that promontory, were simply drowned out, not by reasoned opposition to what he had to say, but by the incidental noise of the celebrity vortex itself.

Life magazine devoted six full pages, with fourteen pictures, to the opening of Eliot's *The Confidential Clerk* in 1954 (Matthews, 'Comedy' 56–64). Had he glanced at the magazine he would have found himself crowded on one side by a photospread on the latest swimsuit fashions ('Hot Weather Warm-Up'), some gaga about the actress Judy Holliday on the other, and the gala launching, a little further on, of the first US Navy atomic submarine at Groton, Connecticut ('A Promising Portent, an Auspicious Future'), not to mention the bright, cheerful bustle of the advertisements for big cars, hair cream, Arrow shirts, pre-cooked Minute Rice, Jell-o and Seagram's Gin. More ominously, a short photospread about French military problems in Indochina and another on the aftermath of the Korean war ('Freedom Scores Joyous Victory') keep the Cold War pressingly in the foreground.

In fact, it is quite easy to see, at this remove, that the style and contents of the magazine have been put together almost entirely according to an ideological subtext written in invisible ink, with an eye to Cold War competition. In this array, Eliot is simply required to play the ideological role of 'our' great author-sage, 'the highest-browed of all literary high-brows' as Matthews impertinently refers to him in the article. Ordinary folk may not really understand what he's saying, but whatever it is, it's deep. It's as if Eliot had finally fallen into the clutches of the enemy, all those grotty little Sweeneys from the 1920s, now cleaned up, sent to college to study *The Waste Land* and civil engineering, and then transposed to suburbia.

The final and numbing irony in this Eliot number of *Life* is an inno-
cent-looking article at the end about education and the building of new
schools, 'New Schools, Economy Too' (74–80). Every educational principle about which Eliot, in the 1950s, was busy lecturing in America (for
example his 'Aims of Education' series at the University of Chicago, in
November 1950) is simply ignored, not deliberately, just simply not taken
into account. Eliot, the venerable sage, remains frozen on his pedestal
just where a sage belongs, but in the world of real schools and real education, about which he had much to say in those years, his words are
drowned out by the optimistic, utopian noises of the American riposte to
the other pretend-utopia in the East. All those social planners, econo-
mists, liberal sociologists, the engineers of the Welfare State, against
whom Eliot's social and cultural polemics in the 1930s and 1940s were
aimed, have simply won the argument at the end of the day, not because
they had better reasons, but because of the political and ideological circumstances of the time. The one final ironic twist in all this is that these
victors were probably avid and respectful students of *Four Quartets*.

In the 1950s these new circumstances and the very popularity of
Eliot's last plays, especially *The Cocktail Party*, made it next to impossible
to understand them. They commanded good audiences and long runs,
but they were generally received with respectful incomprehension.
Desmond Shawe-Taylor in the *New Statesman* thought the original
Edinburgh Festival production of *The Cocktail Party* 'entertainment of
much distinction' but generally found the experience chilling (243). The
Eliot hecklers found their voice in Ivor Brown in the *Observer*, who, speaking from the middle brow and as self-appointed leader of the
'Opposition' to Eliot, found it 'all pretentious mystification and a blether
of words' (quoted in Browne, *Making* 235). Everyone who wasn't already
swept up in the Christian revival of the 1940s seemed to be on guard
against the religious message which the play, though very witty, was
thought to convey, 'the subversive Christian propaganda', or so Peter
Russell called it in *Nine* (28–29). But what that propaganda was all about
was not so clear to contemporary theatre goers.

In New York, the play was on Broadway for about a year and was very
much on people's minds, not that very many listened closely enough to
make much sense of it. Brooks Atkinson in *The New York Times* blinked a
few times and found the play 'a verbose and elusive drama that has to be
respected' (17). James Thurber, in the April Fool's Day *New Yorker*, conveyed humorously what always lies ahead for those caught in the soft
coils of the modern celebrity system. As funny as it is, his piece makes

sad reading when one recalls the importance Eliot had always attached
to his privacy and dignity. Thurber satirized the play's reception by
taking his readers to a fashionable Manhattan cocktail party.

Ever since the distinguished Mr. T. S. Eliot's widely discussed play came to town
I have been cornered at parties by women, and men, who seem intent on
making me say what I think *The Cocktail Party* means, so that they can cry 'Great
God, how naive.' (26)

The mock-courteous 'distinguished', the seemingly ingenuous afterthought 'and men', and the catty, blasphemous expletive convey precisely, and at Eliot's expense, the absurdities of the situation. The words
'Great God, how naive', and the tone of voice which conveys them, also
snares many ironic nuances, not the least of which is the attitude of
world weary cynicism and disillusion which Eliot had taught an earlier
generation to cultivate, now returned as a wry little barb in the hands of
a minor humorist. Stephen Spender, in America teaching and, no doubt,
making his acquaintance with the new masters,[1] confirmed that the play
was the principal topic of cocktail party chatter in New York, the new
cultural capital of the Atlantic world. The ironic overtones of Eliot's predicament were not lost on him either ('After the Cocktail Party' 7).

   The Cocktail Party itself is a curiously elusive play, as any reading in the
voluminous secondary literature very soon makes clear. Even so practised an Eliot 'hand' as Helen Gardner suffers from a little interpretative
strain when taking the play on in 1950 in *Time and Tide* (284–85). The
play's Euripidean sources, contemporary affinities (its relation to the
then fashionable existentialism of Sartre and Camus is a predictable
gambit), the peregrinations of the various Christ-figures, the use of
myth, the presence of Goethe, Jessie Weston, Richard Wagner, Philip
Barry, Kierkegaard, St Paul's Letter to the Philippians and others in the
text, characterize most of the scholarly attention paid to it.

   One interesting early reading of the play is Robert Colby's 'The
Three Worlds of *The Cocktail Party*' in 1954, which tries to locate it within
Eliot's continuing interest in the making of a Christian society. This
approach makes the most sense. Colby is particularly good, though
limited in scope, in bringing our attention to the position of the
Community of Christians within a Christian state from *The Idea of a
Christian Society*. We can say that the play's 'message' is not religious in
some narrow doctrinal sense but dramatizes what a Christian society
might look and feel like, if it actually existed. It also dramatizes the place
that ought to be occupied in such a society by the spiritually luminous.

In order to make more vivid the saint's destiny, Eliot rehearses the now familiar description of the unreality of routine social experience. This is all one might expect of upper middle class people as they preserve the contours of customary society. However, like the satirical portrait of the dotty relatives in *The Family Reunion*, their superficiality and occasional idiocy is no reason to believe they do not deserve their position in society. The play shows, convincingly, an empty round of society, a world of transient feelings, unstable relationships, sophisticated vacancies and privilege, a world in need of spiritual renewal and regeneration.

Critics have often simplified the play by contrasting the cocktail party world with Celia's exemplary sacrifice. Is Eliot saying that one must choose Celia's way and renounce the 'cocktail party'? Hardly. The reconvening of the cocktail party in Act III suggests otherwise. The play at its conclusion affirms the cocktail party; in the same way that Eliot affirms the society of the three Knights in *Murder in the Cathedral*. Certainly the cocktail party world is limited and not to be taken seriously as holding the final answers to the enigmas of existence, but it is manageably honest and it is vital enough. Our invitation to take it seriously is made possible by exemplary sacrifice. This renunciatory action, which costs Celia her life, is intended to revitalize the structure of thought and feeling of the upper middle class elite, whether they understand it or not. In other words, like *Four Quartets*, this is a play of re-assurance and the renewal of confidence. And Celia Coplestone is the benign agent of the seasonable resignation which graciously descends on those she leaves behind.

She is especially interesting as she parallels the Becket and Harry figures in Eliot's earlier plays, the exemplars who redeem Christian society. She begins as a social character in the comic ensemble with which the play opens. She is slowly 'metaphysicalized', especially in her sessions with Reilly in Act II. Her radical sense of solitude, her sense that all her relationships, that is her connections with '*everybody*' (*Plays* 186), are at an end, and her radical sense of sin, lead her mysteriously to the desire to atone and, from there, her final redemptive journey towards suffering and death, like the exemplary 'death in the desert' of the French priest, Charles de Foucauld, about whom Eliot wrote so admiringly in 1941.

We are meant to see that her death is not her affair alone, but the focus of a redemptive pattern that concerns society as a whole, like Becket's or Harry's agonies in their plays. A Christian society must learn to protect and nourish such 'triumphant' (*Plays* 210) sensibilities which, when they appear, make us conscious of the presence of God in the world. Edward and Lavinia's resolve to carry on with their marriage, vouchsafed by the sacrifice of Celia, becomes, like Lavinia's final compliance to carry on with the new cocktail party, their 'appointed burden' (212). And Peter's resignation to the making of his films falls into the same category. The cocktail party world stays its course; it is the world 'we' know. The party must go on no matter what, because it is the 'appointed burden' of 'our' lot, 'our' class. It almost goes without saying that the play assumes we know all this without knowing it.

The counsel of renunciation in *Four Quartets*, in its special sense as an exclusively inward affirmation, is carried over to *The Cocktail Party* as resignation, in the face of what is to be borne by the privileged (cf. Peschmann, 'Links' 55). For the clever and well-to-do audiences in the West End and on Broadway, slowly regaining their composure after the deluge of war and despair, a renunciatory programme which ends up by leaving the privileged world essentially intact – marriages, films, power – certainly cannot hurt. For Eliot the image of the world as 'cocktail party' was his way of underlining the superficialities of merely social existence in the face of Celia's exemplary triumph before God. It was never intended as an attack on that world. As long as we understand its limitations, in the larger spiritual sense, it is a perfectly fine world, in fact we are better off simply accepting it as our own, as every other earthly possibility is more limited and banal.

The Cocktail Party, whether we like it or not, was Eliot's own world. His sense of his own fate is reflected in the characters: Reilly is the calm professional shepherd of lost souls, the dramatized version of the ministering voices in *Four Quartets*. Celia is an ideal of sacrifice he never himself reached. Edward is the world weary man of affairs resigned to the steady round of business, marriage, social life, lunches in Monmouth Street, weekends in the country, or *The Times* crossword undertaken on the journey from Chelsea to Russell Square. Reilly's presence, the interventions of the Guardians, Celia's change of heart are the manifest guarantees of the divine presence in routine existence.

For his audiences, who had learned the tactical schizophrenia necessary to survive politicized society, namely the ability to 'know' that the cocktail party was a symbol of the ephemeral, and to agree and to laugh about it, yet also to 'know without knowing' that the cocktail party really did matter in a political world without gods. The trick to survival was learning how to keep the two knowledges as far apart as possible, to forget that one even knew that such a separation existed. The entirely inadvertent legacy of *Four Quartets* was to teach the servants of the power elite how to survive this forgetting.

We might say of this political amnesia in the Cold War context the very same thing that Jacques Derrida has said about Western metaphysics in general in 'White mythology: metaphor in the text of philosophy'. I mean the comment that 'Abstract notions always hide a sensory figure' (210). Derrida here is referring to some remarks about the origin of language by Anatole France, that 'a purity of sensory language' characterizes the origin of the word and that this sensory language takes metaphor as its originary figure. This becomes the *etymon*, then, of 'a primitive sense [which] always remains determinable, however hidden it may be' (210–11). France considers the passage from metaphorical sensuousness, that is the physical and sensory purity of the word, to metaphysical abstraction as a degradation of language. Derrida expands the point:

The primitive meaning, the original, and always sensory and material, figure . . . is not exactly a metaphor. It is a kind of transparent figure, equivalent to literal meaning (*sens propre*). It becomes a metaphor when philosophical discourse puts it into circulation. Simultaneously the first meaning and the first displacement are then forgotten. The metaphor is no longer noticed, and it is taken for the proper meaning. A double effacement. Philosophy would be this process of metaphorization which gets carried away in and of itself. Constitutionally, philosophical culture will always have been an obliterating one. (210)

This and Derrida's further critique of European metaphysics as erasing 'within itself the fabulous scene that has produced it, the scene that nevertheless remains active and stirring, inscribed in white ink, an invisible design covered over in the palimpsest' (213) may be unacceptable philosophy and intolerable anthropology, but it is excellent *Ideologiekritik*, and especially relevant to the cultural ethos of the NATO world in the first decades of the Cold War.

Subjects were immersed in a culture of persistent and well-policed amnesia, a culture whose primary operating procedure seems to have been the systematic obliteration of the primal scene of its begetting. The emphasis in Atlantic culture on art as universalist, affirmative, metaphysical, and as a symbolic arena for resolving conflict by recourse to notions of aesthetic harmony,[2] effaces the unassimilable material 'figure', which scratches out its own disruptive history in 'white ink' beneath the surface cohesiveness of a positive ideology. This is a history which composes, beneath the formal affirmations of a confident and high-minded 'neohumanist' culture (a humanism without humans), the

melancholy, and sometimes incoherent inscriptions of a captive mandarinate, patiently learning how to serve the ends of power in 'reactionary' times: 'Read *The New Yorker*, trust in God; / And take short
views' (Auden, 'Under Which Lyre' *CSP* 226). It is also a history about
learning to forget, learning to overlook 'the fabulous scene' in the early
1940s, when, shaken and exhausted by nihilism, by contingency, and by
the final dissolution of 'Man' as the subject of history, they listened to the
voice of the master begin his concluding lecture. I suppose it is not very
surprising that Eliot's last two plays are essentially about 'forgotten'
pasts, which return to haunt the protagonists. But these dramas of
memory restored rigorously confine themselves to family relations
within the protected enclaves of upper class life. By the mid 1950s the
public sphere had settled down to the fixed routines of the Cold War,
and especially so in its upper reaches. Eliot's plays are about sorting out
the family skeletons in order to allow their distinguished protagonists to
get on with their deaths, minimally afflicted by guilt. They are plays
about the disclosure and accommodation of past fault, and about
resignation to one's lot, easy enough on one level when one's lot is a good
one.

The gist in *The Confidential Clerk* (1953) comes early on when Sir Claude
Mulhammer tells Colby Simpkins, the man he believes to be his son, 'If
you haven't the strength to impose your own terms / Upon life, you must
accept the terms it offers you' (*Plays* 234). And although Sir Claude is
'punished' later, when it is revealed that Colby is not his son at all, and
that the young man will go off to be a church organist, with possibly a
religious calling awaiting him in his new vocation, Sir Claude's words at
the end of Act I still seem true enough. Colby, of course, is the last, faint
exemplar in the Beckett-Harry-Celia line. In fact it is rather interesting
how these exemplary figures grow less distinct in the development of
Eliot's drama, beginning with Beckett in sharp focus at the centre of
Canterbury Cathedral, and fading out with an essentially anonymous,
but clean-limbed young man headed for some remote rural church to
which 'Good organists don't seem to want to come' (289). In his last play,
The Elder Statesman (1958), Eliot having discovered domestic happiness
late in life after his re-marriage, abandons the Christ-figure altogether,
and offers instead the kindly attentions of a young woman for a man preparing himself for death, by helping him make peace with his past.

These two late plays, however, have not lost their connection with the
darkened world which gave birth to *Four Quartets*. Even in the matter of
art as the safe refuge, they bring us back to the concerns of the 1940s. In

The Confidential Clerk, both Sir Claude, the private collector of ceramics, and Colby, the aspiring musician, are given long speeches, where they confess to a love of art as sanctuary from the world. Sir Claude is willing to acknowledge that his collection, kept in a 'private room' of the mansion, offers him escape, 'Escape', he says, 'from a sordid world to a pure one' (236). And Colby Simpkins only plays for himself, because he cannot believe he can communicate to others what only he can hear internally, when he plays the music of the great composers (238). Sir Claude acknowledges at the end of these speeches that it is the appreciation of his ceramics, what he calls his 'agonising ecstasy', that 'makes life bearable' (238). He concludes that the world may have extraordinary people in it, the religious and 'the men of genius', but

> There are others, it seems to me, who have best to live
> In two worlds – each a kind of make-believe.
> That's you and me.   (*Plays* 238)

By the mid-1950s the difficult lessons which the 'sea-waifs', the mandarin 'you and me', had learned a decade earlier, had now become part of an unremarkable and even obvious routine. Perhaps, *The Times* in London in 1946 had anticipated it all perfectly when, in its wisdom, it commissioned Cecil Day Lewis to begin to prepare the file copy of Eliot's obituary.

Notes

1 *ASH-WEDNESDAY* AND THE TRANSITION TO THE LATE CANDOUR

1　Tom Driberg, the *Express* columnist 'William Hickey' in the 1930s, communist, fellow traveller, and, later, Labour member of Parliament, offers another kind of pastiche of Eliot's work in the 1920s. He demonstrates the impact Eliot had on the younger generation, especially those passing through Oxbridge in the twenties. Francis Wheen writes, 'most of [Driberg's] poetry at the time . . . was still all too recognizably written under the influence of Eliot'. He quotes a few verses from a poem called 'Hell' by way of illustration.

> Climb all these stairs, rocketing, buzzing, blind.
> Climb, there, inveterate dizziness.
> This is his lordship's room, and here he often sits, Most bloody and most
> 　　rich.
> Dead Youth surrounds him, rouged corpses attend him.
> Will you await him, having climbed these stairs?
> That is the colonel's chair.　　　　　　　　　　　　　　　　　　　(64)

The extent of Eliot's influence in creating a taste for this kind of poetry is further demonstrated by the fact that Edith Sitwell found Driberg's dreadful pastiches worthy of encouragement. She wrote to Driberg about 'Hell' on 17 January 1928, 'The poem, as usual, shows this remarkable unfolding power of yours . . . I have such great hopes for your future as a poet' (quoted in Wheen, *Tom Driberg* 63). And if this isn't embarrassing enough, she was still touting Driberg, this time to Eliot himself, in 26 June 1935, 'I have just read the unpublished poems of a young man called Thomas Driberg. They seem to me to show really remarkable promise, and, at moments, achievement. He is very greatly under your influence (though not in form; he needs more shaping). But then, who is not?' (Raffel 34). Including, one might add, Sitwell herself.

2　Of course Eliot occasionally did comment *en passant* on his own celebrity as in his famous and often quoted reference to the popularity of *The Waste Land* in 'Thoughts After Lambeth' (*SE* 324). His self-effacing disapproval of contemporary critics who did not really understand the poem or tried to identify him with a bohemia from which he increasingly wished to distance himself is immaculately conveyed by the fact that his remarks are held at arm's length, contemptuously pinched in parentheses. I think this is fairly typical of Eliot's distaste of himself as a public spectacle. Indeed, Vivien probably understood her husband's anxieties in this department very well, which perhaps accounts for her desperate attempts, in the 1930s, to confront him by making a bit of a spectacle of herself at his public appearances (Sencourt, *Memoir* 137; Ackroyd 232). In later years Eliot's deprecating self-references grew more goodnatured: 'As I have a reputation for affecting pedantic precision, a reputation I should not like to lose, I will add . . . ' and so forth (*TCC*, 'American Literature and the American Language' 46).

3 In *Men Without Art* ('T. S. Eliot: The Pseudo-Believer'), Lewis does not directly accuse Eliot of these breaches of decency. He takes greater delight in recording the spectacle of Eliot as the astonished prisoner of I.A. Richards's critical regimen: 'Am I here accusing Mr. Eliot of being a 'humbug' then? – No: rather he is *pseudo* everything, and he has found his theorist to explain and justify him, namely, Mr. I.A. Richards' (77). At the same time, it is difficult to ignore the personal *animus* running through the whole essay and in Lewis's references to Eliot's 'slyness' (68), his 'snobbish veneer' (77), and the scruffy collection of fawning disciples at the *Criterion* (95) (cf. Ackroyd 290). At the time, Lewis particularly delighted in setting Eliot's genuine-seeming professions of belief against Eliot's own earlier theories (especially his famous view of the poet as the writer of 'impersonal' verse), and holding up to public ridicule the resulting contradictions. Richards, it seems, having fallen for Eliot's earlier ptolemyan theories, was forced to devise intricate critical epicycles to save the appearances of the old system (his theory of poetry as the province of pseudo-statement and pseudo-belief, for example). The master's unexpected copernican apostasy in the period of his Anglican conversion, where the matter of 'belief' takes on a new gravity, was seen by Lewis to be zigging of some magnitude, while Eliot's admirers were still busily zagging. The resulting confusion no doubt appealed to the satirist in Lewis. Much of what Lewis has to say in *Men Without Art* may have simply been the result of envy; after all, Eliot began his London career as the new kid in the Vortex, so to speak, where Pound and Lewis were already the senior figures. Was it galling for Lewis to have to admit that in the twenty years since the first *Blast* there was no person with greater influence on English and American letters than T. S. Eliot? Yes, it probably was.

Virginia Woolf's many references to Eliot in her letters also often communicate her amusement at his progress in society. She was particularly diverted by the matter of Eliot's personal manners. His brittle decorousness, on the one hand, subverted by his occasional comic collapses, 'He will, no doubt, be sick in the back room; we shall all feel ashamed of our species' (letter to Roger Fry, 16 October 1928). However, Woolf's remarks, taken as a whole, also convey a slightly different kind of interest, the sly amusement of someone who might be watching with a sardonic eye the intricate manoeuvres of a fraud: 'The question is, will he drop Christianity with his wife, as one might empty the fishbones after the herring' (letter to Francis Birrell, 3 September 1933).

4 Eliot's success and influence as an editor and publisher is a fascinating aspect of his literary work that needs further study. Peter Ackroyd merely whets the appetite with his few paragraphs on this theme in his life of the poet (222–25). Frank Morley's comments in 'T. S. Eliot as a Publisher' in the March and Tambimuttu tribute are more interesting and I will return to them in chapter 4. In addition, there are plenty of personal reminiscences of Eliot as a publisher from colleagues and friends, but most are smarmy and fawning (see, for example, Peter du Sautoy, 'Reminiscences' 75–84) and say very little about the publishing policies of the Faber company and Eliot's part in their formulation and implementation.

5 Although *Ash-Wednesday* has never had the kind of attention paid to it that *The Waste Land* and *Four Quartets* have received, there are nonetheless a number of important studies. Although my treatment of the poem's rhetorical contexts takes me in a different direction, I have learned a great deal about the poem itself from a small group of exemplary readings. Allen Tate's 'Irony and Humility' from 1931 and E.E. Duncan Jones's lucid exposition in her 'Ash Wednesday' (1947) are both still worthy of close study. Helen Gardner's 'The Time of Tension' in *The Art of T. S. Eliot* (1950) and, more recently, David Moody's treatment of the poem in 1979 and Ronald Bush's chapter in his 1984 book on Eliot are important critical statements. It is a bit of a surprise that Paul Murray's *T. S. Eliot and Mysticism* (1991) has so little to say about *Ash-Wednesday* for such a long book on the right subject. And finally who can overlook Christopher Ricks's seven or eight pages on the poem in his *T. S. Eliot and Prejudice* (1988). As the master practical critic of his generation, Ricks gets very close to the words indeed. Many of his insights about the poem's tone and its wordplay are inspired, although these are strangled, now and then, in a prose that sometimes chokes in its own energetic windings: 'The differences between *Ash-Wednesday* and 'The Hollow Men' are immense, and yet we are invited to try to measure them, since the later poem so sets itself to redeem the earlier one, not by rescinding it but by seeking the benign form of the energies which were there so malignly cauterizing as to leave the hollow men unable to muster even the perilous energies of malignancy' (222–23).

6 By 'post-Nietzschean nihilism' I am referring to the Heideggerian reading of Nietzsche's place in the history of Western metaphysics, that is, as marking its end. I have in mind particularly an observation by Heidegger in his fourth volume of lectures on Nietzsche (1940), namely that European nihilism is not merely a philosophical concept, a particular episode in the course of intellectual history, but that 'Nihilism *is* history', that it constitutes history's 'inner logic' and meaning. For Heidegger, this meant coming to terms with nihilism not only as the unhappy dead end of contemporary scepticism, but as the inner meaning of modernity's difficult, one-way journey towards 'the

devaluation of . . . values' as well. Nihilism epitomizes, Heidegger writes, the essential 'lawfulness of events' that brings us to the negation of *all* values, even the highest ones. It is the task of the philosophy of the future to think 'beyond decline', past 'the initial devaluation' towards the dawn of 'the inevitable revaluation' (*Nietzsche* 53). The encounter with nihilism defines the hermeneutic horizon of the literature of our period, including Eliot's works. But his reluctance to push on past Christian metaphysics represents a rearguard action, an intellectual conservatism that makes him rather more properly the contemporary of Newman and Arnold, Bradley and Baudelaire, than of Kafka and Beckett, Céline and Gombrowicz.

7 We only have to recall the famous photograph taken in the Faber offices in the 1950s to understand Eliot's position in the literary history of England in this century. It shows Eliot, Spender, Auden, MacNeice and the tertiary modernist Ted Hughes quietly sipping Chablis together, the happy, proud editor with his stable of smiling authors.

8 The 'crisis' which Gordon examines can be felt in the occasional bitter, gibing sarcasm of the important critical statement, 'The Function of Criticism,' which, significantly, follows 'Tradition and the Individual Talent' in *Selected Essays*. In 'The Function of Criticism' the shape of Eliot's future social and political commitments comes clearly into view for the first time.

9 See especially Eliot's comments in *For Lancelot Andrewes* on Thomas Hobbes (27–38), the Tory historian Keith Feiling (34) and Matthew Arnold (59).

10 In 1939 Eliot acknowledged that he was not unfamiliar with Tawney's revisions of the history of seventeenth-century England (*Idea* 67).

11 Virginia Woolf, for one, was initially rather doubtful about Eliot's new direction: 'He has written some new poems,' she wrote to Roger Fry, 16 October 1928, 'religious, I'm afraid, and is in doubt about his soul as a writer'. Her wry fun at Eliot's expense turned to irritation and disgust by the time of the mounting of the *The Rock* in 1934. 'I couldn't go and see it', she wrote to Stephen Spender, 10 July 1934, 'and in reading, without seeing, perhaps one got the horror of that cheap farce and Cockney dialogue and dogmatism too full in the face. Roger Fry, though, went and came out in a rage'.

12 One thinks particularly of a certain peevishness of tone and a general irritability in texts of the time such as 'The Function of Criticism', *For Lancelot Andrewes*, 'Thoughts After Lambeth', and *After Strange Gods*.

13 Auerbach's comments on Augustine are expanded in *Literary Language* 27–66.

14 See my 1985 review of Perloff in *Ariel*.

15 I have in mind those – Alldritt 120–121 for example – who argue that *Four Quartets* represents a culminating achievement in the *symboliste* tradition.

2 PROVISIONAL DELUSIONS: CRISIS AMONG THE MANDARINS

1 The best brief account of Eliot's American qualities remains A.D. Moody's essay 'T. S. Eliot: The American Strain' (1991) which examines those ways in

which Eliot was an American both by 'genetic and genealogical' inheritance and by the inescapably American 'music' of his writing (88). I think Moody's lucid exposition should put to rest the parochial view, occasionally still heard in America, that Eliot, *for* America, was not a healthy example for the evolution of American culture, a view that mars Richard Poirier's otherwise very fine book, *The Renewal of Literature: Emersonian Reflections* (1987).

2 Charles Morgan was a prominent English Francophile in those years. A Fellow of the Royal Society of Literature, he was drama critic for *The Times*, 1921–39. His services to the propagation of French culture were recognized by his being named to the Legion of Honour. He was the author of the nostalgic-patriotic *Ode to France* in 1942.

3 All the statistics used here can be found in Gallup.

4 The de luxe edition of *Selected Essays* published at the same time as the trade edition was limited to 115 signed copies and was sold for a steep 52s. 6d. When we recall that in the 1930s a 'fifty shilling tailor' could produce a man's business suit for what Eliot's essays cost, it helps put the matter of prices into perspective.

5 One might add that this is a story that is not well known enough. David Trotter's immensely interesting *The Making of the Reader* (1984) touches on what the relationship between Eliot and the poets of the Thirties might depend, giving special attention to the ways in which Auden and Eliot go about constructing a readership (110–129). Steven Ellis also makes reference to the Eliot-Auden relationship. He sees in it a kind of reverse influence, the senior writer comes under the artistic influence of the junior. This may be so in the matter 'of [Eliot's] abundant use of the definite article' as a result of his contact with Auden (144–45), but it leaves out the huge debt Auden owed Eliot as the impresario of the younger man's career. I think that Eliot's assistance is well illustrated by his ability to keep a sharp eye on the readers for the benefit of his authors and, in particular, his editorial regulation of the youthful Auden's avid self-absorbtion. The older man's 'inscrutable aplomb', for example, in emending 'fucked hen' to 'June bride' in the 'Journal of an Airman' section of *The Orators* (1932) before publication (Trotter 113) underlines the point. Eliot's assiduous realism in his shrewd weighing of the susceptibilities of readers provided precisely the sort of guidance his younger 'stars' needed (cf. Cunningham, *Thirties* 22). But, from the very beginning, he worried privately about Auden's ethics, wishing him rather 'less flashy' and in possession of 'more character' (letter to Herbert Read, 11 December 1930, University of Victoria Library Special Collections).

6 The easy contentments of a sequestered mandarinate of 'professional men – lawyers, doctors, public officials, journalists, professors, and men of letters' close to power, was doubly seductive in England because of the absorption of the prosperous middle class families of the industrial bourgeoisie into the upper class ethos and to a comfortable and comforting gentrification: 'The peculiar flexibility of the English aristocracy snatched a

class victory from the brink of defeat, and helped alter the course of national development. At the moment of its triumph, the entrepreneurial class turned its energies to reshaping itself in the image of the class it was supplanting' (Weiner 14 and *passim*). For the Oxbridge trained mandarinate, the attenuation of class tensions between the newly gentrified middle class capitalists and the old landed families made serious rebellion more difficult.

In other European countries, where social and cultural differences between the wealthy bourgeoisie and the landed aristocracy remained sharply etched in political and economic terms, a middle class intelligentsia could occupy positions of political opposition and critique of the old aristocratic order more easily, and, to some extent, was expected to do so. In England the aristocracy, Bertrand Russell quipped, had invented 'the concept of the gentleman . . . to keep the middle classes in order' (quoted in Weiner 13). The bourgeois generation which came of age in the 1930s and 1940s, individuals who had been traumatized by World War One as children and by the Depression as young adults, were really the last to attempt to break free of that cosy relationship with the governing classes for which their families' aspirations, their public schools, Oxbridge and the old-boy networks in London had trained them. Bloomsbury, of all the metropolitan groupings, personified this dilemma most clearly as Raymond Williams has suggested in his superb essay 'The Bloomsbury Fraction', in *Problems in Materialism and Culture* (1980).

7 Francis Wheen, Driberg's biographer, illustrates the nature of the protection someone like Driberg might come to expect from the powerful by an incident early in his career. In November of 1935 Driberg tried to seduce two unemployed Scots miners he had encountered in the street late at night. They immediately went to the police. Lord Beaverbrook, the proprietor of the *Express*, successfully kept the possible scandal out of the papers, although Driberg did go to trial. There, Wheen tells us, his upper class witnesses swayed the jury in his favour by vouching for his character. It was impossible to escape 'the suspicion', Wheen notes drily, 'that the case was being decided by what one might call 'class justice'' (97–98).

8 This is not a poem to which an extensive critical literature is devoted, but Cleanth Brooks in a 1988 essay on Eliot gives Auden's poem its due, though he is careful to say that it is not one of the poet's best. He credits Auden for recognizing Eliot's importance as a mentor and guide in a troubled time, a time which Brooks generalizes as one emptied of metaphyscial significance by science, technology and secularization. In the light of this philosophical generality, Auden's poem is as relevant to 1888 as it is to 1948. My sense of the poem's relevant context draws its play of reference more tightly around the post-war situation. Brooks insists on the wider metaphysical relevance as referring in a general sense to the fate of Western civilization in a secular and scientist epoch. To clinch this point he refers the reader to other poems on the same 'theme' by Auden from the post-war period, 'The Fall of Rome', 'Memorial for the City', 'The Chimeras', and especially, he says, 'A

Walk After Dark' (116–17). All these poems seem to me to be engaged urgently with both the personal fall-out of the 'low dishonest decade' of the 1930s and the even more numbing experiences of war, holocaust, atom bomb, and paranoia in the 1940s.

> For the present stalks abroad
> Like the past and its wronged again
> Whimper and are ignored,
> And the truth cannot be hid;
> Somebody chose their pain,
> What needn't have happened did.
> ('A Walk After Dark,' *CSP* 232)

Brooks's wider, baggier reading of lines like these is not wrong, just not very interesting. It seems to me that when we are asked to consider the plight of the whimpering 'wronged', whose pain was chosen and administered by 'Somebody' else, and we are asked to think about these things in 1947, our more sensible response is to suppose that Auden has something rather definite in mind, something definite like Buchenwald, and not some airy abstractions about science.

9 In this matter I concur completely with Michael North's superb characterization of the political significance of Eliot's concept of the man of letters. '[T]he man of letters stands as Eliot's triumphant solution to the central theoretical problem in his politics, the achievement of a system 'capable of disciplining the individual and at the same time increasing his possibilities of development as an independent member of society' [*Criterion* 10 (January 1931): 314]. For the man of letters these two imperatives, discipline and individual self-fulfilment, are not in conflict but rather in necessary collusion. Not only does this resolution soothe Eliot's own personal anxiety as an uprooted intellectual, but it also dispels the all-too-popular notion that letters are irrelevant to society. Eliot can see this very irrelevance as the primary strength of letters, empowered by its very distance from practical considerations. Thus Eliot proves an even more subtle Hegelian than Bradley, for he makes the very isolation and separation of the conservative into his centrality, as he makes the independence of letters the basis of its social utility (112).

10 In 1937, Eliot had already connected the figure of Arjuna to the dilemma of an uncommitted person contemplating the Spanish Civil War: (*Criterion* [January 1937]: 289–90). But cf. Bush 223.

11 When all was said and done, the backtracking was not all that difficult; indeed, one might have come to expect it (as did Louis MacNeice) on the evidence of people's actual behaviour. See MacNeice's sardonic little anecdote about oysters, posh restaurants, and 'Oxonian' leftists in *Strings* 168–69.

12 In Eliot's conservatism, the restoration of the past is the 'traditionalism' of a thoroughly bourgeois and familiar type. I hope that I am not overstating the point if I suggest that this conservatism parallels totalitarian forms of aesthetic and cultural restoration. Nazi neo-classicism, for example, and

Stalinist socialist realism, for all the revolutionary bravado of their sponsors, are merely harkings back to bourgeois forms of expression that were already subjects of parody and pastiche in Flaubert's time. Both regimes brought to an end, in the 1930s, incomparably fruitful modernisms in Germany and the Soviet Union. Soviet and Nazi restorations are *petite bourgeoisie* imitations of the same *haute* frame of mind that led Eliot and other cultural conservatives in the twentieth century, in their more civilized ways, to similar libidinal investments in the classical past.

Fear was the spur in all cases, fear of the present but, more importantly, of a future that threatened always to slip out of the grasp of the governing class, or the directive elites, or the *nomenklatura*, or the company men, or the party bosses, all of them enjoying the attendance of their mandarin servants. The tragedy of the twentieth century lies in the fact that the new revolutionaries 'in power' simply reproduced, more nakedly, the same structures of fear and domination inherited from the past, but on a monstrous scale. The farcical culmination of this restorative process can be seen in central Bucharest today, where Nicolae Ceaucescu managed, in the erection of his elephantine palace, to re-stage Versailles in burlesque, revealing not 'the glorious arrival of the Communist millennium', but the utterly fitting, yet unconscious, self-exposure of the lumpenproletarian Sun King.

The failure in all cases is certainly one of imagination, and, perhaps, of courage. Eliot embodies, at the end of the day, the principal theme in the bourgeois encounter with modern times, the abject rejection of the future, except as the domain of what already exists. East or West, Right or Left, communist, fascist, or democrat, finally, no one in power has dared tamper with the primary microstructures of domination within bourgeois society in general, without threatening his own privileged position within it. The need for a mandarin enclave in any one of these societies is clear enough. Each developed its own ideological covering. But whether the culture of the modestly comfortable *dacha* outside Moscow enjoyed by the intelligentsia during private respites from surveillance in the Soviet years is all that different, psychologically speaking, from a weekend at the cottage or country house in the world of the North Atlantic mandarinate is a story that will no doubt be told in time.

13   Eliot properly epitomizes Leo Strauss's assertions that the 'philosophers', in order to work comfortably within the system of power, must take care not to seem to subvert the traditional beliefs and mores of the 'city', even as they are sometimes forced to criticize particular instances of unsatisfactory behaviour ('the philosophers' must satisfy 'the city that [they] are not atheists, that they do not desecrate everything sacred to the city'). They must not seem to be 'irresponsible adventurers but good citizens and even the best of citizens' in order to be taken seriously by the people and by the governors (205–206). Strauss's point here is central to my discussion of *Murder in the Cathedral* in the next chapter.

3 THE SOCIETY OF THE MANDARIN VERSE PLAY

1 I am referring to Peter Ackroyd's life of the poet and Lyndall Gordon, *Eliot's New Life*. E. Martin Browne's *The Making of T. S. Eliot's Plays* provides the most important material survey of the genesis, composition and production of the plays. Ashley Dukes, London impresario, sketches Eliot's early years in the theatre in 'T. S. Eliot in the Theatre' in March and Tambimuttu, 111–18. Carol H. Smith's *T. S. Eliot's Dramatic Theory and Practice* and David E. Jones's *The Plays of T. S. Eliot* remain the most comprehensive critical explorations of the plays, though both are now somewhat dated. Arnold Hinchliffe's collection of critical essays in *T. S. Eliot: Plays* brings together the fruit of thirty years of academic criticism. Valuable general studies that attempt to place Eliot in the history of contemporary British drama have been written by William V. Spanos, *The Christian Tradition in Modern British Verse Drama* and Denis Donoghue, *The Third Voice*. There are many studies of individual plays and particular aspects of Eliot's writing for the theatre.

2 I am thinking of early sociologists and social thinkers such as Vilfredo Pareto, Gaetano Mosca, Max Weber, Antonio Gramsci, Julien Benda, Karl Mannheim, Leo Strauss and others.

3 See Eliot's comments to Nevill Coghill about the play reported by Coghill in 'Sweeney Agonistes: (An anecdote or two)' (85–87) in the March and Tambimuttu tribute. Eliot described Sweeney to Coghill in the following terms: 'I think of him as a man who in younger days was perhaps a professional pugilist, mildly successful; who then grew older and retired to keep a pub' (86). Eliot here neatly dams the dangerous current of Rupert Doone's 1934 production which seemed to suggest (to Coghill at least) that every man has a bit of the sadistic killer in him. Eliot's final comment nicely diverts Coghill's unease and any further inquiry in that direction. Of course, we must also take into account the fact that the Oxford don has deliberately cast himself in the role of wide-eyed simpleton in telling the anecdote and, by this stratagem, probably intends to communicate not only his sly delight in Eliot's discomfort but also his admiration of the poet's aplomb in controlled response. The sadism in the play also plays a central role in Francis Bacon's remarkable 'Triptych inspired by T. S. Eliot's Poem "Sweeney Agonistes"' (1967) (Leiris illus. 47).

4 I understand that my very short account of *Sweeney Agonistes* approaches the play from only one limited direction and does not exhaust the play's meanings. There is a small but growing critical literature that sees the play in wider dramatic and intellectual contexts. David Galef and William V. Spanos ('God and the Detective'), not very surprisingly, notice a unifying Christian (or mythic) subtext to the fragments; Barbara Everett positions the playlet in the relevant satiric traditions; Morris Freedman and Carol Smith hear the rhythms of jazz in the verbal texture, and T. H. Thompson detects clues in all the Sweeney texts that 'prove' Sweeney is a murderer. The best compilation of views about 'the Sweeney zone' in all its incarna-

tions is *Critical Essays on T. S. Eliot: The Sweeney Motif*, edited by Kinley E. Roby. Of course, for the purposes of my argument, I am interested in the play from the perspective of Eliot's representation of the lower orders, as one of Eliot's final excursions into what Desmond MacCarthy, reviewing the Group Theatre production in London in November 1934 for the *Listener*, called 'the impulse to contemplate the sordid' and the 'commonplace' (80–81). Other critical approaches are certainly very interesting and no doubt plausible, but not particularly relevant to my aim.

5 Ortega y Gasset's *The Revolt of the Masses* (1930) condensed in a single work a good deal of the paranoia of demos that permeated the conservative intellectuals of Europe all through the later part of the nineteenth century and well into the twentieth. The mistrust, and even hatred, of the masses in power increased in scope and intensity as the popular political organizations of mass society increasingly challenged the sway of the established oligarchies in modern Europe. Fear and loathing of the masses came to characterize conservative political thinking. In England W. H. Mallock's *Aristocracy and Evolution* (1898) sounded the warning and mounted the first specifically modern defence of political elitism (O'Sullivan 116). It is Mallock's reworking, on a new basis, of the conservative defense of inequality and the social necessity of privilege which surfaces again and again in British political debate in the twentieth century, most recently as the 'new' political science of Thatcherism. In the area of anti-democratic vilification of 'the masses' and of 'mass-society' by conservative cultural critics in the 1930s specifically, no one has written more ably than Valentine Cunningham in his *British Writers of the Thirties*. His chapter, 'Movements of Masses' includes many shrewd comments about Eliot's attitudes at the time (277–78, 282). More recently John Carey's *The Intellectuals and the Masses: pride and prejudice among the intellectuals, 1880–1939* (1992) surveys the field very well and makes many telling points. It might be a more valuable piece of work if Carey did not feel obliged to pander to the contempt of intellectuals which for more than a decade of Thatcherite populism has disfigured Britain.

6 Roger Kojecky's enormously helpful research into the micropolitics of Eliot's engagement with the Moot Group and particularly with that energetic apostle of planning in modern times, Karl Mannheim, remains the definitive account of Eliot's detailed and consistent opposition to the sociological fashions of the 1930s and 1940s, especially in the matter of social engineering. We learn from his *T. S. Eliot's Social Criticism* that much of the discussion at the meetings of the Moot led directly to the formulations in *Notes towards the Definition of Culture*. The writings of Richard Chace and Michael North explore the intellectual contexts of Eliot's activity more thoroughly than does Kojecky, who seems to have cast himself somewhat in the role of Eliot's apologist.

7 The play was commissioned by George Bell, the Bishop of Chichester, for the 1935 Canterbury Festival. The socially and politically active Bell first met Eliot after the publication of *Ash-Wednesday*. He was responsible for

introducing Eliot to E. Martin Browne, Bell's Director of Religious Drama at Chichester, who would be a central figure in Eliot's later engagement with the theatre. Bell and Eliot enjoyed cordial relations for many years. During the war, Eliot, along with Bell, was part of the British group that flew to Sweden in 1942 in order to promote political and cultural contacts. It was during the month spent in Scandanavia that Bell (and Eliot as well) met the German opposition to Hitler in the persons of Hans Schoenfeld and Dietrich Bonhoeffer. The Germans wanted to establish secret contact with the British government. Bell reported on his conversations in Stockholm to Anthony Eden, the Foreign Secretary, but nothing came of it. It may seem odd that Bell, a well-known liberal and anti-fascist in the 1930s, would have commissioned Eliot, a conservative, to write a play for Canterbury. But there is nothing odd about this. The play is not an apology for fascist ideas as such. The political reading I am attempting is as relevant to the political culture of class-divided democracies as it is to a variety of totalitarian states. The politics of the play engage, at different levels, with the articulations of power in society and power is certainly not an exclusively fascist obsession.

8 Michael North's incisive critique of Eliot's concept of the Community of Christians in *The Idea of a Christian Society* illuminates this issue indirectly. He asks, with deliberate ingenuousness, how would the Community of Christians be constituted? By another prior Community, 'perhaps [a] Community of Community of Christians?' This line of thought, as North points out, leads nowhere (116–17). North's aim seems to be to disclose the contradictory character of Eliot's ideas in this respect. But the solution to the question has really nothing to do with ideas at all. It seems to me that Eliot simply assumes that the political executives of the governing class would superintend the formation of a mandarin elite from their dominant position of power: for example, the Community of Christians, he writes, 'would include some of those who are ordinarily spoken of . . . as intellectuals' (*Idea* 38), and, one assumes that, correspondingly, it would *not* include some others. Who would decide? Clearly, as North asserts, some sort of national selection board is not what Eliot has in mind. The simple sociopolitical solution to the question is that the governors would pick and choose whomever *they* wanted. One assumes it would be those who are most reliable in serving the interests of their class, interests which the governors believe, and which their class ideology projects, correspond to the interests of the whole society. Certainly the minor inmates of Wishwood assume that society exists for their benefit and are merely bewildered and irritated when the possibility that this is not the case is raised (see Gerald's comment about 'communists' in the play [100]). What Eliot's thinking lacks in consistency and elegance is, practically speaking, beside the point. His silence on this practical matter in *The Idea of Christian Society* is either the blithe blindness of a man who thinks the solution is so obvious it hardly needs comment or a deliberate stratagem to slide past a very difficult sticking point, which if

raised, would attract a rather predictable response from his liberal and socialist opponents. I'm not sure Eliot's strengths as a controversialist, in social or literary matters, ever lay in the direction of argumentative consistency. He was a master of polemic because of his preternatural awareness of the mental habits and tolerances of his readers. It was in the end what he most admired in F.H. Bradley (it was all that was left to admire after G.E. Moore's demolition in the 1904 essay 'The Refutation of Idealism') and, closer to home, what he admired in contemporaries, like the clergyman Bishop Hensley Henson (*Idea* 78–9).

9 The patrician 'our' agrees rather well with Eliot's views about servants in the 1930s as recorded by George Orwell. 'Here is T. S. Eliot on the servant-problem as seen from the Anglo-Catholic standpoint: 'I do not like the situation (i.e. of having only one servant) . . . I should prefer to employ a large staff of servants, each doing lighter work but profiting by the benefits of the cultured and devout atmosphere of the home in which they lived'. That bit about the cultured and devout atmosphere reminds me, as Samuel Butler said of a cracked church bell he heard somewhere, of the smell of a bug' (letter to Brenda Salkeld, 7 March 1935, *CEJP* I:175).

10 Letter to John Betjeman, 18 September 1939, University of Victoria Library Special Collections.

4 REPRESENTING *FOUR QUARTETS*: THE CANONIZERS AT WORK

1 In the 1950s, Eliot always downplayed his role in the early phase of literary modernism, the 'men of 1914' years (Hall 56–58, and see Ackroyd 290–91). It is difficult to see why he did so. Perhaps, it was his usual reticence at revealing anything of himself. Possibly, genuine humility: he didn't need to blow his own trumpet. Possibly also, a kind of wariness by self-effacement: in the 1950s, it was perhaps wise to delicately distance oneself from the unsavouriness of Ezra Pound and, to a lesser extent, from the still snarly Wyndham Lewis, although this wasn't always possible, as in the case of Pound's Bollingen Prize in 1949 and his final release from St Elizabeth's ten years later, episodes in which Eliot stood fast by his old comrade in the face of a good deal of vicious criticism (see for example, Hillyer).

2 Frank Morley, in his short account of Eliot as a publisher in the March and Tambimuttu tribute, speaks of Faber productions exhibiting 'a recognizable character' over time. Richard de la Mare's genius for book design, for one thing, developed into what became the familiar, successive mutations of the house style over the decades, making each Faber book a recognizable physical object. But the Faber 'character' went beyond that. It could be found, Morley writes, in 'some intrinsic quality . . . some aspect of truthfulness or beauty' that went beyond mere commercial calculation (65–66). Of course the commercial factors were not ignored either, but, in Morley's good-natured reminiscence 'among friends', truth and beauty make better copy. What makes the Faber & Faber story so very interesting, however, is

the company's long term wager that, marketed properly, modernist culture would sell. And so it seems it did, handsomely.

3   The Christian revival in Britain in the interwar years is an important and often overlooked aspect of the ideological struggles of the times. The principal focus in the study of the two decades has normally been on the politics of Left and Right. In many, but less glamorous, ways, the various Christian societies, clubs and associations touched many more people's lives than the activities of the ideologues of Right and Left. R.H. Tawney, a crucial figure in those years, was certainly a socialist, but he was a *Christian* socialist. We tend to forget that he reflected a powerful inclination within the Church of England. Archbishop William Temple's Conference on Christian Politics, Economics and Citizenship (COPEC) was organized in 1924 and provided a focus for specifically Christian political action among professionals; Tawney was an important influence here. There were other organizations as well, such as Conrad Noel's Catholic Crusade, the League of the Kingdom of God, the National Guilds League, and the influential Christendom Group. This last reached its apogee of visibility at the Malvern Conference of 1941 which met, under the auspices of the Archbishop of York 'to consider how far the Christian faith and principles based upon it afford guidance for action in the world to-day' (Gallup 128). Eliot attended and spoke on the theme of 'The Christian Conception of Education', a subject he would return to again in the late 1940s and 1950s. See Angus Calder's *The People's War* 483–88 for an account of the conference. Martin Weiner 115–18, E.R. Norman 245 and *passim* and John Oliver *passim* provide summary accounts of the vitality of Christian social thought in the interwar years. Literary intellectuals like C. S. Lewis, Charles Williams, J.R.R. Tolkien, Dorothy Sayers, and others contributed much to the revival (see Carpenter, *Inklings*). Lewis's *The Screwtape Letters* (1942) remained a bestseller for decades and offered a trenchant programme of consolation in dreadful times to educated middle brows. It functioned, on its level, in the same way as Eliot's loftier ministrations directed at the higher mandarin plateaux.

4   On the Pound-Bollingen Prize controversy in 1948 see Noel Stock's *Life of Ezra Pound* (545–47). The poet and critic Allen Tate was a Fellow in American Letters of the Library of Congress in November 1948 when Pound was awarded the Prize. As one of the jury, he voted with the majority in the matter of *The Pisan Cantos*. During the nasty controversy that ensued, he wrote a personal *apologia* of his decision to vote for Pound, for *The Partisan Review* special number on the Pound dispute, reprinted in *The Man of Letters in the Modern World* (1955). After some to-ing and fro-ing about Pound, the last paragraph of this short piece turns to the general question of the relation of 'the civilized intelligence' to the 'the men who run the state', the very issue I have been tracing in Eliot's work. Tate writes that the 'task of the civilized intelligence is one of perpetual salvage' in a situation in which 'the businessman and the politician, the men who run the state' are in no posi-

tion to know what the responsibility of the 'man of letters' actually consists of. The maintenance of the health of language defines the responsibility of the literary intellectual. The men of power are hardly aware of language at all and, therefore, inevitably abuse it (cf. Wright Mills 350 and *passim*). '[P]art of our responsibility', Tate writes, 'is to correct the monism of the statesman who imagines that what he says is scarcely said in language at all, that it exists apart from the medium in a 'purity' of action which he thinks of as "practicality"' (266–67). This passage echoes the political purport of Eliot's *Murder in the Cathedral*, that the mandarin class must learn to serve power in various ways, sometimes by direct advice and instruction, sometimes by courageous admonition, as in the case of Becket, or possibly Pound and, Tate implies, even of Tate himself.

5 *FOUR QUARTETS*: THE POEM PROPER

1 My sense of *Being and Time* as a work profoundly influenced by the general moral and political crisis of Germany in the 1920s, was princially formed in conversation with my colleague Steven Taubeneck in the course of a Heidegger reading group in Vancouver during the period from the Autumn of 1992 to the Spring of 1994. The group included Kay Stockholder, Roger Seamon and Richard Fatechand. But see also Steiner, *Heidegger* 74–75 and Sheehan, 'Reading a Life' 77–78.

2 The ambiguous position of 'inwardness' with respect to its political fate in the modernized societies of surveillance is well summarized by Adorno. 'Terminologically, inwardness becomes a value and possession behind which [the subject] entrenches itself; and it is surreptitiously overcome by reification. It becomes Kierkegaard's nightmare of the 'aesthetic world' of the mere onlooker, whose counterpart is to be the existential inwardly man. Whatever wants to remain absolutely pure from the blemish of reification is pasted onto the subject as a firm attribute. Thus the subject becomes an object in the second degree, and finally the mass product of consolation: from that found in Rilke's 'Beggars can call you brother and still you can be a king' to the notorious poverty which is the great inward gleam of the spirit' (*Jargon* 73).

3 See especially volume four of Heidegger's *Nietzsche: Nihilism*, Keiji Nishitani, *The Self-Overcoming of Nihilism*, and Gianni Vattimo, *The End of Modernity*.

4 The presence in the mass media of the Atlantic world of cultural workers with leftist inclinations in the 1930s is a well-known story. Of course, communist sympathizers and fellow-travellers in the media did not go unchallenged; their story is one of conflict with the emerging conservatism that would take hold of the public media after the war. It is certainly not a story of their pervasive control of the public means of mass communication. Although political conservatives to this day promote opportunistically the myth of such control. The most famous example of the presence of leftists in the mass media occurred in the Hollywood of the 1930s. They were dealt

with in the ideological cleansing of America by the witch-hunters of the
1940s and 1950s.

5   Reviewers of *Collected Poems, 1909–1935*, with 'Burnt Norton' as the one
important new item, had by 1936, when the volume appeared, come to
accept Eliot's 'acquisition of faith' as no longer an obstacle to appreciation,
indeed Peter Quennell, in the *New Statesman*, wrote that it had 'added to the
delicacy . . . of Mr. Eliot's poetic method', even though it had had a more
deleterious effect on his critical work (Grant I 343). The outpouring of positive reviews both in England and America maps the enormous change in
Eliot's position, and in the public reactions to the fact of his Christianity.
See reviews by Edwin Muir, Cyril Connolly, Marianne Moore, D.W.
Harding, Louis Untermeyer and R.P. Blackmur and others in Grant, vol. 1
(335–68). Even the review in *New Masses*, by Rolfe Humphries, one more
mandarin intelligence flirting with the class struggle in the 1930s, does not
dismiss out of hand the scribblings of a class 'enemy', but urges the magazine's readers to pay close attention to a man who possesses a 'poetic
authority too great to be questioned' (Grant I 359). Those already feeling
their way back from the radicalism of the 1930s towards respectibility in the
1940s and beyond, no doubt read with particular care. Later, Humphries,
like Day Lewis and Warner, would find his way back into the post-war mandarinate by quietly translating classic authors, namely, Ovid and Lucretius.

6   The crisis I am referring to has been authoritatively described by Anthony
Giddens in *Modernity and Self-Identity* (1991). For Giddens, modernity is a
culture of risk in social environments characterized by uncertainity and
choice. As post-traditional society, modernity has not replaced the 'sureties
of tradition and habit' by 'the certitude of rational knowledge' (3). The
importance of Giddens's work is that it locates the radical doubt and scepticism of the modern philosophical tradition as also a shaping, institutional
factor in the making of ordinary social life. One may make claims about this
or that, but all claims 'are in principle always open to revision and may at
some point have to be abandoned'. What is true of ideas in modernity, is
true also for the very constituents of social being, the self for example. 'In
the settings of what I call 'high' or 'late' modernity – our present-day world
– the self, like the broader institutional contexts in which it exists, has to be
reflexively made' (3). The perplexed radicals of the 1930s, on their way back
to the bourgeois society from which, for a time, they had exiled themselves
politically and psychologically, experienced the concrete consequences of
living 'amid a puzzling diversity of options and possibilities', some of them
dangerous, and each requiring the fabrication of an appropriate self. In this
environment of high risk, it is perhaps not surprising that former radicals, in
England at least, were drawn again and again to their early experiences in
the public schools they attended as adolescents. These institutions may have
had their repulsive sides, but, at least, they had carried something of an
older, traditional world deep into the new culture of risk and dread. On this
latter point see especially Edmund Wilson on Denton Welch (*Europe* 10).

The sometimes irresistible seductions of totalitarian politics and parties are also part of the same psychological nexus.

7 See his *English Public Schools* (1945). And see Edmund Wilson's comments on the importance of the public school ethos in the lives of Warner's generation. While in London, in the Spring of 1945, Wilson 'listened, at a literary party, to a conversation between two writers who were comparing notes about their experiences in the volunteer fire brigades. They had both been to public schools, and they agreed it was quite different from 'school'. I gathered that what was lacking was the spirit of the old school team: the cockneys who were sometimes in command merely counted on people to do the right thing in a more matter-of-fact way' (9–10).

8 This hunger for an inner composure after the posturing and the disarray, a composure very much like that which Eliot identifies in Virgil, must surely lie at the heart of Rex Warner's and C. Day Lewis's rebirth in the war years as classicists and translators of ancient Greek and Roman texts. Day Lewis's quixotic turn to the translation of Virgil's *Georgics* in the early 1940s may be read as a personal project of private rehabilitation and public contrition, perfectly attuned to the ideological identification of essential Englishness with the rural shires in wartime. The cultural importance of Virgil in the 1940s for a broken Europe was not an English obsession alone. It was pan-European in scope; see, for example, Paul Valéry's verse translation *Les Bucoliques de Virgile*, composed from 1942 to 1944, in *Oeuvres I* (207–81). See also Jeffrey M. Perl's very interesting comments on *The Aeneid* and its hero: 'The modernists viewed their time as an odyssey, when the best they could hope for, in a time such as theirs, was to live an Aeneid. Our century has been blessed with the wrong epic. The image of Aeneas – counting his dead, declining to credit the pleadings of Providence – is a more apt emblem than Odysseus of postwar pathology' (151).

9 See the work of John R. Harrison, Roger Kojecky, Richard Chace and the Eliot chapter in Michael North's *The Political Aesthetic of Yeats, Eliot, and Pound*.

10 In addition to the early critical response to the poem by F.R. Leavis discussed in chapter four, there are a number of scholars who read *Four Quartets* (and most of Eliot's other work) as a poem of metaphysical, primarily ontological, interests: Eric Thompson, J. Hillis Miller, Jitendra Kumar, Lewis Freed, see especially Freed's comments about the objective correlative and immediate experience (67); Anne Bolgan, Armin Paul Frank, Keith Alldritt, Jeffrey M. Perl, especially chapter three.

11 This phrase in 'Burnt Norton' must remind us of Heidegger's concept of 'idle talk' (*Gerede*) in *Being and Time* 213. But see also Adorno, *Jargon* 101–103.

12 It's not as if the central characters in my story were not themselves aware of the state of psychological affairs I am describing. Some, indeed, were very candid about it. Goronwy Rees, a friend of Day Lewis and personally acquainted with several of the Cambridge traitors in the 1930s, did not mince his words about this matter of the coherence of one's self-identity. 'It has always surprised, and slightly bewildered me', he writes in *A Bundle of*

Sensations, 'that other people should take it so much for granted that they each possess what is usually called 'a character'. That is to say, a personality with its own continuous history . . . I have never been able to find anything of that sort in myself; and in the course of my life this has been the source of many misunderstandings, since other people persist in expecting of one a kind of consistency – which they really have no right to demand.' An indignant A.L. Rowse, who quotes this passage in his *Glimpses of the Great* (154–55), loftily disapproves of such notions as evidence of Rees's deplorable lack of 'character' in the old sense. Eliot, 'the invisible poet', was certainly capable of understanding what Rees was talking about. After all, it was precisely these very qualities which for Eliot composed the triumph and depravity of Byron (*OPP* 203, 205). It was part of Eliot's triumph as a major figure in a literary scene that he was capable of psychologically enveloping the sensibilities of both a Rowse *and* a Rees, and the several, morally slippery senses of the word 'character' which divided them.

13 These passages on Spender were written before the appearance of Ian Hamilton's 'Spender's Lives' in the 28 February 1994 number of *The New Yorker*. Hamilton's reflections on Spender's active personas provide ample, general support, I think, for my interpretation of the usefulness of Eliot for the making of the 'new' Spender in the 1940s.

14 The theory and practice of social intimacies in modernity have been well described by Anthony Giddens in *Modernity and Self-Identity* (88–98). Giddens's work is not restricted to an account of the politics of intimate experience among intellectuals; his work is of larger scope. However, the styles of life and the lifeplans of the intelligentsias and mandarinates of the early twentieth century, the Auden generation, say, in the 1930s and 1940s, anticipate social and psychological developments that have trickled down to the population at large in post-modernity.

15 See also Stephen Spender, *The Destructive Element* (149–52). Spender believed that Eliot was working in a musical mode derived from Beethoven's quartets as early as *Ash-Wednesday*.

16 Some of Eliot's contemporaries, from various intellectual traditions, were also preoccupied by a similar revisioning of time, history and revelation. Cf. Walter Benjamin's formulation of the intersection of time and eternity, 'History is the subject of a structure whose site is not homogeneous empty time, but time filled by the presence of the now (*Jetztzeit*)' (263 and 263n). Or Heidegger's more pessimistic declaration, 'Not only have the gods and the god fled, but the divine radiance has become extinguished in the world's history' ('What are poets for?' 91).

17 See 'Appendix B: Indian Section programmes produced by George Orwell' in *Orwell: The War Broadcasts* (284–88).

18 Eliot's two most important critical engagements with John Milton, one in 1936 and the second in 1947, are collected in *OPP* (138–61).

19 Eliot's mentoring style is well conveyed in the sketches and reminiscences of many of the younger writers with whom Eliot associated in the 1930s and

1940s. This is very clearly the case in the memoir of Hugh Sykes Davies, 'Mistah Kurtz: He Dead' (in Tate, *T. S. Eliot* 355–63). Many of the younger contributors to the March and Tambimuttu *Symposium* in 1948 confirm Sykes Davies's impressions, Auden, Nicholas Moore, Ronald Bottrall, Tambimuttu himself, Kathleen Raine, Spender and several others, including William Empson, whose sardonic remarks are made to sound oddly unappreciative by the surrounding tide of warm praise.

6 WHITE MYTHOLOGY: THE COMEDY OF MANNERS IN NATOPOLIS

1 The picture that Ian Hamilton paints of Spender after his deft political rehabilitation during the 1940s is of a man assiduously 'working the cultural networks' and socializing with the 'Big-money names' on both sides of the Atlantic, and, of course, particularly in America. The rich and the powerful 'pepper the pages of his diaries', Hamilton writes. 'When he is not lodging at Michael Astor's Oxfordshire estate, he is cruising the Mediterranean on Hansi Lambert's yacht. In America, he hobnobs with Anne Cox Chambers and Drue Heinz.' The reward for his new political reliability and for being 'so amusing' and for retailing, from the past, 'such wonderful stories about such interesting people' (David Plante, quoted in Hamilton) is a successful career as a mandarin in the cultural institutions of the Cold War and the honour of having none other than Philippe de Rothschild himself lay on the claret on the occasion of his seventieth birthday (Hamilton 80). Whether any final literary recognition or creative achievement would have given Spender more delight, at the end of the day, than the enjoyment of the Baron's favour is difficult to say.

2 Eliot and the New Critical formalists in America would have thought of this ideological function of art in that familiar, depoliticized, critical abstraction characteristic of the 1950s, namely that artworks impose order on chaos. Music, in that formulation, served as a powerful metaphor for aesthetic integration. See, for example, Auden's 'Anthem for St Cecilia's Day' and also his charming homage to Mozart in 'Metalogue to the Magic Flute':

> *Basta*! Maestro, make your minions play!
> In all hearts, as in our finale, may
> Reason & Love be crowned, assume their rightful sway. (*CSP* 279)

Works cited

Abse, Dannie. *A Poet in the Family*. London: Hutchison, 1974.

Ackroyd, Peter. *T. S. Eliot*. London: Abacus-Sphere Books, 1985.

Adorno, Theodor. *Introduction to the Sociology of Music*. Trans. E. B. Ashton. New York: Continuum, 1989.

The Jargon of Authenticity. Trans. Kurt Tarnowsky. Evanston: Northwestern University Press, 1973.

Minima Moralia: Reflections from Damaged Life. Trans. E. F. N. Jephcott. London: Verso, 1984.

Negative Dialectics. Trans. E. B. Ashton. London: Routledge, 1990.

Prisms. Trans. Samuel and Shierry Weber. Cambridge, Mass.: The MIT Press, 1982.

Age of Austerity: 1945–1951. Eds. Michael Sissons and Philip French. Harmondsworth: Penguin Books, 1964.

Aiken, Conrad. 'After "Ash-Wednesday"'. *Poetry* 45 (December 1934): 161–65.

Alldritt, Keith. *Eliot's Four Quartets: Poetry as Chamber Music*. London: Woburn Press, 1978.

Arnold, Matthew. *Culture and Anarchy*. 1869; rpt. edn. J. Dover Wilson. Cambridge University Press, 1955.

Atkinson, Brooks. 'At the Theatre'. *The New York Times* 23 Jan. 1950: 17.

Auden, W. H. *Collected Shorter Poems, 1927–1957*. London: Faber, 1966.

The English Auden: Poems, Essays and Dramatic Writings, 1927–1939. Ed. Edward Mendelson. London: Faber, 1977.

Auerbach, Erich. *Literary Language and Its Public in Late Latin Antiquity and in the Middle Ages*. Trans. Ralph Mannheim. New York: Pantheon, 1965.

Mimesis: the Representation of Reality in Western Literature. Trans. Willard Trask. Princeton University Press, 1974.

Ayers, Robert W. '*Murder in the Cathedral*: A "Liturgy Less Divine"'. *Texas Studies in Literature and Language* 20 (Winter 1978): 579–98.

Barford, Philip. *The Keyboard Music of C.P.E. Bach*. London: Faber & Faber, 1965.

Barrett-Ayres, Reginald. *Joseph Haydn and the String Quartet*. London: Barrie & Jenkins, 1974.

Barry, Kevin. *Language, Music, and the Sign: a study of aesthetics, poetics, and poetic practice from Collins to Coleridge*. Cambridge University Press, 1987.

Bateson, F. W. 'The Poetry of Learning'. In *Eliot in Perspective: A Symposium*. Ed. Graham Martin. London: Macmillan, 1970: 31–44.

Beehler, Michael T. '*Murder in the Cathedral*: the Countersacramental Play of Signs'. *Genre* 10.3 (Fall 1977): 329–38.

Belli, Angela. *Ancient Greek Myths and Modern Drama: A Study in Continuity*. New York: New York University Press, 1969.

Benjamin, Walter. *Illuminations*. Trans. Harry Zohn. New York: Harcourt, Brace & World, 1968.

Berger, Peter L. and Thomas Luckmann. *The Social Construction of Reality: a Treatise in the Sociology of Knowledge*. Harmondsworth: Penguin Books, 1979.

Blythe, Ronald (ed.). *Components of the Scene: Stories, Poems, and Essays of the Second World War*. Harmondsworth: Penguin Books, 1966.

Bogan, Louise. 'Review of *Four Quartets*'. *The New Yorker* 23 May 1943: 19–21.

Bolgan, Anne C. *What the Thunder Really Said: A Retrospective Essay on the Making of 'The Waste Land'*. Montreal: McGill-Queen's University Press, 1973.

Boulton, J.T. 'The Use of Original Sources for the Development of a Theme: Eliot in *Murder in the Cathedral*'. *English* 11.61 (Spring 1956): 2–8.

Boutwood, Arthur. *National Revival: A Re-Statement of Tory Principles*. London: Herbert Jenkins, 1913.

Brooks, Cleanth. 'The Serious Poet in a Secularized Society: Reflections on Eliot and Twentieth-Century Culture'. In *The Placing of T. S. Eliot* (1991): 109–18).

Browne, E. Martin. 'From *The Rock* to *The Confidential Clerk*'. In *T. S. Eliot: A Symposium for his Seventieth Birthday*. Ed. Neville Braybrooke. London: Rupert Hart-Davis, 1958: 57–69.

The Making of T. S. Eliot's Plays. Cambridge University Press, 1969.

Burger, Peter. *The Theory of the Avant-Garde*. Trans. M. Shaw. Minneapolis: University of Minnesota Press, 1984.

Burke, Kenneth. *The Philosophy of Literary Form: Studies in Symbolic Action*. 1941; rev. edn. New York: Vintage Books, 1957.

Bush, Ronald. *T. S. Eliot: A Study in Character and Style*. New York: Oxford University Press, 1984.

Calder, Angus. *The People's War: Britain 1939–1945*. New York: Pantheon Books, 1969.

Carey, John. *The Intellectuals and the Masses: Pride and Prejudice among the Intellectuals*. London: Faber, 1992.

Carpenter, Humphrey. *The Brideshead Generation: Evelyn Waugh and his Friends*. London: Faber, 1990.

The Inklings. London: Allen & Unwin, 1978.

Carpentier, Martha C. 'Orestes in the Drawing Room: Aeschylian Parallels in T.S.Eliot's "The Family Reunion"'. *Twentieth Century Literature* 35.1 (Spring 1989): 17–42.

Chace, William M. *The Political Identities of Ezra Pound and T. S. Eliot*. Stanford University Press, 1973.

Chapman, Guy. *A Kind of Survivor: The Autobiography*. London: Gollancz, 1975.

Clubb, Merrel D. 'The Heraclitean Element in Eliot's *Four Quartets*'. *Philological Quarterly* 40 (January 1961): 19–33.

Coats, R. H. 'An Anchor for the Soul: a Study of Mr. T. S. Eliot's Later Verse'. *The Hibbert Journal* 44.2 (January 1946): 112–18.

Coghill, Nevill. 'Sweeney Agonistes: (An anecdote or two)'. In March and Tambimuttu: 82–87.

Colby, Robert A. 'The Three Worlds of *The Cocktail Party*: The Wit of T. S. Eliot'. *University of Toronto Quarterly* 24.1 (October 1954): 56–69.

Condon, James P. 'Notes on T. S. Eliot's "What is a Classic?": The Classical Norm and Social Existence'. *Classical Journal* 73 (1977–78): 176–178.

Connolly, Cyril. *Enemies of Promise*. 1938; rev.ed. New York: Macmillan, 1948.
  Ideas and Places. London: Weidenfeld & Nicolson, 1953.
  The Unquiet Grave: a Word Cycle by Palinurus New York: Harper, 1945.

Cooper, John Xiros. Rev. of Perloff 1981. *Ariel* 16.1 (January 1985): 91–96.
  T. S. Eliot and the Politics of Voice: the Argument of 'The Waste Land'. Ann Arbor: UMI Research Press, 1987.

Cunningham, Valentine. *British Writers of the Thirties*. Oxford University Press, 1988.
  'Marooned in the 30s'. *The Times Literary Supplement* 19 August 1994: 4

Daniells, Roy. 'The Christian Drama of T. S. Eliot'. *Canadian Forum* 16 (August 1936): 20–21.

Davidson, Clifford. 'T. S. Eliot's *Murder in the Cathedral* and the Saint's Play Tradition'. *Papers on Language and Literature* 21.2 (Spring 1985): 152–69.

Davie, Donald. *These the Companions: Recollections*. Cambridge University Press, 1982.

Dawson, Christopher. *It Shall Not Happen Here*. London: Sword of the Spirit Publications, 1947.

Day Lewis, C. 'At East Coker'. In Tate (1966): 114–15.
  Collected Poems 1954. London: Cape, 1954.
  'Foreword'. *The Georgics of Virgil*. London: Cape, 1940.

Deacon, Richard. *The Cambridge Apostles: A History of Cambridge University's Elite Intellectual Secret Society*. New York: Farrar, Straus & Giroux, 1986.

Derrida, Jacques. *Margins of Philosophy*. Trans. Alan Bass. University of Chicago Press, 1982.

Donoghue, Denis. *The Ordinary Universe: Soundings in Modern Literature*. New York: The Ecco Press, 1987
  The Third Voice: Modern British and American Verse Drama. Princeton University Press, 1959.

Dowden, Edward. *Essays Modern and Elizabethan*. London: Dent, 1910.

Dreyfus, Hubert, L. 'Heidegger on the connection between nihilism, art, technology, and politics'. In *The Cambridge Companion to Heidegger*. Ed. Charles B. Guignon. Cambridge University Press, 1993: 289–316.

Driberg, Tom. *Ruling Passions*. London: Cape, 1977.

Dukes, Ashley. 'T. S. Eliot in the Theatre'. In March and Tambimuttu, 111–18.

Du Sautoy, Peter. 'T. S. Eliot: Personal Reminiscences'. In Olney: 75–84.

Eagleton, Terry. *Criticism and Ideology: A Study in Marxist Literary Theory*. London: NLB, 1976.

Edwards, Thomas R. *Imagination and Power: A Study of Poetry on Public Themes*. New York: Oxford University Press, 1971.

Eliot, T. S. *Knowledge and Experience in the Philosophy of F. H. Bradley* (1915). London: Faber, 1964.

'*Ulysses*, Order and Myth'. *Dial* 75 (November 1923): 483.

For Lancelot Andrewes: Essays on Style and Order. 1928; rpt. London: Faber, 1970.

Anabasis: a poem by St-John Perse. 1931; rev. 1949; 3rd. ed. London: Faber, 1959.

Selected Essays: New Edition. 1932, 1950; rpt. New York: Harcourt, Brace & World, 1964.

After Strange Gods: A Primer of Modern Heresy. New York: Harcourt, Brace, 1934.

The Idea of a Christian Society. 1939; rpt. London: Faber, 1962.

'Towards a Christian Britain'. In *The Church Looks Ahead: Broadcast Talks*. London: Faber, 1941: 106–117.

'Preface'. *The Dark Side of the Moon*. London: Faber, 1946.

Notes towards the Definition of Culture. 1948; rpt. London: Faber, 1972.

Poetry and Drama. The Theodore Spencer Memorial Lecture, Harvard University, 21 November 1950. London: Faber, 1951.

Collected Plays. 1962; rpt. London: Faber, 1968.

Collected Poems, 1909–1962. 1963; rpt. London: Faber, 1968.

To Criticize the Critic and Other Writings. 1965; rpt. London, Faber, 1988.

Letters, 1898–1922. Vol. I. Ed. Valerie Eliot. San Diego: Harcourt Brace Jovanovich, 1988.

Ellis, Steve. *The English Eliot: Design, Language and Landscape in 'Four Quartets'*. London: Routledge, 1991.

Empson, William. 'The Style of the Master'. In March and Tambimuttu: 35–37.

Everett, Barbara. 'The New Style of *Sweeney Agonistes*'. *Yearbook of English Studies* 14 (1984): 243–63.

Fenton, James. *All the Wrong Places: Adrift in the Politics of the Pacific Rim*. New York: Atlantic Monthly Press, 1988.

Fergusson, Francis. *The Idea of a Theater*. Princeton University Press, 1949.

Flint, R. W. 'The *Four Quartets* Reconsidered'. In *T. S. Eliot, Four Quartets: a Selection of Critical Essays*. Ed. Bernard Bergonzi. London: Macmillan, 1969: 107–18.

Florio, John. *The Essayes of Michael Lord of Montaigne*. 1603; rpt. New York: The Modern Library., n.d.

Forster, E. M. *Nordic Twilight*. Macmillan War Pamphlet 3. London: Macmillan, 1940.

Review of *Notes towards the Definition of Culture*. *The Listener* 20 Jan. 1949: 253.

Frank, Armin Paul. 'T. S. Eliot's Objective Correlative and the Philosophy of F.H. Bradley'. *Journal of Aesthetics and Art Criticism* 30 (Spring 1972): 311–17.

Freed, Lewis. *T. S. Eliot: The Critic as Philosopher*. West Lafayette, Ind.: Purdue University Press, 1979.

Freedman, Morris. 'Jazz Rhythms and T. S. Eliot'. *South Atlantic Quarterly* 51 (July 1952): 419–35.

'The Meaning of T. S. Eliot's Jews'. *South Atlantic Quarterly* 55 (April 1956): 198–206.

Freeman, Kathleen. *Ancilla to The Pre-Socratic Philosophers: A complete translation of the Fragments in Diels, 'Fragmente der Vorsokratiker'*. Oxford: Basil Blackwell, 1956.

Galef, David. 'Fragments of a Journey: the Drama in T. S. Eliot's *Sweeney Agonistes*'. *English Studies* 69 (December 1988): 481–96.

Gallup, Donald. *T. S. Eliot: A Bibliography*. London: Faber, 1969.

Gardner, Helen. *The Art of T. S. Eliot*. 1950; rpt. New York: E. P. Dutton, 1959.

'The Cocktail Party'. *Time and Tide* 25 March 1950: 284–85.

The Composition of Four Quartets. London: Faber, 1978.

Giddens, Anthony. *Modernity and Self-Identity: Self and Society in the Late Modern Age*. Stanford University Press, 1991.

Gombrowicz, Witold. 'On Art and Revolution: excerpts from *Le Journal 1953–56*'. Trans. June Guicharnaud. *The Drama Review* 14.3 (1970): 97–101.

Good, Graham. 'Orwell and Eliot'. In *George Orwell: A Reassessment*. Ed. Peter Buitenhuis and Ira Nadel. London: Macmillan, 1988: 139–156.

Gordon, Lyndall. *Eliot's Early Years*. Oxford University Press, 1977.

Eliot's New Life. New York: The Noonday Press, 1989.

Gramsci, Antonio. *Selections from the Prison Notebooks*. Trans. Quintin Hoare and Geoffrey Nowell Smith. New York: International Publishers, 1983.

Grant, Michael (ed.). *T. S. Eliot: The Critical Heritage*. 2 vols. London: Routledge & Kegan Paul, 1982.

Graves, Robert and Alan Hodge. *The Long Week-end: a Social History of Great Britain, 1918–1939*. London: Faber, 1940.

Green, Martin. *Children of the Sun: A Narrative of the Decadence in England after 1918*. New York: Basic Books, 1976.

Hall, Donald. 'T. S. Eliot'. Interview. *Paris Review* (Spring/Summer 1959): 44–68.

Hamilton, Ian. 'Spender's Lives'. *The New Yorker* 28 February 1994: 72–84.

Harding, D.W. 'The Rock'. *Scrutiny* 3 (September 1934): 180–83.

'We have not reached conclusion'. *Scrutiny* 11 (Spring 1943): 216–219.

Harrison, John R. *The Reactionaries: A Study of the Anti-Democratic Intelligentsia*. New York: Schocken Books, 1967.

Hay, Eloise Knapp. *T. S. Eliot's Negative Way*. Cambridge, Mass.: Harvard University Press, 1982.

Hayward, John. *Prose Literature Since 1939*. London: Longmans Green, for The British Council, 1947.

Heaney, Seamus. *North*. London: Faber, 1975.

Heath, Carl. *The Redemption of Europe*. York: Northern Friends' Peace Board, 1947.

Heidegger, Martin. *Being and Time*. Trans. John Mcquarrie & Edward Robinson. New York: Harper & Row, 1962.

    Nietzsche: Nihilism. Vol. 4. Trans. Frank A. Cappuzzi. Ed. David Farrell Krell. San Francisco: HarperCollins, 1982.

    'What Are Poets For?' In *Poetry, Language, Thought*. Trans. Albert Hofstadter. New York: Harper Colophon, 1975: 91–142.

Heppenstall, Rayner. 'I am not in favour of the Working Class'. In *New Road, 1944: New Directions in European Art and Letters*. Eds. Alex Comfort and John Bayliss. London: The Grey Walls Press: 217–222.

Herwitz, Daniel. *Making Theory / Constructing Art: On the Authority of the Avant-Garde*. University of Chicago Press, 1993.

Hill, Geoffrey. *Collected Poems*. Harmondsworth: Penguin Books, 1985.

    'Of diligence and jeopardy'. Review article. *Times Literary Supplement* 17–23 November 1989: 1273–1276.

Hillyer, Robert. 'Treason's Strange Fruit'. *Saturday Review of Literature* 11 June 1949: 9–11, 28.

    'Poetry's New Priesthood'. *Saturday Review of Literature* 18 June 1949: 7–9, 38.

Hinchliffe, Arnold P. (ed). *T. S. Eliot: Plays*. London: Macmillan, 1985.

'Homo Sapiens'. 'Blue Print for an "Internationale of Science"'. In *Solidarity*. Volume IV. London: Harrap, 1943: 22–40.

Howard, Anthony. 'We Are the Masters Now'. In *Age of Austerity*. 15–34.

Howard, Brian. 'Mr. Eliot's Poetry'. *New Statesman* 8 November 1930: 146.

Howarth, Herbert. 'Eliot, Beethoven, and J.N.W. Sullivan'. *Comparative Literature* 9 (Autumn 1957): 322–32.

Hughes, H. Stuart. *Consciousness and Society: The Reorientation of European Social Thought, 1890–1930*. New York: Vintage Books, 1958.

Hughes, Ted. *A Dancer to God: Tributes to T. S. Eliot*. London: Faber, 1992.

Hulme, T.E. *Speculations: Essays on Humanism and the Philosophy of Art*. Ed. Herbert Read. London: Kegan Paul, Trench, Tubner, 1936.

Hynes, Samuel. *The Auden Generation: Literature and Politics in England in the 1930s*. London: The Bodley Head, 1976.

Jackson Knight, W.F. *Roman Vergil*. London: Faber, 1944.

Jay, Martin. *Adorno*. Cambridge: Harvard University Press, 1984.

    The Dialectical Imagination: A History of the Frankfurt School and the Institute of Social Research, 1923–1950. Boston: Little, Brown, 1973.

Jenkins, Nicholas. 'The errant elitist'. *The Times Literary Supplement* 5 August 1994: 9.

Jones, David E. *The Plays of T. S. Eliot*. University of Toronto Press, 1960.

Jones, E. E. Duncan. 'Ash Wednesday'. In *T. S. Eliot: A Study of his Writings by Several Hands*. Ed. B. Rajan. London: Dennis Dobson, 1947: 37–56.

Jones, Grania. 'Eliot and History'. *Critical Quarterly* 18.3 (Autumn 1976): 31–48.

Kendon, Frank. *The Time Piece: A Poem*. Cambridge University Press, 1945.

Kenner, Hugh. *The Invisible Poet*. London: Methuen, 1966.

    The Pound Era. Berkeley: University of California Press, 1971.

Keown, Eric. 'At the Play'. *Punch* 13 Nov. 1946: 434–35.

222 *Works cited*

Kermode, Frank. *The Sense of an Ending*. London: Oxford University Press, 1966.
'T. S. Eliot on Poetry'. Rev. of *On Poetry and Poets*. *International Literary Annual*
(1958): 133–135.
Kirk, G. S. and J. E. Raven. *The Presocratic Philosophers: a Critical History with a
Selection of Texts*. Cambridge University Press, 1960.
Kirk, Russell. *Eliot and his Age: T. S. Eliot's Moral Imagination in the Twentieth Century*.
New York: Random House, 1971.
Kojecky, Roger. *T. S. Eliot's Social Criticism*. London: Faber, 1971.
Kumar, Jitendra. 'Consciousness and its Correlates: Eliot and Husserl'.
Philosophy and Phenomenological Research 28 (March 1968): 332–52.
Kwan-Terry, John. 'The Structure of Rhythm and Meaning in "Ash
Wednesday"'. *Literary Half-Yearly* 20.2 (1979): 155–166.
Leavell, Linda. 'Eliot's Ritual Method: *Ash Wednesday*'. In Olney: 145–52.
Leavis, F. R. *D. H. Lawrence, Novelist*. 1955; rpt. Harmondsworth: Penguin Books,
1970.
Education & and the University: a Sketch for an English School. 1943; rpt. London:
Chatto & Windus, 1965.
The Living Principle: 'English' as a Discipline of Thought. New York: Oxford
University Press, 1975.
New Bearings in English Poetry: a Study of the Contemporary Situation. London:
Chatto & Windus, 1932.
Thought, Words and Creativity: Art and Thought in Lawrence. New York: Oxford
University Press, 1976.
Leiris, Michel. *Francis Bacon: Full Face and Profile*. New York: Rizzoli, 1983.
Lewis, C. S. *The Screwtape Letters*. 1942; rpt. London: Fount, 1982.
Lewis, Wyndham. *Men Without Art*. London: Cassell, 1934.
Lucas, F. L. Review of *The Waste Land*. *New Statesman* 3 November 1923: 116–118.
Lukes, Steven. *Power: A Radical View*. London: Macmillan, 1978.
MacCarthy, Desmond. 'Some Notes on Mr. Eliot's New Play'. *New Statesman* 25
March 1939: 455–56.
'Sweeney Agonistes'. *The Listener* 9 Jan. 1935: 80–81.
MacNeice, Louis. *Collected Poems, 1925–1948*. London: Faber, 1949.
The Strings Are False: An Unfinished Autobiography. New York: Oxford University
Press, 1966.
MacVean, Jean. 'In Argos or in England'. *Agenda* 23.1/2 (Spring–Summer 1985):
111–130.
Mannheim, Karl. *Man and Society in an Age of Reconstruction: Studies in Modern Social
Structure*. London: 1940; rpt. Routledge & Kegan Paul, 1966.
March, Richard and Tambimuttu (eds.). *T. S. Eliot: A Symposium*. London:
Editions Poetry, 1948.
Marcuse, Herbert. *Negations: Essays in Critical Theory*. Trans. Jeremy J. Shapiro.
Boston: Beacon Press, 1968.
Matthews, T. S. 'T. S. Eliot Turns to Comedy'. *Life*. 1 February 1954: 56–64.
McCarthy, Patrick A. 'Eliot's *Murder in the Cathedral*'. *Explicator* 33.1 (September
1974): 7.

Miller, J. Hillis. *The Poets of Reality*. Cambridge, Mass.: Harvard University Press, 1966: 131–89.

Miller, Vincent. 'Eliot's Submission to Time'. *Sewanee Review* 84 (Spring 1976): 448–64.

Mills, C. Wright. *The Power Elite*. New York: Oxford University Press, 1957.

Milosz, Czeslaw. *The Captive Mind*. Trans. Jane Zielonko. New York: Vintage Books, 1955.

Moody, A. D. 'T. S. Eliot: The American Strain'. In *The Placing of T. S. Eliot* (1991): 77–89.

    Thomas Stearns Eliot: Poet. Cambridge University Press, 1979.

Morley, F. V. 'T. S. Eliot as a Publisher'. In March and Tambimuttu: 60–70.

Mulhern, Francis. *The Moment of 'Scrutiny'*. London: Verso, 1981.

Murray, Paul. *T. S. Eliot and Mysticism: The Secret History of Four Quartets*. London: Macmillan, 1991.

Nairn, Tom. 'The English Literary Intelligentsia'. *Bananas*. Ed. Emma Tennant. London: Quartet Books, 1977: 57–83.

New British Poets: An Anthology. Ed. and Intro. Kenneth Rexroth. n.c. [Norfolk, Conn.]: New Directions, n.d. [1948].

Newton, Scott and Dilwyn Porter. *Modernization Frustrated: The Politics of Industrial Decline in Britain since 1900*. London: Unwin Hyman, 1988.

Nicodemus (pseud.). *Midnight Hour*. London: Faber, 1941.

Nicolson, Harold. *Comments, 1944–1948*. London: Constable, 1948.

    '"My Words Echo"'. In *T. S. Eliot: A Symposium for his Seventieth Birthday*. London: Rupert Hart-Davis, 1958: 34–35.

Nishitani, Keiji. *The Self-Overcoming of Nihilism* (1949). Trans. Graham Parkes and Setsuko Aihara. Albany: State University of New York Press, 1990.

Norman, E. R. *Church and Society in England, 1770–1970: An Historical Study*. Oxford University Press, 1976.

North, Michael. *The Political Aesthetic of Yeats, Eliot, and Pound*. Cambridge University Press, 1991.

Oldham, J. H. 'Christian Humanism'. In *Humanism: Three BBC Talks*. London: Watts, 1944.

Oliver, John. *The Church and Social Order: Social Thought in the Church of England, 1918–1939*. London: Mowbray, 1968.

Olney, James (ed.). *T. S. Eliot: Essays from the 'Southern Review'*. Oxford: Clarendon Press, 1988.

Ophuls, Marcel. *Hotel Terminus: The Life and Times of Klaus Barbie*. Film. 1988.

Ortega y Gasset, Jose. *The Revolt of the Masses*. Trans. Anthony Kerrigan. Notre Dame, Ind.: University of Notre Dame Press, 1985.

Orwell, George. *The Collected Essays, Journalism and Letters*. 4 vols. Harmondsworth: Penguin Books, 1970.

    Nineteen Eighty-Four. Harmondsworth: Penguin Books, 1969.

Orwell: The War Broadcasts. Ed. W.J. West. London: Duckworth/British Broadcasting Corporation, 1985.

O'Sullivan, Noel. *Conservatism*. London: Dent, 1976.

Palmer, Herbert E. *Cinder Thursday*. London: Ernest Benn, 1931.

Perl, Jeffrey M. *Skepticism and Modern Enmity: Before and After Eliot*. Baltimore: The Johns Hopkins Press, 1989.

Perloff, Marjorie. *The Poetics of Indeterminacy: Rimbaud to Cage*. Princeton University Press, 1981.

Peschmann, Hermann. '*The Cocktail Party*: Some Links Between the Poems and Plays of T. S. Eliot'. *The Wind and the Rain* 7.1 (Autumn 1950): 53–58.

Placing of T. S. Eliot, The. Ed. Jewel Spears Brooker. Columbia: University of Missouri Press, 1991.

Poggioli, Renato. *The Theory of the Avant-Garde*. New York: Harper and Row, 1971.

Preston, Raymond. *Four Quartets Rehearsed: a Commentary on T. S. Eliot's Cycle of Poems*. London: Sheed & Ward, 1946.

Prichard, William H. *Seeing Through Everything: English Writers, 1918–1940*. New York: Oxford University Press, 1977.

Pryce-Jones, David. 'Towards the Cocktail Party'. In *Age of Austery*: 216–239.

Purdy, Anthony (ed.). *Literature and Money*. Amsterdam: Rodopi, 1993.

Raffel, Burton. *Possum and Ole Ez in the Public Eye: Contemporaries and Peers on T. S. Eliot and Ezra Pound*. Hamden, Conn.: Archon Books, 1985.

Rainey, Lawrence. 'The Price of Modernism: Publishing *The Waste Land*'. In *T. S. Eliot: The Modernist in History*. Ed. Ronald Bush. Cambridge University Press, 1991: 91–133.

Read, Herbert. *The Politics of the Unpolitical*. London: Routledge, 1946.

'Reassuring Sir Humphrey'. *The Economist* 19–25 March 1994: 67–69.

Reeve, N. H. *The Novels of Rex Warner: An Introduction*. London, Macmillan, 1986.

Reeves, Gareth. *T. S. Eliot: a Virgilian Poet*. New York: St. Martin's Press, 1989
'T. S. Eliot, Virgil and Theodor Haecker: Empire and the Agrarian Ideal'. *Agenda* 23.3/4 (Autumn–Winter 1985/86): 180–201.

Reibetanz, Julia Maniates. *A Reading of Eliot's Four Quartets*. Ann Arbor: U.M.I. Research Press, 1983.

Richards, I. A. 'On TSE'. in Tate (1966): 1–10.

Ricks, Christopher. *T. S. Eliot and Prejudice*. London: Faber, 1988.

Roby, Kinley E.(ed.) *Critical Essays on T. S. Eliot: The Sweeney Motif*. Boston: G. K. Hall, 1985.

Rorty, Richard. *Contingency, Irony, and Solidarity*. Cambridge University Press, 1989.

Rosenberg, Harold. *The Tradition of the New*. New York: McGraw-Hill, 1965.

Rousset, David. *L'univers concentrationne*. Paris: Edition du Pavois, 1946.
A World Apart. Trans. Yvonne Moyse and Roger Senhouse. London: Secker and Warburg, 1951.

Rowse, A. L. *Glimpses of the Great*. London: Methuen, 1985.

Russell, Peter. 'A Note on T. S. Eliot's New Play'. *Nine* 1 (October 1949): 28–29.

Samuelson, Scott. 'The Word as Sword: Power and Paradox in *Murder and the Cathedral*'. *Literature and Belief* 7 (1987): 73–81.

Sayers, Dorothy L. *The Mysterious English*. Macmillan War Pamphlet 10. London: Macmillan, 1941.

Schwartz, Delmore. 'The Literary Dictatorship of T. S. Eliot'. *Partisan Review* (February 1949): 119–37.

Sencourt, Robert. *T. S. Eliot, a Memoir*. Ed. Donald Adamson. New York: Dodd, Mead, 1971.

Sergeant, Howard. 'Man Meeting Himself'. *New Road 5*. Ed. Wrey Gardiner. London: Grey Walls Press, 1949: 83.

Shawe-Taylor, Desmond. Review of *The Cocktail Party*. *New Statesman* 3 Sept. 1949: 243.

Sheehan, Thomas. 'Reading a life: Heidegger and hard times'. In *The Cambridge Companion to Heidegger*. Ed. Charles B. Guignon. Cambridge University Press, 1993.

Sisson, C. H. *English Poetry, 1900–1950: An Assessment*. New York: St. Martin's Press, 1971.

The Spirit of British Administration and some European Comparisons. London: Faber, 1959.

Smith, Carol H. *T. S. Eliot's Dramatic Theory and Practice*. Princeton University Press, 1963.

Smith, Grover. *T. S. Eliot's Poetry and Plays: A Study in Sources and Meaning*. 2nd ed. University of Chicago Press, 1974.

Smith, Stevie. 'History or Poetic Drama?' In *T. S. Eliot: A Symposium for his Seventieth Birthday*. Ed. Neville Braybrooke. London: Rupert Hart-Davis, 1958: 170–175.

Spanos, William V. *The Christian Tradition in Modern British Verse Drama*. New Brunswick, NJ: Rutgers University Press, 1967.

'God and the Detective: the Christian Tradition and the Drama of the Absurd'. *Newsletter of the Conference on Christianity and Literature* 20.2 (1971): 16–22.

Spencer, Theodore. 'On "Murder in the Cathedral"'. *Harvard Advocate* 125 (December 1938): 21–22.

Spender, Stephen. 'After the Cocktail Party'. *The New York Times Book Review* 19 March 1950: 7, 20.

The Creative Element. London: Hamish Hamilton, 1953.

The Destructive Element: A Study of Modern Writers and Beliefs. London: Cape, 1936.

European Witness. London: Hamish Hamilton, 1946.

The New Realism. London: The Hogarth Press, 1939.

Returning to Vienna 1947: Nine Sketches. n.c. [New York]: Banyan Press, 1947.

The Still Centre. London: Faber, 1939.

Steiner, George. *Heidegger*. London: Fontana, 1989.

Stern, James. *The Hidden Damage*. New York: Harcourt, 1947.

Stock, Noel. *Life of Ezra Pound*. New York: Pantheon Books, 1970.

Strauss, Leo. *On Tyranny*. Revised and expanded edition. Ed. Victor Gourevitch and Michael S. Roth. New York: The Free Press, 1991.

Sutherland Boggs, Jean. Radio Interview. *Arts National*. Canadian Broadcasting Corporation, 29 April 1988.

Tate, Allen. 'Irony and Humility'. *Hound and Horn* (Jan.–March 1931): 290–97.

'Ezra Pound and the Bollingen Prize'. *The Man of Letters in the Modern World: Selected Essays: 1928–1955*. New York: Meridian Books, 1955: 264–67.

(ed.). *T. S. Eliot: The Man and his Work*. New York: Delacorte Press, 1966.

Tawney, R. H. *The Agrarian Problem in the Sixteenth Century*. 1912; rpt. New York: Harper and Row, 1967.

Religion and the Rise of Capitalism: A Historical Study. 1926; rpt. Harmondsworth: Penguin Books, 1977.

Thielicke, Helmut. *Nihilism: Its Origin and Nature – with a Christian Answer*. Trans. John W. Doberstein. London: Routledge & Kegan Paul, 1962.

Thomas, R. Hinton. 'Culture and T. S. Eliot'. *Modern Quarterly* 21 (Spring 1951): 147–62.

Thompson, Eric. *T. S. Eliot: The Metaphysical Perspective*. Carbondale: Southern Illinois University Press. 1963.

Thompson, T. H. 'The Bloody Wood'. *London Mercury* 29 (January 1934): 233–39.

Thurber, James. 'What Cocktail Party?' *The New Yorker* 1 April 1950: 26–29.

Tomlin, E. W. F. *T. S. Eliot: A Friendship*. London: Routledge, 1988.

Trotter, David. *The Making of the Reader: Language and Subjectivity in Modern American, English and Irish Poetry*. London: Macmillan, 1984.

Unger, Leonard. *T. S. Eliot: Moments and Patterns*. Minneapolis: University of Minnesota Press, 1966.

Valéry, Paul. *Oeuvres I*. Ed. Jean Hyter. Paris: Gallimard, 1957.

Vattimo, Gianni. *The End of Modernity: Nihilism and Hermeneutics in Postmodern Culture*. Trans. Jon R. Snyder. Baltimore: Johns Hopkins University Press, 1988.

Vidler, Alec R. *Secular Despair and Christian Faith*. London: SCM Press, 1941.

Warner, Rex. *The Cult of Power: Essays*. 1947; rpt. Port Washington, N.Y.: Kennikat Press, 1969.

English Public Schools. London: Collins, 1945.

The Professor. 1938; rpt. Harmondsworth: Penguin Books, 1945.

Weiner, Martin J. *English Culture and the Decline of the Industrial Spirit, 1850–1980*. Cambridge University Press, 1981.

Wertheim, Albert. 'The Modern British Homecoming Play'. *Comparative Drama* 19 (Summer 1985): 151–165.

West, Rebecca. *The Meaning of Treason*. 1949; rpt. Harmondsworth: Penguin Books, 1965.

Wheen, Francis. *Tom Driberg: His Life and Indiscretions*. London: Chatto & Windus, 1990.

Williams, Raymond. *Culture and Society, 1780–1950*. Harmondsworth: Penguin, 1961.

Politics and Letters: Interviews with New Left Review. London: Verso, 1981.

Problems in Materialism and Culture: Selected Essays. London: Verso, 1980.

Wilson, Edmund. *Europe without Baedeker: Sketches, among the Ruins of Italy, Greece, and England.* London: Secker and Warburg, 1948.

Wilson Knight, G. 'T. S. Eliot: Some Literary Impressions'. In Tate (1966): 245–61.

Winton, J. R. *Lloyds Bank, 1918–1969.* London: Oxford University Press, 1982.

Woolf, Virginia. *The Letters.* 6 vols. London: Hogarth Press, 1975–80.

Zabel, Morton D. 'The Still Point'. In Grant 282–85.

Index

Ackroyd, Peter, 28, 100, 183, 200n, 206n
Adorno, Theodor, 49, 63, 184
  Jargon of Authenticity, 49, 52, 123, 211n, 213n
  Minima Moralia, 109, 124, 130, 132, 136, 184–6
  Negative Dialectics, 122
  Sociology of Music, 163, 165, 168
  with Max Horkheimer, *Dialectic of Enlightenment*, 186
Aeneas, 4–5, 142–44
Aeschylus, *The Orestia*, 86, 88, 91, 92, 93
affirmative culture, 47–8
Alexander the Great, 55
Alldritt, Keith, 162–4, 166, 210n, 213n
Andrewes, Lancelot, 4, 6, 9, 11, 18, 19–21, 26
Anglo-Catholic Prayer Book, The, 16
Anglo-Catholicism, 9, 22
anthropology, 8
Antin, David, 25
Aristotle, 55
Arjuna, 204n
Arnheim, Rudolf, 106
Arnold, Matthew, 5, 55, 201n
Artaud, Antonin, 5, 62
Ashbery, John, 3
Astor, Michael, 215n
Atkinson, Brooks, 191
Auden, W. H., 29, 34, 35, 45, 52, 137, 138, 154, 201n, 215n
  'Anthem for St Cecilia's Day', 162, 215n
  'August for the people', 170
  'The Chimeras', 203n
  'A Communist to Others', 87
  'The Fall of Rome', 90, 203n
  'In Praise of Limestone', 52–4
  'Memorial for the City', 181, 189–90, 203n
  'In Memory of Ernst Toller', 137–8
  'In Memory of Sigmund Freud', 114
  'In Memory of W.B. Yeats', 108, 136, 137, 163
  'Metalogue to the Magic Flute', 215n
  'Music is International', 162
  The Orators, 65, 202n

'To T. S. Eliot on his Sixtieth Birthday', 45, 203n
  'September 1, 1939', 108, 162, 204n
  'Spain', 48, 105
  'Under Which Lyre', 196
  'A Walk After Dark', 204n
Auden, W. H., and Christopher Isherwood, 62, 92, 172
Auden generation, the, 8, 64, 104, 105, 214n
Auerbach, Erich, 16, 109, 210n
Augustans, the, 24
Augustine, St, 16, 201n

Bacon, Francis, 206n
Bank of England, 128
Barbie, Klaus, 128
Barker, George, 105
Barnes, Djuna, 105, 107
Barrett-Ayres, Reginald, 163, 165
Barry, Kevin, 167–8
Barry, Philip, 192
Bartók, Bela, 162, 168
Bataille, Georges, 5
Baudelaire, Charles, 4, 24, 51, 154, 201n
Bazin, René, 79
Beat poets, 25
Beaverbrook, Lord, 203n
Beckett, Samuel, 201n
Beethoven, Ludwig van, 168, 214n
Bell, Daniel, 157
Bell, George, the Bishop of Chichester, 207–8n
Benda, Julien, 32, 206n
Benjamin, Walter, 214n
Benn, Gottfried, 42
Berlin, Fall of, 42
Betjeman, John, 106, 112, 209n
Bhagavad Gita, 173, 204n
Bible, The (King James), 26
Birrell, Francis, 200n
Blackmur, R. P., 212n
Blake, WIlliam 116

228

Blast, 101, 199n
Blitz, 8, 24, 110
Bloomsbury, 64, 203n
Blunt, Anthony, 40
Bogan, Louise, 140
Boggs, Jean Sutherland, 109
Bohemia, 92
Bolgan, Anne, 213n
Bollingen Prize, 113, 209n, 210–1n
Bonhoeffer, Dietrich, 208n
Book of Common Prayer, The, 16, 26
Bottrall, Ronald, 215n
Boulton, J.B., 74
Boutwood Lectures, 34
Bowra, Maurice, 140, 155
Bradley, F. H., 9, 134, 201n, 204n, 209n
Brecht, Berthold, 55, 62
Britain, Battle of, 24
British Broadcasting Corporation, 106, 173
Broadway, New York, 100, 194
Brooks, Cleanth, 203–4n
Brown, Ivor, 191
Browne, Martin, 92, 206n, 208n
Burger, Peter, 96
Burgess, Guy, 40
Bush, Ronald, 5, 6, 89, 91, 145, 200n
Butler, Samuel, 209n
Byron, 214n

Calder, Angus, 210n
Cambridge University, 34, 111, 188, 198, 203n,
    213n
Cambridge University Press, 291
Camus, Albert, 112, 125, 192
Canterbury Cathedral Festival, 61, 73, 207n
Cape, Jonathan, 103
Carey, John, 207n
Caribbean, 102
Catholic Crusade, 210n
Cavalcanti, Guido, 6, 17
Ceaucescu, Nicolae, 205n
Cecchi, Emilio, 126–7
Céline, Ferdinand, 62, 210nn
Chace, William, 94, 213n
Chapman, Guy, 36
Chatterton, Thomas, 79
Cheapside, 80, 81
Chicago, University of, 191
Chichester, Dean of, 171, 178
Christendom Group, 210n
Christian News Letter, The, 182
Christian Revival, 210n
Church of England, 8, 9–10, 11, 20, 26, 61, 63,
    73, 128, 210n
Civil War, English, 175

Civil War, Spanish, 48–9, 204n
class, 37–8, 44
Clynes, J. R., 171
Coats, R. H., 145–6
Coghill, Nevill, 206n
Colby, Robert, 192
Cold War, The, 31, 33, 49, 50, 51, 117, 148, 157,
    180–1, 186, 187–8, 190, 195–6, 215n
Coleridge, Samuel Taylor, 96
Communist Party, 128
Community of Christians, 32, 96–8, 208–9n
concentration camps, 8, 22, 126–7, 204n
Conference on Christian Politics, 210n
Congress of Cultural Freedom, 157
Connolly, Cyril, 33, 35, 100, 189, 212n
    Enemies of Promise, 33, 35
    Horizon, 100
    Ideas and Places, 129
    The Unquiet Grave, 100, 153
Conrad, Joseph, 127
Conservative Party, 8, 11, 12, 36, 59
contextual criticism, 62
Cooper, Duff, 172
Coriolanus, 66
Coward, Noel, 62
Cox Chambers, Anne, 215n
Crashaw, Richard, 175
Creeds, 26
Cripps, Stafford, 64
Cunard, Nancy, 105
Cunningham, Valentine, 207n
Curtius, Ernst Robert, 109
Czechoslovakia, 34

Daily Mail, The, 12
Dante, 4, 6, 16, 17, 158, 174, 178
Darkness at Noon, 76
David, Hugh, 154
Davies, Hugh Sykes, 34, 108–9, 178, 215n
Dawson, Christopher, 131
Day Lewis, Cecil, 45, 58, 138, 159, 197, 212n,
    213n
    'O Dreams, O Destinations', 170
    'At East Coker', 45, 101
    'A Letter from Rome', 172
    The Magnetic Mountain, 58, 87
    translation of Virgil's *Georgics*, 213n
    Word Over All, 138, 153
de Foucauld, Charles, 4, 78–9, 91, 193
de la Mare, Richard, 209n
Delhi, 32
denazification, 42
Derrida, Jacques, 195
Dial, The, 9
Dido, 143–4

Diels, Hermann, 149
Dittersdorf, Karl Ditters von, 163
Dodds, E. R., 35
Donne, John, 4, 20
Donoghue, Denis, 73–4, 135, 206n
Doone, Rupert, 206n
dramatic monologue, 2, 61
Dresden, 22
Driberg, Tom (William Hickey), 40–1, 198n,
    203n
Dru, Alexander, 43
du Sautoy, Peter, 200n
Dukes, Ashley, 206n
Durbin, Evan, 36

Eden, Anthony, 208n
Edinburgh Festival, 191
Editions Poetry (London), 32
Eliot, T. S., as American, 28, 70–1, 85–6, 87,
    201–2n
  as Anglican convert, 4, 9, 14, 15, 16, 17, 21,
    26, 200n
  aestheticism, 9–10, 11, 23, 24, 25, 55, 154, 190
  as 'best-selling' author, 29–32
  as businessman, 3, 6, 8, 101–4, 200n
  candour, 2, 6–7, 16, 133, 176–80
  as celebrity, 1–2, 3, 4, 5, 15, 23, 26–7, 72, 99,
    100–1, 104, 177, 182, 185–6, 190–2, 198–9n
  classicism, 24–6, 142–5, 146–7, 177
  as 'confessional' writer, 2–5, 6, 16, 18–19,
    176–80
  conservatism, 10–14, 37–8, 47, 58, 63–4, 66–7,
    76, 88, 94, 98, 111–2, 182, 186–8, 204–5n
  as controversialist, 6, 73, 95, 99, 187
  cultural unity of Europe, 42–4, 49–51, 183–4
  as dramatist, 61, 73–4
  as English, 4, 12–13
  history as theme, 169–71, 173, 174–6
  impersonality, 2, 4, 102, 199n
  as influential figure, 28–32, 42, 72, 100–4,
    111
  as ironist, 1, 2, 6–7, 14, 15, 18, 27, 114
  'the man of letters', 9, 46, 51, 204n
  mastery, 18–19, 111, 176–7
  the Moot group, 37, 39, 207n
  Nobel Prize, 100
  Order of Merit, 100
  as 'pétainiste', 100–1, 112, 113
  as publisher, 6, 8, 55, 104–8, 136, 145, 185,
    201n, 209–10n
  relationship to Auden, 202n
  as sage, 32, 99, 100, 108, 191
  as social climber, 4, 5, 6, 8, 9, 23, 63, 103
  tradition, 44, 55
  violent crimes, 63, 77

POETRY AND PLAYS:
  Anabasis, 30, 65–6, 68
  Ariel poems, 2, 5, 30
  Ash-Wednesday, 1, 2, 4, 5–7, 8, 15–27, 30, 95,
    98, 110, 131, 139, 160, 180, 200n, 207n,
    214n
  'Aunt Helen', 55
  'Burnt Norton', 15, 29, 69, 120, 133, 135,
    139–40, 141–2, 148–62, 166, 169, 170, 177,
    179, 212n, 213n
  'Choruses from *The Rock*', 70–3
  The Cocktail Party, 29, 60, 79, 94, 98, 100, 188,
    191–4
  Collected Poems, 1909–1935, 29, 73, 103–4,
    212n
  The Confidential Clerk, 31, 98, 190, 196–7
  'Coriolan', 61, 65, 66–70, 74, 78
  'Cousin Nancy', 55
  'The Dry Salvages', 28, 29, 50, 63, 112, 120,
    141–2, 164, 170, 173–4, 177, 179
  'East Coker', 10, 12, 29, 110–2, 119–20, 134,
    135, 141, 155–6, 161, 169, 170–1, 172, 175–7,
    179
  The Elder Statesman, 6, 98, 196–7
  'Eyes that last I saw in tears', 5
  The Family Reunion, 60, 79, 84–94, 155, 193
  Four Quartets, 1, 8, 22, 23, 24, 25, 29, 31, 33, 45,
    49, 71, 73, 89, 96, 98–9, 109–21, 122–81,
    185, 188, 189, 190, 193, 194, 196, 200n,
    201n, 213n
  'Gerontion', 23
  'The Hippopotamus', 14–15
  'The Hollow Men', 5, 127, 200n
  'Hysteria', 18
  'Landscapes', 73
  'Little Gidding', 10, 29, 118, 142, 169, 173,
    174–6, 177, 178–80
  'The Love Song of J. Alfred Prufrock', 7, 18
  'Mr Apollinax', 55
  Murder in the Cathedral, 60, 61, 69, 73–84,
    89–90, 93, 93–4, 138, 142, 193, 205n,
    211n
  'Portrait of a Lady', 7, 18, 55
  The Rock, 54, 61, 70–3, 201n
  Selected Poems, 29
  Sweeney Agonistes, 5, 61, 62–4, 100, 190, 206–7
  The Waste Land, 1, 2–3, 7, 8, 9, 13, 14, 18, 23,
    25, 27, 30, 63, 64, 95, 108, 127, 134, 139,
    142, 190, 198–9n, 200n
  'The wind sprang up at four o'clock', 5
PROSE:
  After Strange Gods, 18, 61, 94, 111, 134, 147,
    201n
  'The Christian Conception of Education',
    210n

Clark Lectures (1926), 6
The Criterion, 13, 30, 34, 42–3, 46, 61, 102, 109,
    111, 134, 199n, 204n
To Criticize the Critic, 28
Die Einheit der Europaischen Kultur, 42–51, 129
For Lancelot Andrewes, 9, 10, 11, 14, 18, 19–21,
    111, 134, 147, 171, 201n
'The Function of Criticism', 201n
The Idea of a Christian Society, 13, 32, 34, 39, 56,
    59, 66–7, 71, 77, 79–80, 87, 88, 94, 96–8,
    133, 170, 192, 208–9n
*Knowledge and Experience in the Philosophy of
    F. H. Bradley*, 9
'The Literature of Politics', 59
'Marie Lloyd', 13, 63
'Milton II', 175–6
Notes towards the Definition of Culture, 37–8, 39,
    42, 56, 59, 61, 71, 85, 113, 127, 169, 170, 182,
    187–8, 207n
'The *Pensées* of Pascal', 4
Poetry and Drama, 61
Points of View, 30
'Preface', *The Dark Side of the Moon*, 182–4
Selected Essays, 13, 30, 31, 201n, 202n
Selected Prose, 30
'Thoughts after Lambeth', 63, 131, 134, 198n,
    201n
'Towards a Christian Britain', 79
'Tradition and the Individual Talent', 169,
    201n
'What is a Classic?', 4–5, 25, 142–8, 177
Eliot, Valerie, 102, 196
Eliot, Vivien, 3, 143–4, 182, 199n, 200n
elites, governing, 22, 32, 33, 35, 36, 37–8, 55,
    56–9, 62, 74–6, 85, 86, 92, 136
    reform of, 77–84
Elizabeth I, queen of England, 10
Ellis, Steven, 202n
Elyot, Thomas, 172–3
Emma, Jane Austen, 85
Empson, William, 8–9, 215n
Encounter, 157
England, 10, 12–14, 44
Enlightenment, the, 71, 94
Erastianism, 77
Ernest Benn, Ltd, 1
Euripides, 192
Everett, Barbara, 206n
existentialism, 125, 160–1
Express, The, 203n

Faber & Faber, Ltd., 8, 29, 55, 65, 102, 103–9,
    112, 136, 140, 145, 156, 183, 200n, 201n,
    209–10n
Faber & Gwyer, 102, 103

Faber, Geoffrey, 105
Fabians, 36, 64
Fatechand, Richard, 211n
Feiling, Keith, *History of the Tory Party*, 11–12,
    201n
Fenton, James, 42
'fifty shilling tailor', 202n
Flaubert, Gustave, 205n
Fleet Street, 41, 64
Flint, R.W., 112, 118
Florio, John, 16
Fluchère, Henri, 127
Forster, E. M., 100–1, 113, 171, 172
France, Anatole, 195
France, Fall of, 41, 44
Frank, Armin Paul, 213n
Frankfurt School, 62
Freed, Lewis, 213n
Freedman, Morris, 206n
French Revolution, 94
Freud, Sigmund, 8
Fromm, Erich, 52
Fry, Roger, 199n, 210n
Furtwängler, Wilhelm, 42

Galef, David, 206n
Gallup, Donald, 202n
Gardner, Helen, 5, 74, 89, 116–18, 120, 162,
    165–7, 168, 192, 200n
Garnett, Edward, 103
General Election (1945), 36, 109, 188
General Strike (1926), 11
Germany, 37, 43–4, 46, 51–2, 54, 205n
Germany, Federal Republic of, 49
Gestapo, 23, 128
Giddens, Anthony, 212n, 214n
Gide, André, 52
Girouard, Mark, 90
God, City of, 72
Goethe, Johann Wolfgang von, 192
Gollancz, Victor, 188
Gombrowicz, Witold, 201n
Gordon, Lyndall, *Eliot's Early Years*, 7, 134,
    201n
    Eliot's New Life, 5, 24, 28, 72, 74, 84, 86,
    91, 93, 155, 206n
Gramsci, Antonio, 44, 206n
Great Depression, 33
Grierson, John, 106
Gropius, Walter, 106
Group Theatre, 206n
Guillen, Nicolas, *Espana*, 105

Haecker, Theodore, 43
Hale, Emily, 3

Hamilton, Ian, 214n, 215n
Hamlet, 61
Harding, D. W., 101, 115, 212n
Harrison, J. R., 94, 213n
Harvard University, 100, 103, 109
Haydn, Josef, 163
Hayward, John, 30, 33, 101, 117
Heaney, Seamus, 124
Heath, Carl, 127
Heidegger, Martin, 42, 45
    Being and Time, 122–3, 125, 148, 150, 164, 169, 211n, 213n
    Nietzsche, 200–1n, 211n
    'What are poets for?', 109, 129–30, 135, 139, 214n
Heinz, Drue, 215n
Hellman, Lillian, 154
Hendry, J. F., 154
Henry II, king of England, 76
Henson, Bishop Hensley, 209n
Heppenstall, Rayner, 160–1
Heraclitus, 149–51, 154, 172, 189
Herbert, A. P., 171
Herwitz, Daniel, 96
Hill, Geoffrey, 49, 50
Hillis Miller, J., 213n
Hinchliffe, Arnold, 206n
Hiroshima, 22, 89
Hitler, Adolf, 92
Hobbes, Thomas, 201n
Holliday, Judy, 190
Holocaust, 22, 108, 126
homosexuality, 40, 40–1
Hopkins, Gerard Manley, 71
Hotel Terminus, 129
Howard, Brian, 41
Howl (Allen Ginsberg), 3
Hughes, Ted, 54, 201n
humanism, 8, 13, 14, 16–17, 19, 22–3, 26, 27, 42, 56, 145
Humphries, Rolfe, 212n
Huxley, Julian, 39
Hymnal, 16
hysteria, 8

imagism, 16, 20–1
Imperial Airways, 106
Indochina, 190
Institut d'Etudes Anglaises (Paris), 28–9
Institute of Contemporary Art, 113
Instone, Ralph, 111
intellectuals, see mandarinate
intelligentsia, see mandarinate
Isaiah, 69
Isherwood, Christopher, 33

James, Henry, 33
Joad, C. E. M., 171, 178
Job, The Book of, 126
John of the Cross, St, 157, 158
Jones, David, 105, 109
Jones, E. E. Duncan, 200n
Joyce, James, 9, 101, 105, 107
Juliana of Norwich, 189
Junger, Ernst, 41
Juvenal, 185

Kafka, Franz, 201n
Kendon, Frank, 161
Kenner, Hugh, 5
Kermode, Frank, 170
Kierkegaard, Sören, 7, 192, 211n
Kipling, Rudyard, 59
Kirk, Russell, 40
Knox, Ronald, 171
Kojecky, Roger, 94, 207n, 213n
Korean War, 190
Kumar, Jitendra, 213n

Labour Party, 128
Laforgue, Jules, 4
Lambert, Hansi, 215n
Lambeth Conferences, 63
Langland, William, 116
Laski, Harold, 36, 64, 171
Lawrence, D. H., 101, 102
Lawrence, T. E., 92, 172
Le Carré, John, 50
League of the Kingdom of God, 210n
Leavis, F. R., 110–11, 114–15, 118, 148, 169, 213n
    New Bearings in English Poetry, 78
Leavitt, David, 154
Legion of Honour (France), 202n
Lehmann, John, 117
Lévi-Strauss, Claude, 97–8
Lewis, C. S., 210n
Lewis, Wyndham, 3, 5, 33, 101, 144, 209n
    Men Without Art, 5, 33, 199n
Life, 31, 190–1
Lindsay, Kenneth, 39
Listener, The, 101, 113, 207n
Litvinoff, Emmanuel, 113
Lloyds Bank, 102
London School of Economics, 36
Lucretius, 212n

MacCarthy, Desmond, 92, 207n
MacDiarmid, Hugh, 109
MacDonald, Ramsay, 11
McGrath, Raymond, 106

Machiavelli, Niccolò, 4, 134
Maclean, Donald, 40
Macmillan War Pamphlets, 171
MacNeice, Louis, 34, 40, 58, 64, 210n
   Autumn Journal, 34
   'Epitaph for Liberal Poets', 161
   The Strings Are False, 58, 139, 204n
Madison Avenue, 31
Mallarmé, Stéphane, 8, 24, 154
Mallock, W.H., 207n
Malvern Conference (1941), 210n
mandarinate, 8, 10, 22, 23, 28, 30, 36–7, 38,
   39–40, 42, 44, 45, 51, 55, 62, 64, 67, 68, 70,
   73, 75, 95, 109
   anxiety in, 49, 51–2, 52–4, 59–60, 118, 146,
     164
   consolation of, 45, 89, 108–9, 118–21, 123,
     151–2, 175, 178
   definition of, 31–4, 46, 57, 76, 146
   disillusionment of, 50, 88–9, 114, 139–40,
     148, 175
   domestication of, 153, 165, 173, 180–1, 186,
     189, 197, 212–13n
   German, 42, 44, 47, 51–2, 122–3, 208n
   relationship to power, 50, 54, 56–9, 62, 75,
     82–3, 96–8, 120, 123–5, 163, 189–90, 205n,
     211n
   revolt of, 36–7, 38, 39–41, 74–6
Mannheim, Karl, 37–8, 39, 206n, 207n
   Man and Society in an Age of Reconstruction, 37
March, Richard, 32, 100, 200n, 215n
Marks and Spencer, Ltd, 39
masses, the, 33, 54, 63, 64, 66–7, 87, 88, 95–6,
   136, 207n
Matthews, T. S., 31, 190
Maurras, Charles, 54
Mengele, Josef, 22
Métadier, Jacques, 38
Metaphysical poets, 6
Mexico City, 32
Milne, A. A., 171
Milosz, Czeslaw, 183
Milton, John, 71, 176, 214n
modernism, 2, 8, 21, 24–5, 117, 124, 136, 151,
   205n, 209n, 213n
Montaigne, 16
Montreal, 32
Moody, David, 5, 17, 66, 89, 200n, 201–2n
Moore, G.E., 209n
Moore, Marianne, 212n
Moore, Nicholas, 154, 215n
Moravia, 92
Morgan, Charles, 29, 202n
Morley, Frank, 101, 103, 200n, 209n
Morrell, Ottoline, 3

Mosca, Gaetano, 206n
Moscow, 205n
Mosley, Oswald, 39
Mont Blanc restaurant, 103
Mozart, Wolfgang Amadeus, 163, 215n
Muir, Edwin, 212n
Munich conference (1938), 34, 89, 92, 133–4
Murray, Paul, 200n
music, 24, 25, 54, 117, 162–6, 186
myth, 8, 9, 26

Nagasaki, 89
Nassau, 102
National Gallery, Ottawa, 210n
National Guilds League, 109
Naziism, 204–5n
Nehemiah, 70
New Apocalypse, the, 154
New Deal, 39
New English Weekly, The, 110, 134
New Left Review, 188
New Masses, The, 212n
New Statesman, The, 191, 212n
New York Times, The, 191
New Yorker, The, 191, 196, 214n
Newman, John Henry, 5, 210n
Nicholson, Max, 39
Nicolson, Harold, 129, 141
Nietzsche, Friedrich, 17, 21, 132, 200–1n
nihilism, 7–8, 21, 22, 45, 51, 53, 109, 114, 125–35,
   140, 145, 149, 190, 196, 200–1n
Nine, 191
Nishitani, Keiji, 131–2, 211n
NKVD, 23
Nobel Prize (1948), 100
Noel, Conrad, 210n
Noica, Constantine, 76
Norman, E.R., 210n
North Atlantic Treaty Organization, 180–1
North, Michael, 9, 204n, 208–9n, 213n

O'Hara, Frank, 25
Observer, The, 191
occult, 8
Oldham, J. H., 131, 133
Oliver, John, 210n
Ophuls, Marcel, 129
Ortega y Gasset, José, 207n
Orwell, George, 32–3, 110, 112, 118, 209n
   at the BBC, 173, 214n
   Homage to Catalonia, 139
   Nineteen Eighty-Four, 48, 57, 58, 60, 77, 126,
     164–5, 184–5, 188, 189
Ovid, 212n
Oxford University, 103, 198n, 203n, 204n

Palinurus, see Connolly, Cyril, 153
Palmer, Herbert, 1–2
Paradise Lost, 65
Pareto, Vilfredo, 55, 206n
Partisan Review, The, 210n
Pascal, Blaise, 4
Pater, Walter, 33, 117
Paul, St, 192
Paz, Octavio, 32
Penguin Books, 29–30
Perl, Jeffrey, 125, 213n
Perloff, Marjorie, 201n
Perse, St-Jean, 65
Philby, Kim, 40
Plante, David, 215n
Plath, Sylvia, 3, 79
Poetry London, 100, 110
Poggioli, Renato, 96
Poirier, Richard, 202n
Poland, 41, 183
Postan, M. M., 36
Pound, Ezra, 3, 8, 101, 102, 103, 105, 107, 113,
  182, 209n, 210n
  The ABC of Reading, 146
  The Cantos, 71, 106, 109, 210n
  Hugh Selwyn Mauberley, 71
Powell, Anthony, 41
Powell, Michael, 171
Powers, Eileen, 36
Preston, Raymond, 115–16, 117, 149
Priestley, J.B., 171, 178
Prospero, 18

Quennell, Peter, 212n

Raine, Kathleen, 215n
Read, Herbert, 106–7, 127–9, 202n
Redgrave, Michael, 93
Rees, Goronwy, 213–4n
Reeve, N. H., 141
Reeves, Gareth, 43
Richards, I. A., 102, 199n
Ricks, Christopher, 200n
Rilke, Rainer Maria, 51
Rimbaud, Arthur, 25
Robbins, Lionel, 36
Roby, Kinley E., 207n
romanticism, 94, 144, 146–7
Rome, 32, 66
Rorty, Richard, 126
Rosenberg, Harold, 153, 186
Rotha, Paul, 106
Rothermere family, the, 102
Rothschild, Baron Philippe de, 215n
Rousset, David, 126, 127, 129

Rowse, A. L., 214n
Royal Academy of Art, 107, 128
Royal Society of Literature, 202n
Russell, Bertrand, 203n
Russell, Peter, 191

Sadler's Wells, 73
saint, the, 79, 96–7
Salkeld, Brenda, 209n
Salter, Arthur, 39
Sartre, Jean-Paul, 112, 192
Sayers, Dorothy, 171, 172, 210n
Schoenfeld, Hans, 208n
Schwartz, Delmore, 40
SCM Press, 112
Scrutiny, 100
Seamon, Roger, 211n
Sergeant, Howard, 152–6
Shakespeare, William, 16, 17, 171, 172
Shamley Green, 24
Shawe-Taylor, Desmond, 191
Sheed & Ward, 112
Shostakovitch, Dmitri, 164
Sieff, Israel, 39
Sigg, Eric, 28
Sikorska, Helena, 183
Sikorski, General Wladyslaw, 183
Sisson, C.H., 15, 22, 46–7
Sitwell, Edith, 198n
Smart, Christopher, 116
Smith, Carol H., 206n
Smith, Grover, 89, 91
Smith, Stevie, 82
Solidarity, 38–9
Somme, Battle of the, 23
Sophocles, 126
South Africa, 71
Southern Review, The, 112
Soviet-Nazi Pact, 89
Soviet Union, 51, 205n
Spanos, William V., 206n
Spencer, Stanley, 93
Spender, Stephen, 34, 126, 127, 138, 152–3, 155,
  192, 201n, 214n, 215n
  The Destructive Element, 156, 214n
  European Witness, 51–2, 53, 57, 127, 129
  Forward from Liberalism, 141
  The New Realism, 152–3
  Returning to Vienna, 158
  T. S. Eliot, 168
  The Still Centre, 156–8
  World Within World, 158
Spottiswoode, Raymond, 106
Stalinism, 81, 205n
Stead, William Force, 9

Stern, James, 129
Stock, Noel, 210n
Stockholder, Kay, 211n
Stockholm, 208n
Stokes, Adrian, 106
Strachey, John, 64
Strachey, Lytton, 33
Strauss, Leo, 45, 55, 64, 205n, 206n
style, 5–6, 11, 14, 15–17, 18–21, 24, 25–7, 33, 95, 187
subjectivity, 6–7, 17, 22, 27, 31, 33, 49–50, 54, 108–9, 129, 135, 145, 177
Sweden, 208n
Sweeney, James Johnson, 111, 118

Tambimuttu, 32, 100, 200n, 215n
Tate, Allen, 200n, 210–1n
Taubeneck, Steven, 211n
Tawney, R. H., 10–1, 12, 13, 36, 201n, 210n
Tempest, The, 18
Temple, William, Archbishop of York, 210n
Thatcher, Margaret, 187, 207n
Thielicke, Helmut, 130–1, 132–3, 146
Thirty-Nine Articles, The, 16
Thompson, Eric, 213n
Thompson, T. H., 206n
Thurber, James, 191–2
Time and Tide, 192
Times, The, 12, 104, 128, 197, 202n
Tolkien, J. R. R., 210n
Toller, Ernst, 137–8
Tom Jones, 85
Tomlin, E. W. F., 28–9, 34
Toronto, University of, 109
Traherne, Thomas, 116
Treece, Henry, 154
Trotter, David, 202n
Tudor England, 10, 11–12, 13–14, 56, 175

UNESCO, 184
Untermeyer, Louis, 212n
Upanishads, 173

Valéry, Paul, 31, 51, 126, 213n
Vanderbilt University, 112

Vattimo, Gianni, 211n
Vaughan, Henry, 116
Versailles, 116
Vidler, Alec, 134
Virgil, 33, 72, 138, 146, 150, 213n
    Aeneid, 4–5, 69, 142–4, 146, 147, 213n
    The Georgics, 58, 71–2
Vortex (London), 8, 199n

Wagner, Richard, 192
Walpole, Hugh, 171
Wanhal, Johann Baptist, 163
Warner, Rex, 35, 212n, 213n
    The Cult of Power, 35
    The Professor, 58, 141
Waugh, Evelyn, 87, 139
Weber, Max, 206n
Week-End Review, 39
Wehrmacht, 41
Weimar, 123
Weiner, Martin, 36, 203n, 210n
Welch, Denton, 212n
Wertheim, Albert, 84
West, Rebecca, 36
West End, London, 100
Westminster Theatre, 92
Weston, Jessie, 192
Wheen, Francis, 198n, 203n
Whistler, James McNeill, 117
Whitehall, 33, 41
Wilenski, R. H., 106
Williams, Charles, 210n
Williams, Raymond, 187, 188, 203n
Williams, William Carlos, 25
Wilson, Edmund, 213n
Wilson Knight, G., 171, 172
Woolf, Virginia, 101, 171, 199–200n, 210n
Wordsworth, William, 116
World War One, 8, 23, 66
World War Two, 24, 31, 32, 41–2, 48, 50, 89, 98
Wright Mills, C., *The Power Elite*, 56–7, 59, 75

Yeats, J. B., 47
Yeats, W. B., 51, 65, 68